THE YORK BOOK

THE YORK BOOK

A history of York in a concise
A to Z format

Edited by Antonia Evans

Contributors:
Michael Bennett
Antonia Evans
Timothy Hebbert
Siân Jay
Matthew Lund
Christopher Summerville

BLUE BRIDGE

THE YORK BOOK

Published in 2002 by Blue Bridge, PO Box 609,
York YO31 8WA

Edited by Antonia Evans
Contributors: Michael Bennett, Antonia Evans,
Timothy Hebbert, Siân Jay,
Matthew Lund & Christopher Summerville

© Blue Bridge 2002

Lines from *Twelve Songs* © The Estate of W.H. Auden

Cover design by Timothy Hebbert
Cover photography by Christopher Summerville

ISBN 0954274903

A catalogue record for this book is available from the British Library

Printed and bound by Sessions of York

THE YORK BOOK

This first edition of *The York Book* aims to offer a comprehensive encyclopaedia of the city of interest to both residents and visitors. To some there may appear to be unjustified inclusions, to others serious omissions. Furthermore, history is frequently open to interpretation, facts debatable, and even dates disputable. At the time of writing all the information contained in this book is believed to be correct. However, with York being a constantly developing city, clearly some information can be rapidly superseded. We welcome any comments upon, and contributions to, the information contained in this book, to ensure that the second edition is even more accurate than the first. Please write to Blue Bridge, PO Box 609, York YO31 8WA.

ACKNOWLEDGEMENTS

We would like to thank the following for their help and support:

Jo Cameron-Symes, Paula Czaczkowska, Peter Day, Paul Doughty, Bryn Evans, Sister Gregory IBVM, Ewa Haren, Janet Hewison, Chris Houseman, Ray Kershaw, Anna Kesteven, Martin Lacy, Tony Lawton, Roger and Ileana McMeeking, Andrew McMeeking, Jeremy Muldowney, Richard Pollitt, Dr W.J.Sheils, Bob Sissons, Ulla Valentiner, Professor James Walvin, Kathryn Washington, Phyllis Woodward.

INTRODUCTION

The York Book is the first book of its kind, a concise history of York in an A-Z format that includes intriguing detail about all aspects of the city.

The idea of *The York Book* came about one day at Waterstone's bookshop in York, when Chris Summerville and I were asked, once again, for a short paperback history of the city. There were books available full of photographs but little history, books about Romans, Vikings, railways, guidebooks for tourists, but nothing which covered the entire history of York in an accessible format. We were being asked for a particular book which we decided to write ourselves. Our aim was to create an amalgam of an encyclopaedia and a guidebook that would be suitable for visitors and residents alike. Above all, the visitor should appreciate the breadth of York's history and the resident should have a deeper understanding of the city.

We have endeavoured to make sense of York by cross-referencing all the entries, making everything lead to something else of interest. The links to other entries are in capital letters. If a person's full name is in capital letters (such as JOSEPH SEEBOHM ROWNTREE or THOMAS FAIRFAX) it is because there is more than one person with the same surname included in the book. Information about them is therefore included under their surname. A few entries are italicised, signifying that they do not refer particularly to York but should be explained because of their historical relevance. We have included few buildings or places that no longer exist, except when relevant to the modern city.

All six contributors to this book have read countless books about York. Consequently there are too many references to mention. However, we would like to thank in particular the Borthwick Institute, the Reference Library, the Minster Library and the City Archives, as they have all been invaluable sources of information.

Antonia Evans
York 2002

THE CITY OF YORK

York was founded by the **Romans** in AD71 and named Eboracum. It was the capital of the north of Britannia. The Roman occupation lasted until cAD410, when the island was formally abandoned. **Anglo-Saxons** from Germany then began to settle in York, calling it Eoforwic. Little of the city's history is recorded between the Roman withdrawal and AD627, the period known as the Dark Ages.

In AD866 the city was captured by Scandinavian **Vikings**, who renamed it Jorvik. Following the death of the last Viking king of Jorvik in AD954, York was governed by Anglo-Scandinavian earls. The city was then captured by William the Conqueror from Normandy, northern France, following his victory at Hastings in 1066.

Norman rule lasted until 1154, when a new dynasty, the **Plantagenets**, ruled the country. It is during this period (1154-1485), known as the Middle Ages, that the city was at the peak of its importance. York was the second city of the realm and second only to London in terms of population.

During the **Tudor** period (1485-1603), the city's political importance began to decline. However, during **Stuart** rule (1603-1714) this underwent a brief revival, York being the headquarters of King Charles I during the English Civil War.

With industrialisation largely passing the city by, York became primarily a social centre during the **Georgian/Hanoverian** period (1714-1837), before the emergence of tourism and the railway industry in **Victorian** times (1837-1901). In the twentieth century York gained a university and a reputation for excellence in biotechnology.

YORK

Periods of History

ROMAN
AD71 - c410

DARK AGES
cAD410 - c627

ANGLO-SAXON
cAD400 - 1066

VIKING
cAD866 - 954

NORMAN
1066 - 1154

MEDIEVAL
1154 - 1485

TUDOR
1485 - 1603

STUART
1603 - 1714

GEORGIAN/HANOVERIAN
1714 - 1837

VICTORIAN
1837 - 1901

EDWARDIAN
1901 - 1910

WINDSOR
1910/1917 -

YORK

<u>Principal Historical Attractions</u>
(York telephone code 01904)

YORK MINSTER (Tel. 557216)
Largest gothic cathedral in Northern Europe,
built 1220-1472

CITY WALLS
Two-and-three-quarter miles of medieval wall,
built 1240s-1340s

CASTLE MUSEUM Eye of York (Tel. 653611)
Social history museum with famous Victorian street

JORVIK CENTRE Coppergate (Tel. 643211)
Reconstruction of ninth/tenth-century Viking York

NATIONAL RAILWAY MUSEUM Leeman Road
(Tel. 621261)
World's largest railway museum

YORKSHIRE MUSEUM Museum Gardens
(Tel. 551800)
Archaeological finds and special exhibitions

Other Attractions & Information

ALL SAINTS CHURCH North Street
Exceptional medieval church

THE ARC St Saviourgate (Tel. 654324)
"Hands on" display of archaeological discoveries

ASSEMBLY ROOMS Blake Street (Tel. 637254)
Impressive eighteenth-century building

BAR CONVENT MUSEUM Blossom Street
(Tel. 643238)
Seventeenth-century convent

BARLEY HALL Coffee Yard, off Stonegate
(Tel. 610275)
Superb example of fifteenth-century townhouse

BEDERN HALL Bedern (Tel. 646030)*
Fourteenth-century guildhall

BLACK SWAN INN Peasholme Green (Tel. 686911)
Fourteenth-century building with General Wolfe
connection

BOOTHAM BAR High Petergate
One of York's four main medieval gateways

BRASS RUBBING CENTRE Skeldergate (Tel. 630456)
A chance to sample a unique English craft

BUS TOURS (Tel. 692505 & 640896)
Departing from Exhibition Square every fifteen minutes

CITY ART GALLERY Exhibition Square (Tel. 551861)
Varied exhibitions plus early Italian to modern paintings

CLIFFORD'S TOWER off Clifford Street (Tel. 646940)
Surviving thirteenth-century keep of York Castle

DICK TURPIN'S GRAVE St George's Churchyard,
off George Street, near Fishergate Bar

FAIRFAX HOUSE Castlegate (Tel. 655543)
Fine example of elegant Georgian residence,
dating from 1750

GUILDHALL St Helen's Square (Tel. 613161)
Fifteenth-century hall, rebuilt following World
War Two bombing

HOLY TRINITY CHURCH Goodramgate
Spectacular medieval church with surviving box pews

HOSPITIUM Museum Gardens (Tel. 629745)
Former guesthouse of St Mary's Abbey

KING'S MANOR Exhibition Square (Tel. 433996)
Headquarters of Henry VIII's Council of the North

MANSION HOUSE, St Helen's Square (Tel. 613161)*
Eighteenth-century building, residence of the
Lord Mayor

MERCHANT ADVENTURER'S HALL Piccadilly
(Tel. 654818)
Finest surviving medieval guildhall in Europe

MERCHANT TAYLORS' HALL Aldwark (Tel. 624889)*
Late fourteenth-century guildhall

MICKLEGATE BAR MUSEUM Micklegate
(Tel. 634436)
Medieval gatehouse, a civil and social insight
into York's history

MONK BAR Goodramgate (Tel. 634191)
Medieval gatehouse currently housing the
Richard III Museum

MULTANGULAR TOWER Museum Gardens
Surviving tower from Roman period

REGIMENTAL MUSEUM Tower Street (Tel. 662790)
Over 300 years of military history

RICHARD III MUSEUM Monk Bar, Goodramgate
(Tel. 634191)
Reassessment of the much-maligned king

RIVER TRIPS (Tel. 628324)
Departing from King's Staith and Lendal Bridge
Landing

ROMAN BATH PUB St Sampson's Square
(Tel. 620455)
Pub with remains of a Roman bathhouse in
its basement

ST MARGARET'S CHURCH Walmgate (Tel. 658338)
Home of National Centre for Early Music

ST WILLIAM'S COLLEGE College Street
(Tel. 557233)
Striking fifteenth-century timbered building, formerly
housing chantry priests

SHAMBLES
Located between King's Square and Pavement.
York's most famous street

STONEGATE
Joining St Helen's Square to Minster Gates. Famous
and attractive York Street

THEATRE ROYAL St Leonard's Place (Tel. 623568)
Year-round programme of events and productions

TOWN CRIER (Tel. 634998)
York's current town crier is self-employed and
available for hire

TREASURER'S HOUSE Minster Close (Tel. 624247)
Seventeenth-century building with strong Roman
and medieval links

WALKING TOURS (Tel. Tourist Information 621756)
Free walking tours at 10.15am, 2.15pm and 6.45pm
(summer) from Exhibition Square

WALMGATE BAR Walmgate (Tel. 638777)
The only one of York's four main medieval gateways
to retain its barbican

YORK DUNGEON Clifford Street (Tel. 632599)
Infamous museum of horror

YORK MODEL RAILWAY Tearoom Square York
Railway Station (Tel. 630169)
With landscape scenes and running trains

YORK RAILWAY STATION Station Road
(Tel. 08547 484950 for enquiries)
Opened in 1877, once the largest railway station in
the world

* denotes either no or restricted public access

A

AARON OF YORK (c1180-1268) Leading member of the JEWS of York following the MASSACRE OF THE JEWS in CLIFFORD'S TOWER in 1190. Perhaps surprisingly, a Jewish community remained in the city until 1290. By 1219 Aaron and his father-in-law Leo Episcopus were named among the twelve wealthiest Jews of the kingdom. In 1236, the most prosperous time for the York Jews, Aaron was appointed Archpresbyter of All the Jews of England. He lent substantial amounts of money to HENRY III which the king did not repay. Furthermore Henry imposed such heavy taxes upon Aaron, that, unable to pay them, he was imprisoned in York CASTLE. Thus his great wealth was eroded.

ACKHORNE Pub in St Martin's Lane. The pub is tucked down a narrow alley off MICKLEGATE, next to ST MARTIN-CUM-GREGORY CHURCH. It has been an inn since 1783, originally known as the "Ackhorne" although it was called the "Acorn" for many years. The names are interchangeable, "ackhorne" being the eighteenth-century spelling. The pub reverted to the previous version of its name following major refurbishments in the 1990s.

ACOMB Suburb two miles (3.2km) to the west of York, once a village which became part of the city in 1937. Acomb means "place of the oak trees" in Old English, spelt variously as Achum and Acum in the DOMESDAY BOOK. The whole district was woodland until the late twelfth century, when a farming village was established. In the seventeenth century York Races were held on

Acomb Moor, visited by CHARLES I on his first visit to York in 1633. A Methodist Society was formed by Wesleyan preacher John Nelson at Acomb in 1743, and it became the centre of York Methodism. The main arterial road is Front Street running out of the city, with residential areas to the north and south. St Stephen's church, in York Road, Acomb, contains glass by Henry GYLES dating from 1663.

ACRE *Unit of measurement used in the UK and certain other English-speaking countries. An acre is the equivalent of 4840 square yards (4047 square metres). As a rough guide, a football (soccer) pitch is around two acres.*

AINSTY District adjacent to York to the west, contained between the rivers OUSE, Wharfe and Nidd, with a western boundary across the land from the Nidd by the Ainsty Cross to the Wharfe, east of Wetherby. The city had considerable jurisdiction over this area, particularly in matters of defence.

ALBERT GEORGE (1895-1952) Thirteenth DUKE OF YORK 1920-36. Born on the anniversary of Queen VICTORIA's husband Albert's death (14 December), the future George VI was diplomatically christened after his great-grandfather. Victoria herself was asked to be godmother. Created Duke of York in 1920, he visited the city the same year, receiving its honorary FREEDOM. He bravely overcame his stammer to deliver his famous speech, in which he said "The history of York is the history of England". His 1923 marriage to Elizabeth Bowes-Lyon (the late Queen Elizabeth the Queen Mother) proved popular, his queen becoming the darling of the nation. The couple visited York in the summer of 1925, when Elizabeth unveiled the restored FIVE SISTERS WINDOW in York MINSTER. Albert unexpectedly, and reluctantly, became king following the 1936 abdication of his elder brother, Edward VIII. He chose to use his second name in order to maintain continuity. His decision, along with his queen, to remain in London during the Blitz of WORLD WAR TWO perhaps makes him one of York's bravest dukes.

ALCUIN (AD735-804) Distinguished York scholar. Alcuin was born to a noble family in York and he was sent to Archbishop EGBERT's school which may have later become ST PETER'S SCHOOL. He became a teacher, librarian, and eventually the head of the school in AD776. He described York as "High walled and towered / A merchant town of land and sea / A haven for ships from distant parts / Watered by the fish rich Ouse / A lovely dwelling place". A brilliant scholar, he became Master of the palace school in Aachen (Germany) at the request of Charlemagne (d.814), King of the Franks and Holy Roman Emperor. Alcuin lived in Aachen from 782-90 and 793-6, retiring to become Abbot at Tours in France, where he died. Alcuin and Charlemagne worked towards the creation of a Christian kingdom throughout Europe. The period from 732-780 was known as the ANGLO-SAXON "Golden Age" of learning in York. A college at the UNIVERSITY OF YORK is named after Alcuin.

ALDERMAN *Elder or senior member of a local council, elected by other councillors.*

ALDWARK Street running from GOODRAMGATE to PEASHOLME GREEN, on the line of the ROMAN wall surrounding their PRINCIPIA. A small section of this Roman wall is visible from the city WALLS. The street's name comes from the Old English "old werk", meaning fortification. It is the location of the MERCHANT TAYLORS' HALL (c1400). York's first permanent Methodist Chapel, the Peasholme Green Chapel was based at 60 Aldwark, around the corner from Peasholme Green. In April 1759 John WESLEY preached in "the shell of the new house", which opened as a chapel later that year. However, with the completion of the New Street Chapel in 1805, the Peasholme Green Chapel became redundant and was sold in 1806. By 1829 it was referred to simply as 60 Aldwark and was for a time the lodging of the infamous MINSTER arsonist Jonathan MARTIN. The street was the home of Hunt's Brewery which closed in the 1950s, the demise of which left the city without a brewery until the opening of the YORK BREWERY in 1996. From 1885 until its closure in 1975 there was a synagogue in Aldwark. In 1968 ESHER's report led to new housing being built in Aldwark and the surrounding streets, in order to revitalise the city centre.

ALEXANDER, WILLIAM (1768-1841) QUAKER printer, publisher and bookseller whose business was taken over by William Sessions in 1865. Alexander married Ann Tuke, daughter of WILLIAM TUKE, in 1796. He traded in corn in Suffolk and when his business failed in 1808, he and his wife moved to York to run what eventually became the MOUNT SCHOOL. In 1812, with the assistance of the Tukes, Alexander set up a bookshop in CASTLE-

GATE, and began to publish Quaker works in 1819. He rejected *Ivanhoe* when he was offered the book by Sir Walter SCOTT, saying it was "too worldly".

ALL SAINTS CHAPEL in the Minster Small military chapel in the East End of the MINSTER, to the south of the LADY CHAPEL. In 1923 it was dedicated to the Duke of Wellington's Regiment and is reserved for private services. The chapel contains the recent addition of the RICHARD III window, depicting his coat of arms, installed by the Society of FRIENDS OF RICHARD III in 1997.

ALL SAINTS CHURCH, NORTH STREET One of York's finest medieval churches, with a mid-fifteenth-century tower, across the OUSE from the GUILDHALL. The original church was built in the late eleventh century. The North Chapel was built c1325 and the South Chapel c1340. The church contains some of the best medieval STAINED GLASS in York, including a fourteenth-century window curiously depicting a man wearing spectacles. Major restoration took place in 1866. In 1897 the column bases of a possible Roman temple were discovered. There are three small timber-framed houses alongside the church dating from c1410. There has been considerable restoration of the glass, notably the "Pricke of Conscience" window, depicting the onset of the end of the world.

ALL SAINTS CHURCH, PAVEMENT Medieval church located at the junction of COPPERGATE and PAVEMENT. It is perhaps best known for its octagonal lantern tower, built c1400. For many years a large lantern was placed in the tower and lit at night to guide travellers through the dense FOREST OF GALTRES to the north of the city. In 1782 the original chancel, the location of the altar, was demolished in order to widen Pavement for the market. There is a pulpit dating from c1634, from which John WESLEY preached. All Saints is the GUILD Church of the city and is mentioned in the DOMESDAY BOOK. It has a thirteenth-century door knocker depicting a sinner being eaten by a lion. A fugitive holding the door knocker could claim sanctuary from people pursuing him until he came out of the church.

ALMSHOUSES Public institutions designed as shelters for the poor. York, given its comparatively large population, had several from the sixteenth to the nineteenth centuries. Former almshouses in the city include INGRAM'S ALMSHOUSES in BOOTHAM and LADY HEWLEY'S ALMSHOUSES in ST SAVIOURGATE.

ALTAR in the Minster The NAVE altar is used for occasional services, but the one used most frequently is the HIGH ALTAR in the CHOIR.

ANDREW, DUKE OF YORK (1960-) Second son of Queen ELIZABETH II who became the fourteenth DUKE OF YORK in 1986. York gained both a Duke and a Duchess on 23 July 1986, as Prince Andrew was created Duke of York in the morning and married Sarah Ferguson in the afternoon. During the Falklands War in 1982, Andrew flew a helicopter on active service with the Royal Navy. In 1987 he became the fifth successive Duke to receive the FREEDOM OF THE CITY and his wife became the first Duchess to receive similar rights. The couple divorced in 1996, though the Duchess retains her title.

ANDREWS, GEORGE TOWNSEND (1804-55) Victorian architect responsible for many buildings in York, including the second RAILWAY STATION in 1841, ST LEONARD'S PLACE in 1844, the Station Hotel and renovations to the BAR CONVENT.

ANGLIAN TOWER Small stone tower located close to the MULTANGULAR TOWER, behind the LIBRARY and accessible from the MUSEUM GARDENS. It was originally thought to have been built by the ANGLO-SAXONS, though given the rarity of stone buildings from this period it is now believed more likely to be ROMAN. The layers of York's defences, showing the appropriate ground levels over the centuries, are displayed in the ramparts alongside the city WALLS. The tower was buried cAD900 and rediscovered in 1839 by workmen. It was restored to its present condition in 1969-71. Archaeologist Jeffrey Radley died in an accident on site in July 1970.

ANGLO-SAXONS Name commonly used since the eighteenth century for the related groups from North Germany (Angles, Saxons, Jutes, Frisians and others) who invaded ROMAN Britain from the third century onwards. They settled in what is now England from the fourth century onwards, effectively conquering it by cAD650. They formed seven kingdoms, East Anglia, Kent, Essex, Sussex, Wessex, Mercia, and NORTHUMBRIA, of which York was the capital. Several kings including EDWIN of

Northumbria and ATHELSTAN periodically claimed rule over the whole Anglo-Saxon people. Northumbria was under VIKING rule from AD866 to 954. A full-scale Scandinavian invasion of 1015 saw CANUTE of Denmark recognised as king of England. In 1043 Saxon rule was restored under Edward the Confessor. Saxon Earl Harold GODWINSON became the real power in the land until the NORMAN Conquest of 1066. Despite the Anglo-Saxon period being referred to as the "Dark Ages", great scholars such as BEDE and ALCUIN flourished.

ARAM, EUGENE (executed 1759) Yorkshire schoolmaster who was condemned on circumstantial evidence and hanged at TYBURN in 1759, for the murder of his friend Clarke fourteen years earlier. Despite defending himself skilfully in court, he was found guilty, and later confessed his crime while imprisoned at York CASTLE. His case became the subject of Edward Bulwer-Lytton's bestselling novel *Eugene Aram* (1832).

ARC Archaeological Resource Centre in ST SAVIOUR-GATE, located in ST SAVIOUR'S church. Set up by the YORK ARCHAEOLOGICAL TRUST in 1990, the ARC allows visitors to see a working archaeological unit and lets them handle and sort archaeological finds.

ARCHBISHOP OF YORK Along with Canterbury, York, probably due to its importance under the ROMANS, was one of the two Archbishoprics to be established in England by the Pope in AD735. EGBERT was the first Archbishop. Other famous Archbishops include William Fitzherbert (ST WILLIAM), Walter DE GRAY, Thomas

Wolsey (Archbishop 1514-31) and RICHARD SCROPE. The original ARCHBISHOP'S PALACE was thought to be located in BISHOPHILL. From c1230 the palace was situated in DEAN'S PARK and from c1250 the Archbishop's country residence was BISHOPTHORPE PALACE. Following the DISSOLUTION OF THE MONASTERIES, the palace at Bishopthorpe became the chief residence. Seven Archbishops of York, most recently Donald Coggan (Archbishop 1961-74) have subsequently become Archbishops of Canterbury. The Archbishop's signature is his Christian name followed by Ebor, from EBORACUM.

ARCHBISHOP HOLGATE'S SCHOOL Comprehensive school, a grammar school until 1985, located in Hull Road one mile (1.6km) east of York's city centre. The school was founded by ARCHBISHOP OF YORK Robert HOLGATE in 1546, based initially in MINSTER CLOSE before moving to a site in OGLEFORTH in 1547. The original Ogleforth building was rebuilt in 1667. The school continued on this site until it amalgamated with the Yeoman School in 1858 and transferred to LORD MAYOR'S WALK. The Ogleforth building became a public bathhouse and a private dwelling before being demolished in 1929. The school occupied part of the current premises of YORK ST JOHN COLLEGE in Lord Mayor's Walk from 1858 to 1963, before moving to Hull Road. Perhaps the best-known old boy is Labour MP Frank DOBSON.

ARCHBISHOP'S PALACE *See* BISHOPTHORPE PALACE

ART GALLERY York's main public gallery in EXHIBITION SQUARE, built by Edward Taylor for the Yorkshire Fine Art and Industrial Exhibition of 1879. The site chosen for the present Art Gallery was in the grounds of ST MARY'S ABBEY. In 1892 the gallery, together with an important bequest of over a hundred British paintings from John Burton, was sold to the CITY OF YORK COUNCIL and became the City Art Gallery. In 1931 Dr W.A.Evelyn's vast collection of prints, drawings and watercolours depicting York was bought by public subscription. The gallery was supported by DEAN Eric Milner-White who donated paintings and studio pottery, and F.D.Lycett Green donated over a hundred European paintings in 1955. There are works in the gallery by Bellotto, ETTY, Courbet, Fantin-Latour, Gore, LOWRY, MOORE and Turner, and glass panels by William PECKITT. The monument to William Etty outside the gallery is by George Walker Milburn and dates from 1911. The gallery was rebuilt between 1948 and 1952 after sustaining war damage. Twenty paintings with a value of approximately £700,000 were stolen in an armed robbery in January 1999. These included an 1820s watercolour of Rievaulx Abbey by Turner, valued at £450,000. Four months later all the paintings, largely undamaged, were recovered in Rotherham, South Yorkshire, and those responsible subsequently imprisoned.

ARTHUR (cAD500-c537) Legendary king of Wessex who is said to have kept the first Christmas (Mass of Christ) in Britain in York. He reputedly stayed afterwards to complete the rebuilding of damaged churches.

ASKE, ROBERT (executed 1537) Landowner and leader of the PILGRIMAGE OF GRACE in opposition to HENRY VIII's REFORMATION. Robert Aske was a lawyer who practised in London and Yorkshire and organised an efficient army. The rebels gathered in York then marched to Pontefract in West Yorkshire where Lord Thomas Darcy guarded the Castle with only about 300 men. He surrendered to Aske as he was outnumbered, and he too became a Pilgrim. In 1537 Aske was tricked into capture by Henry VIII and hung in chains from CLIFFORD'S TOWER. It took him a week to die, his body being left there for a year as an example to other "traitors".

ASKERN, THOMAS (1816-78) York's last hangman, who like William "Mutton" CURRY was himself a convicted criminal, being a debtor. He is said to have been the last hangman to hold a provincial post in Britain.

ASKHAM BRYAN COLLEGE Agricultural and horticultural college located at Askham Bryan, four miles (6.4km) west of York. The college was founded in 1948 and has 3200 students. It has recently begun to offer a wider range of courses.

ASSEMBLY ROOMS Georgian building on BLAKE STREET, designed by Lord BURLINGTON. It was built between 1730 and 1735 as a meeting place for the local gentry, and based on the Italian architect Palladio's Egyptian hall. Assemblies were a form of winter entertainment in the seventeenth and eighteenth centuries, usually consisting of card games and dancing. Eventually they came to be associated with York Races. Assemblies became less popular after 1750 and over the next 200 years the Assembly Rooms were only occasionally used for dancing and concerts, until they were restored in 1951. The building is currently a restaurant.

ASSIZE COURTS Now York Crown Court on the EYE OF YORK, alongside the CASTLE MUSEUM. The building was designed by John CARR, taking four years to build and opening in 1777. Courts of Assize were visiting sessions of the High Court of London, held regularly in the counties to try the most serious crimes. Before travelling to York's courts, the judges would visit the Mayoress who presented them with a collection of herbs meant to ward off the foul smells of festering prisoners. On arrival at court the judges were announced by two trumpeters. The Judges of Assize sat here until 1971 when Assize Courts were abolished. Until 1806 the judges would stay at JUDGES' COURT and thereafter at the JUDGES' LODGINGS. There are public galleries to enable people to attend trials at the Crown Court.

ASSIZE OF ALE Event dating from the thirteenth century which takes place in York every August. HENRY III mandated the SHERIFF of York to check the beer sold in each of the city's taverns annually, as many publicans were fond of weakening the ale to maximise profits. The GUILD of Scriveners, or copyists and drafters of legal documents, who have existed since at least 1487, generally organise the Assize. The day now consists of a colourful pub crawl for charity.

ASTRONOMICAL CLOCK in the Minster Distinctive clock in the NORTH TRANSEPT of the MINSTER, created by craftsmen of the Royal Greenwich Observatory in London. There is a gold cross above the clock in the form of a blazing sun. The clock is a memorial to the 18,000 airmen who lost their lives flying from north-eastern bases during WORLD WAR TWO. It was dedicated in the presence of the Duke of Edinburgh in 1955.

ATHELSTAN (AD895-939) Grandson of Alfred the Great and the first ANGLO-SAXON king of all England. Legend has Alfred placing the regalia of kingship on Athelstan as a child. In 925 Athelstan became king of Wessex and Mercia in the southern half of England, and began extending his rule over the rest of the country. Athelstan seized York in 927 from the rebellious supporters of the late Danish king Sihtric ("the squint-eyed"), his brother-in-law. He had first gained York by marrying his sister to Sihtric in 926, with the agreement that Sihtric would adopt Christianity. In reality Athelstan spent little time in York, but may have visited during his climactic campaign against his enemies in 937. That year he defeated the combined forces of the Irish Vikings and the SCOTS at the battle of Brunanburh, a site never satisfactorily identified in northern England.

ATKINSON, KATE (1951-) York-born novelist and former pupil of the (now closed) Queen Anne Grammar School off BOOTHAM. Her debut novel *Behind the Scenes at the Museum*, set in York, won the Whitbread Prize in 1995.

ATKINSON, THOMAS (1729-1798) Architect and rival of John CARR, with whom he dominated architecture in York in the eighteenth and early nineteenth centuries. Atkinson's best work is the Chapel of the BAR CONVENT (1765-69) and its façade (1787-89). He rebuilt BISHOPTHORPE PALACE in 1763 with stone thought to have come from Cawood Castle, ten miles (16km) from York.

ATKINSONS Prolific York architects of the eighteenth and nineteenth centuries. Peter Atkinson Senior (1735-1805) took over John CARR's practice and in 1801 it became Peter Atkinson & Son, with Peter Atkinson Junior (c1776-1843). They built The RETREAT hospital in 1796. FOSS BRIDGE (1811) and OUSE BRIDGE (1820) were built by Peter Atkinson Junior. In turn Peter Atkinson Junior's sons William Atkinson (c1810-1886) and John Bownas Atkinson (1807-1874) joined the firm, which became J.B. & W. Atkinson. The firm was responsible for the present Waterstone's bookshop (formerly a bank, built in 1839) on the corner of Nessgate and High Ousegate, the GRANGE (a former Workhouse) in Huntington Road (1848-49), the COUNTY HOSPITAL in MONKGATE (1849-51), the chapel of ST PETER'S SCHOOL (1861-62), the DEAN COURT HOTEL (1865) and the ELM BANK HOTEL (1870). The firm carried out restoration work all over the city. J.B. & W. Atkinson were joined by Walter BRIERLEY in 1885. The practice is now Brierley Groom & Associates, based in LENDAL. An archive of the firm's plans and documents is in the BORTHWICK INSTITUTE.

AUDEN, W. H. (1907-1973) Poet and playwright Wystan Hugh Auden was born on 21 February 1907 at 54 BOOTHAM. His father was a doctor in York and they moved to Solihull, West Midlands, when Auden was a child. Auden later lived in Berlin before WORLD WAR TWO and in the USA for many years, but he spent his last years in Oxford as Professor of Poetry (1956-61). Perhaps his best-known lines feature in the 1994 film *Four Weddings and a Funeral*: "He was my North, my South, my East, my West / My working week and my Sunday rest / My noon, my midnight, my talk, my song / I thought that love would last forever: I was wrong" (Number IX of *Twelve Songs*) He was a powerful influence on twentieth-century literature and in the 1930s he led an influential left-wing group which included the writers Louis MacNeice, Stephen Spender and Cecil Day-Lewis.

B

BAEDEKER BLITZ Most destructive of eleven German bombing raids on York in WORLD WAR TWO. York was perceived to be a legitimate target, with all troop movements north and south passing through the RAILWAY STATION. During the night of 28/29 April 1942 twenty aircraft attacked York in one of the raids on historic British cities. In response to a British raid on Lübeck, Hitler allegedly ordered the destruction of English cities appearing in the *Baedeker* tourist guidebook. (The publishing company of Karl Baedeker, established in the nineteenth-century, produced guidebooks covering most of Europe.) York's Railway Station was hit, with damage to the roof and the destruction of an empty troop train. The GUILD-HALL was burnt out and the church of ST MARTIN-LE-GRAND ruined. The BAR CONVENT was hit and five nuns killed. POPPLETON ROAD SCHOOL suffered a direct hit. Over seventy people died and some 200 were injured. Over 9000 properties were listed as suffering damage greater than broken glass. In the aftermath of the raid 3000 people attended a memorial service at the MINSTER. One German plane was shot down by a French pilot, Yves Mahé, who was rewarded with the *Croix de Guerre* and a reception at the MANSION HOUSE.

BAILE HILL Site of one of the two CASTLES built in York by WILLIAM THE CONQUEROR in 1068-9, the other castle being what is now CLIFFORD'S TOWER. Situated at the end of SKELDERGATE possibly on earlier VIKING fortifications, this wooded hill was the site of a NORMAN wooden motte-and-bailey castle. Its military role was short-lived and by the start of the thirteenth century it was owned by the ARCHBISHOP OF YORK who used it as a PRISON. During the SIEGE OF YORK it was used as a gun emplacement, and from 1807 until the 1880s it was the location of one of the city prisons. Apart from London, York is the only place to have two castles built by William the Conqueror.

BAKER, JOHN (1942-) Crime writer whose novels include *Poet in the Gutter* and other books set in York. He was born in Hull, East Yorkshire, but has lived in York for over twenty years.

BAR CONVENT Convent and school in BLOSSOM STREET, founded on this site by followers of Mary WARD in 1686. During an anti-Catholic riot in 1696, the convent was allegedly saved by an apparition of St Michael. The school opened in 1699. Thomas ATKINSON rebuilt the house in 1765-69. A domed chapel built by Atkinson was hidden from the outside, containing a priest's hiding hole and eight doors to facilitate a quick exit. Joseph HANSOM was baptised in the chapel in 1803. After the French Revolution many French priests came to York, where they were given shelter by the Bar Convent. The clock on the front of the building was made by Henry Hindley and dates from 1790. The central courtyard of the Convent was covered by a glass roof by George Townsend ANDREWS, who also added the Poor School on the corner in 1844. During WORLD WAR ONE Belgian refugee children and wounded soldiers were cared for here. In 1942, during the BAEDEKER BLITZ, the Bar Convent suffered a direct hit, the east wing destroyed and five nuns killed. The school now forms part of All Saints School and part of the Convent is open to the public as a museum. The Convent is also a conference venue and pastoral centre, St Bede's.

BAR WALLS *See* WALLS, CITY

BARBICAN Protrusion of the defence of a gate or drawbridge. All of York's four main BARS, and possibly FISHERGATE BAR, originally had barbicans, effectively a long tunnel for additional defence. The theory was that, in the event of attack, the enemy would be trapped in the tunnel. All of York's barbicans were removed in the nineteenth century for traffic purposes, except for the one at WALMGATE BAR, which remains intact. The word is Arabic or Persian in origin.

BARBICAN CENTRE *See* PARAGON STREET

BARKER TOWER Medieval tower alongside LENDAL BRIDGE, part of the defences of the city WALLS. This conically roofed tower takes its name from the leather industry, a "barker" (or tanner) being one who prepares animal skins. TANNER ROW and TANNERS' MOAT are located nearby, and were at the centre of York's leather trade. In medieval times a chain was hung across the OUSE from this tower to LENDAL TOWER, theoretically to prevent ships entering or leaving York without paying their fees. In reality the chains were ineffective with a number of shipowners sailing blithely through the city without paying a penny in dues. Barker Tower is currently an artist's studio.

BARLEY HALL Restored medieval townhouse, located in COFFEE YARD off STONEGATE. Today the hall is open to the public, illustrating York life in the fifteenth century when William SNAWSELL, a friend of RICHARD III, owned the hall. Barley Hall is a typical fifteenth-century timber-framed house, and earlier buildings on its site were used as a monastic hospice. Over forty monasteries had halls in York, but Barley Hall is the only survivor. The monks began leasing the hall to private tenants in the fifteenth century. Restoration was carried out in the 1990s by the YORK ARCHAEOLOGICAL TRUST at vast expense, its new name coming from Professor Maurice Barley, the Trust's first Chairman. The main dining hall can be viewed from Coffee Yard through a giant window. An audio tour, featuring the voices of Judi DENCH and Robert Hardy, is included in the entrance fee.

BARRY, JOHN (1933 -) Oscar-winning composer born in York. John Barry Prendergast's father was Jack Xavier

Prendergast, who owned several CINEMAS and theatres in the city. The family lived at 167 Hull Road and later moved to FULFORD. John Barry attended the BAR CONVENT Junior School and from the age of eleven, ST PETER'S SCHOOL. He was at the Bar Convent the afternoon before the BAEDEKER RAIDS, in which five nuns were killed and the building was severely damaged. He became a jazz fan and joined the Modernaires dance band as a trumpet-player, often playing at the DE GREY ROOMS. He worked as a film projectionist and after National Service he formed a successful band, The John Barry Seven, but he always wanted to be a film composer. In 1962 the producers of the first James Bond film, *Dr No*, asked him to work on the music. Since then he has gone on to score several Bond films, including *Goldfinger*. His other scores include the Oscar-winners *Born Free*, *The Lion in Winter*, *Out of Africa* and *Dances with Wolves*. He has also produced several albums of instrumental music. He now lives in Long Island, USA. In 2002 he received the FREEDOM OF THE CITY of York.

BARS BOOTHAM BAR, MONK BAR, WALMGATE BAR and MICKLEGATE BAR are the four main medieval gateways into York through the city WALLS. There is also FISHERGATE BAR, dating from the early fifteenth century, and VICTORIA BAR, created in 1838. The word "bar" is effectively an abbreviation of "barrier". It was impractical to call them "gates", as over forty of York's streets are "gates", *gata* being the VIKING word for street. All four main Bars, and possibly Fishergate Bar, originally had a BARBICAN, yet only Walmgate Bar retains this outer defence. Micklegate Bar remains the entrance generally used by royalty on entering York, and until the eighteenth century it was the Bar most frequently used to display the HEADS of executed traitors.

BARTENDALE, JOHN (survived execution 1634) A musician who was hanged at TYBURN on the KNAVESMIRE on 27 March 1634 for felony. He apparently hung for three-quarters of an hour before being cut down and buried near the gallows. However, a traveller, apparently one of the VAVASOUR family, passing by shortly after, thought he saw the freshly dug earth move. With the help of a servant, he dug Bartendale up alive. The musician, surviving his amazing ordeal, was taken to York CASTLE but obtained a pardon, his sentence theoretically already having been carried out.

BAYEUX, THOMAS OF (d.1100) First NORMAN ARCHBISHOP OF YORK, responsible for the rebuilding of the MINSTER between 1080 and 1100. He was appointed by WILLIAM THE CONQUEROR in 1070, and was the instigator of the system of cathedral administration that still remains. He established a CHAPTER of CANONS with a DEAN at its head, appointed the first TREASURER and built the first TREASURER'S HOUSE. As well as his ecclesiastical work, he was known as an excellent musician and a writer of verse. The verses on the tomb of William the Conqueror, at St Stephen's Abbey at Caen, Normandy, were composed by him. Thomas was described as being "of noble presence, of great excellence in life and possessed of very unusual learning".

BEATLES Legendary Liverpool pop group who played four times in York in 1963 at the Rialto, currently a bingo hall, in FISHERGATE. The first three appearances were merely as a support act, but by their final appearance on 27 November, "She Loves You" was a number one hit and York fans queued all night for tickets.

BEDE (AD673-735) The Venerable Bede was one of the greatest ANGLO-SAXON scholars, and tutor to the first ARCHBISHOP OF YORK, EGBERT. Much of the information on York in this period is from Bede's great *Ecclesiastical History of the English People*, completed in 731. Bede rarely moved from his monastic cells at Jarrow and Monkwearmouth in the north-east of England, but he wrote a long letter to Egbert in 734 warning against being "surrounded by those given over to laughter, jokes, eating, drinking, and other suggestions of the soft life".

BEDERN Small area accessible from ALDWARK, GOODRAMGATE and St Andrewgate. Historian Francis DRAKE believed that the ROMAN PALACE was situated in this area. The name Bedern is derived from the ANGLO-SAXON for "house of prayer". Ealdred (d.1069), ARCHBISHOP OF YORK (1060-69) endowed a dormitory and refectory here for MINSTER priests and a chapel was consecrated in 1066. From 1248 Bedern was the home of the Vicars Choral, priests who led prayers. The only entrance was from Goodramgate, where the restored remains of the chapel still exist. The Vicars disbanded before the REFORMATION, and by the seventeenth century most of their buildings had been demolished. By Victorian times Bedern had become a notorious slum, many poor Irish immigrants living in tenements in terrible conditions. A report of 1852 notes that

300 people in Bedern had only five toilets. Ninety-eight families lived here, sixty-seven of whom occupied just one room each. The slums were cleared in the early twentieth century, but it was not until the 1970s after ESHER's report that the area was redeveloped. The restored Bedern Hall is situated here, used by the GUILDS of Freemen and Master Builders and the Company of Cordwainers. The building dates from the fourteenth century and was the refectory of the Vicars Choral. It was restored in 1984.

BELLS in the Minster The current bells are located in the WESTERN TOWERS of the MINSTER. BIG PETER is in the north-west tower and there are fourteen bells in the south-west tower. New bells were installed in 2000, dedicated to the late Queen Elizabeth, the Queen Mother.

BENEDICT (d.1189) Jewish moneylender who lived in CONEY STREET controlling many properties from c1180 to 1189. He was one of the most important JEWS OF YORK. After RICHARD I was crowned in London in 1189, the king went on a Crusade to the Holy Lands and in his absence countrywide religious fervour led to attacks on Jews. There were violent riots and Benedict was killed while in London. His house in York was looted and his widow murdered in riots, culminating in the MASSACRE OF THE JEWS in CLIFFORD'S TOWER.

BENINGBROUGH HALL Manor house seven miles (11.3km) north-west of York, built in 1716 for the Bourchier family, who also owned MICKLEGATE HOUSE. The original estate was once owned by ST LEONARD'S

HOSPITAL and passed into private ownership after the DISSOLUTION OF THE MONASTERIES in 1539. The hall has belonged to the National Trust since 1958 and is open to the public. During WORLD WAR TWO it was home to RAF bomber pilots from the nearby base at Linton-on-Ouse. Today the house contains a large collection of portraits on loan from the National Portrait Gallery in London.

BEST, MARY ELLEN (1809-1891) York-born painter, whose watercolours of the lost interiors of MICKLEGATE HOUSE are in the ART GALLERY.

BETTY'S TEA ROOMS World-famous tea rooms in ST HELEN'S SQUARE. A Swiss man, Frederick Belmont, established Betty's in Harrogate, North Yorkshire, in 1919. He had come to England from Switzerland in 1907. He arrived in Harrogate having accidentally caught the wrong train from London, but as Yorkshire reminded him of his native Alps he decided to stay. In the 1920s Betty's opened another branch in York, later adding Little Betty's in STONEGATE. The ocean liner *Queen Mary* inspired the décor of the St Helen's Square site after Belmont travelled on her in 1936. During WORLD WAR TWO Royal Air Force crews frequented "Betty's Bar" and inscribed their names on a mirror in the basement. Legend has it that flyers would sign in lipstick before a mission. Those who did not return would have their names erased. This story became a play, *Betty's Mirror*, later performed at the THEATRE ROYAL. Many theories exist as to who precisely Betty was, from the late Queen Mother to a young girl interrupting a meeting to decide the name. Among Betty's specialities is the "Fat Rascal" bun.

BIG PETER in the Minster Also known as Great Peter, the third heaviest bell in the country. The largest bell in the north-west tower of the MINSTER, weighing over ten and three-quarter tons. Big Peter, apparently the deepest-toned bell in Europe, can be heard each day at noon. The Minster is the Cathedral Church of ST PETER, hence the bell's name.

BILE BEANS The large and distinctive advertisement ("Nightly BILE BEANS keep you Healthy, Bright-Eyed and Slim"), located on LORD MAYOR'S WALK, originally dates from the mid-nineteenth century. Bile Beans were a popular laxative. Advertisements were often painted on end terraces, or alongside bridges to maximise their impact. This became more prevalent with the arrival of the RAILWAYS.

BISHOPHILL Part of the city that approximately covers the area of the ROMAN civil town or COLONIA. It lies within the city WALLS south-west of the OUSE, between MICKLEGATE and Bishopgate, to the north of SKELDERGATE. This area of York is thought to be the original site of the first ARCHBISHOP'S PALACE, later located in DEAN'S PARK then BISHOPTHORPE. The area near BAILE HILL once housed a PRISON. Nearby is the GOLDEN BALL pub and the church of ST MARY'S with its pre-NORMAN Conquest tower. VICTORIA BAR provides access through the city walls to Nunnery Lane. The remains of the QUAKER Burial Ground are in Cromwell Road. PRIORY STREET was created in 1854, leading to the redevelopment of the area.

BISHOPTHORPE PALACE Residence of the ARCH-BISHOP OF YORK, in Bishopthorpe, two miles (3.2km) from York alongside the river OUSE. In 1241 Archbishop Walter DE GRAY bought the village of Thorpe St Andrew, known as Bishopthorpe by 1316, and began building a country residence with a chapel which was completed c1250. Some of the medieval building survives. In 1617 JAMES I dined with Archbishop Toby Matthew at the Palace. The Great Hall dates from 1660-64, based on the original thirteenth-century room. The present façade and gatehouse date from the 1760s, designed by Thomas ATKINSON. Only occasionally open to the public, the palace is best viewed from one of the many RIVER TRIPS.

BITCHDAUGHTER TOWER Small round defensive tower in the city WALLS near BAILE HILL. It is mentioned in 1451 and 1566 when stones from the Tower were used to repair OUSE BRIDGE. The inner room with a fireplace dates from 1645 when a guardhouse and gun platform were built here. The origin of the name is unknown.

BLACK BESS One of the more disputable stories connected with York is that Dick TURPIN'S legendary horse, Black Bess, collapsed and expired at the CAVALRY BAR-RACKS in FULFORD Road.(In reality the barracks were not built until 1795.) A tree to the right of the entrance of what is now York's principal POLICE STATION is said to mark the spot. Black Bess is first mentioned in Harrison Ainsworth's 1834 novel *Rookwood* as Turpin's mare.

BLACK HORSE PASSAGE SNICKELWAY leading from STONEBOW towards HUNGATE. Bordered on one side by the ruined wall of a Carmelite priory, the passage provided Victorians with concealed access to Hungate's brothels.

BLACK SWAN Timber-framed pub in PEASHOLME GREEN. This building has had many uses and famous occupants since the fifteenth century. The pub is reputedly one of the most haunted in York, having allegedly been used as a witches' coven in the sixteenth century. Strange faces and skeletal images can be made out in the wooden panelling in the first floor room, perhaps painted by these Tudor witches. Before it became the Black Swan in the 1820s, it was home to the mother of General WOLFE, Henrietta Thompson. Wolfe himself may have visited as a child. Prior to this Sir Martin Bowes, Lord Mayor of London and Treasurer to Queen Elizabeth I, owned the house. There is said to be a secret tunnel linking the pub to ST CUTHBERT'S CHURCH.

BLAKE STREET Street linking DAVYGATE with ST LEONARD'S PLACE, the impressive ASSEMBLY ROOMS are situated here. The street's name originates from an Old Danish word *bleg*, meaning "bleaching". It is thought that Blake Street was used for the VIKING leather trade, bleaching being part of the process of curing skins. It could also be a corruption of *bleke,* meaning "white-paved" street, perhaps referring to an ancient road here.

BLOSSOM STREET Street linking MICKLEGATE BAR to The MOUNT, the location of the BAR CONVENT.

Blossom Street is a link to York's agricultural past, the name being a corruption of the medieval Ploxwaingate, meaning "the ploughman's street". In ROMAN times the street was just outside their civilian COLONIA and many Roman burials have been discovered in this area. Soon after the ODEON CINEMA, the street becomes The Mount.

BLUE BELL Pub in FOSSGATE, perhaps the smallest pub in York. The pub was in the hands of the Robinson family for most of the twentieth century, George Robinson taking over the licence in 1902. One of the first directors of YORK CITY Football CLUB, he held meetings in the Blue Bell which led to the club's formation in 1922. The origins of the pub are unclear, due to records of a much older Blue Bell on the same street in the eighteenth century. The present pub has probably been an inn since the 1780s. It had one of the last three men-only bars in York, the other two being at the FALCON pub in MICKLEGATE and at the BOOTHAM Tavern. They were all opened to women in the 1970s.

BLUE BRIDGE Small footbridge which can be raised, situated at the confluence of the OUSE and the FOSS rivers. The Blue Bridge connects ST GEORGE'S FIELD with the NEW WALK. The first wooden bridge was built in 1738 and was painted blue. The current bridge was built in 1929. Alongside the bridge were two large cannon captured from Sebastopol during the Crimean War in 1855, but they were removed and melted down during WORLD WAR TWO as part of the war effort.

BLUE COAT SCHOOL Residential school for poor boys, often orphans, which existed in York between 1705 and 1947. Its creation, and that of the GREY COAT SCHOOL for girls, which also opened in 1705, was seen as the most important innovation in education in the city. The Blue Coat School was based in ST ANTHONY'S HALL in PEASHOLME GREEN. The pupils wore blue, the name being taken from the long blue coats worn by the boys at Christ's Hospital School in London. The 1944 Education Act meant the school could not be categorised as a primary, secondary or boarding school, and it closed in 1947. The school sustained damage during bombing in both WORLD WAR ONE and WORLD WAR TWO, but there were no casualties.

BOER WAR MEMORIALS There are two WAR MEMORIALS to the Boer War in York. One is set in its own garden in DUNCOMBE PLACE near the MINSTER. It is dedicated to British Legion soldiers from the York area who died fighting the Boers (Afrikaners) in South Africa during the second phase of the Boer War (1899-1902). It was erected in 1905 by their fellow Yorkshiremen. There is also a granite memorial to the Green Howards Regiment located on the roundabout at the Tower Street end of SKELDERGATE BRIDGE. The names of three officers and 188 men of the regiment who lost their lives in the conflict are inscribed on the monument. The memorial was restored by the CITY OF YORK COUNCIL and rededicated in May 2000.

BOOTHAM Principal street from the north into York, running from CLIFTON to BOOTHAM BAR. Its name is derived from *buthum*, the Old Norse word for "at the booths", a booth referring to a stall at a twelfth-century market or fair. Bootham is the location of BOOTHAM PARK HOSPITAL and over the centuries has been involved in many historical events. Chief among these is the SIEGE OF YORK, when the Parliamentary forces mined ST MARY'S TOWER, breaching the Abbey WALLS, and entered an orchard in the grounds of the KING'S MANOR. The poet W.H.AUDEN was born at number 54 in 1907.

BOOTHAM BAR Gateway in the city WALLS between HIGH PETERGATE and BOOTHAM. It stands on the original site of the north-west entrance to the ROMAN PRINCIPIA, the Porta Principalis Dextra. The outer archway is NORMAN, dating from the eleventh century when the Bar was known as Galmanlith. The remainder of the gateway dates mainly from the fourteenth century. In 1501 a doorknocker was installed, as SCOTS were required to knock first to seek permission from the LORD MAYOR to enter the city. The Bar suffered damage during the SIEGE OF YORK in 1644. It was sometimes used to display the HEADS of traitors, with the heads of three rebels opposing CHARLES II's restoration being placed here in 1663. The structure narrowly avoided demolition in the 1830s. The BARBICAN was removed in 1831, and the two outer archways are Victorian. The three statues on the top of the Bar were carved in 1894, and represent a medieval mayor, flanked by a mason and a knight. The mason is holding a model of the newly restored Bar.

BOOTHAM PARK HOSPITAL Imposing building in BOOTHAM which houses the psychiatric hospital formerly known as Bootham Asylum. It was built by John

CARR in 1777 as the first purpose-built County Asylum. At the time Bedlam Hospital in London still exhibited "lunatics" to the public every Sunday and attracted 100,000 visitors annually.

BOOTHAM SCHOOL Independent QUAKER school in BOOTHAM, currently housed in a building designed by Peter ATKINSON Senior in 1804. In 1822 the original school opened in the home of its founder, William Simpson, in a building called "The Appendage" in Lawrence Street, near WALMGATE BAR. WILLIAM TUKE had proposed the founding of a Quaker school for boys in 1818 but died before its establishment. Diseases spreading from the nearby KING'S FISHPOOL forced the school to move to its present site in 1846. In 1899 much of the teaching area was destroyed in a fire caused by a pupil boiling snail shells. The blaze was noticed in the early morning, too late to save the building. The headmaster immediately resigned, and the school was forced to move to Scarborough until 1902. The pupil responsible became a farmer, and was blown up by his own dynamite whilst attempting to uproot a tree. The school is now co-educational with over 400 pupils in modern facilities attached to the original buildings. Joseph ROWNTREE was once a resident of 49 Bootham, now part of the school.

BORTHWICK INSTITUTE Located in St Anthony's Hall in PEASHOLME GREEN, the Borthwick Institute of Historical Research is now part of the UNIVERSITY OF YORK. Following the closure of the BLUE COAT SCHOOL in 1947, the hall was offered to YORK CIVIC

TRUST. Trustees of the estate of the recently deceased William Borthwick of Bridlington, East Yorkshire, decided the proposals were suitable to benefit under his will. The Borthwick Institute was thus officially opened in 1953 by Princess Alice (1897-1965), sister of GEORGE VI. It contains numerous archives, including church records, some dating back to the thirteenth century.

BOSSES in the Minster Decorative circular carvings of wood or stone which cover the intersections of the ceiling vaulting. They are generally gilded and painted. Noteworthy bosses in the MINSTER include the Ascension boss in the NAVE, showing the feet of Christ, and the centre boss in the CENTRAL TOWER, showing ST PETER and St Paul, carved 1470-72. Following the MINSTER FIRE in the SOUTH TRANSEPT in 1984, children's television programme *Blue Peter* ran a competition to design new bosses. Out of 34,000 entries six were chosen, two showing man landing on the moon in 1969.

BOWMAN, ALICE (c1565-unknown) Recusant Catholic at the time of Protestant Queen Elizabeth I, who was imprisoned in MONK BAR's "LITTLE EASE" cell in 1594. The Bar, which now houses the RICHARD III MUSEUM, claims the cell to be the world's smallest, measuring just 5 feet 3 inches (1.6 metres) in diameter. Alice Bowman's precise fate is unknown, the last record of her being when, along with her brother William and his wife Isobel, she was re-imprisoned in 1598. This may have been at Monk Bar, but was more likely to have been at the KIDCOTES on OUSE BRIDGE. A cross in the wall of the Little Ease prison cell may well have been carved by Alice Bowman.

BRASS RUBBING CENTRE *See* YORVIK BRASS RUB-
BING CENTRE

BRIERLEY, WALTER (1862-1926) Prolific architect who
lived and worked in York for most of his life. Among his
most important public buildings in York are HAXBY ROAD
SCHOOL, POPPLETON ROAD SCHOOL, FISHER-
GATE School, Park Grove School, SCARCROFT
SCHOOL and the city LIBRARY. He also built the
Principal's House at the KING'S MANOR, the PUREY-
CUST HOSPITAL, and various houses including
Bishopsbarns, in St George's Place off Tadcaster Road,
for himself. Brierley joined the firm of J.B. & W. ATKIN-
SON & Son in 1885 and took control in 1899. The firm
was founded by John CARR in around 1750. It is now
Brierley Groom & Associates, based in LENDAL. An
archive of the firm's plans and documents is in the
BORTHWICK INSTITUTE.

BRIGANTES (First century AD) Possibly the first settlers
in the York area during the Iron Age, though there is scant
archaeological evidence. If any tribe had a settlement in
the area, it was more likely to have been the Parisi of East
Yorkshire. The word *brigante* means hill- or upland-
dweller, appropriate for these peoples living across the
Pennine hills, to the north-west and west of York. When
the ROMANS first encountered the Brigantes their queen,
CARTIMANDUA, signed a treaty with them cAD45.
However, divisions arose among the Brigantes,
Cartimandua's husband VENUTIUS rebelling against her
and the Romans. The Romans sent the NINTH LEGION
north to enforce peace. They had always intended the

site to be a legionary fortress, and as part of this campaign to subdue the Brigantes the fort of EBORACUM, now York, was built between the OUSE and FOSS rivers. It is likely that both Cartimandua and Venutius were dead by AD71 and by AD250 most of the Brigantes' territory was Roman.

BRONTË SISTERS Literary sisters Anne, Charlotte, Emily and Ellen, perhaps best known for Charlotte's *Jane Eyre* and Emily's *Wuthering Heights*. The sisters were frequent visitors to York from their home in Haworth, West Yorkshire. Charlotte (1816-55) and Anne (1820-49) stayed at the George Inn, CONEY STREET in 1849. Anne Brontë was very ill at the time, and a trip to Scarborough meant a stop in York. Ellen Brontë later wrote: "After a rest at the George Hotel and partaking of dinner which she enjoyed, Anne went out. Her visit to the MINSTER was an overpowering pleasure not for its own imposing and impressive grandeur only, but because it brought to her susceptible nature a vital and overwhelming sense of omnipotence. Emotion stayed her speech and she was hastened to a less exciting scene." Anne died later that year.

BROWN COW Pub in Hope Street, off WALMGATE. Despite redevelopment in the 1930s, the pub kept its original character, continuing to serve the local community. The Brown Cow claims to have hosted a darts match which was broadcast live on the radio in 1939, when it had six dartboards.

BUBONIC PLAGUE *See* PLAGUE

BURGESS, FREDERICK GEORGE (1871-1951) York's first Labour MP, elected in 1929 with a majority of 3,300. In 1992, with a Conservative majority of just 147, York was the country's most marginal seat.

BURLINGTON, RICHARD BOYLE, THIRD EARL OF (1695-1753) London-born politician and architect of York's ASSEMBLY ROOMS. Burlington was an admirer of the Italian architect Andrea Palladio and through his influence made the Palladian style a dominant theme in English building.

BURTON STONE Located on the corner of BOOTHAM and Burton Stone Lane, this curious stone with three carved holes has a number of theories as to its origin and purpose. It is mentioned in the sixteenth century as a meeting place for troops leaving to fight the SCOTS, and may also have been used to mark York's boundary. Burton Stone Lane was one of the "Ridden" boundaries, those ceremonially ridden along by the LORD MAYOR to display the city's authority. The Victorians interpreted the stone as a PLAGUE STONE for the purpose of disinfecting. It seems more likely that the Burton Stone, already in use as a boundary marker with a post in the central hole, was adapted for use as a plague stone later. A similar stone exists on HOB MOOR where huts for PLAGUE victims had been erected.

BUTTER MARKET York became the centre of the lucrative trade in butter from the late seventeenth century until legislation in the mid-nineteenth century permitted cheap Irish imports. The Butter Market was located either in front of the church of ST MARTIN-CUM-GREGORY or behind it, between MICKLEGATE and Fetter Lane. In 1722 an Act of Parliament gave York the right to market Yorkshire's butter. By the end of the eighteenth century all butter sold in London came from York Butter Market.

C

CANON *One of several churchmen on the staff of a cathedral, whose duties include organising services and assisting the DEAN in administration.*

CANUTE (cAD995-1035) Also known as Cnut the Great, king of Norway, Denmark and later England (1016-35). The son of SWEYN FORKBEARD, his fleet landed at Sandwich, Kent, in 1015, subduing most of England and eventually York.

CAP OF MAINTENANCE Also known as the Swordbearer's Hat, worn by the person carrying the SWORD OF STATE in civic ceremonies in York. The Cap used at present dates from 1915 and may have been made from George V's Coronation robes. The Swordbearer may not remove the Cap during civic ceremonies, even in church. There is another Cap, made in 1580, which still exists and has been restored, though it is not in use. This Cap was made because Robert Crippling, then LORD MAYOR, had been imprisoned for unseemly behaviour. Thus the Cap, MACE and Sword of State all had to be replaced having lost their dignity by association with Crippling.

CAPITAL OF ENGLAND York effectively became the country's capital for seven years (1298-1304), during the Scottish Wars of Independence (1290s-1314). King EDWARD I saw York as a convenient base for his campaigns against the SCOTS, transferring both the Treasury and the Courts to the city. In 1392 King RICHARD II stayed in York for six months, bringing his government offices with him. King CHARLES I also established his court in York for six months in 1642, when the city was again regarded as the capital.

CARACALLA (AD186-217) ROMAN Emperor Marcus Aurelius Antoninus. On the death of his father SEPTIMUS SEVERUS in York in AD211, Caracalla and his younger brother Geta returned from EBORACUM (York) to Rome as co-Emperors. To secure sole power Caracalla murdered Geta (AD212) and put to death some 2000 of his supporters. He was later murdered himself.

CARR, JOHN (1723-1807) York architect, born in Horbury, Wakefield. "Carr of York", as he became known, was responsible for some of the finest Georgian architecture in the city and the county. Existing examples of his work in York include FAIRFAX HOUSE (1762), CASTLEGATE HOUSE (1762-3), BOOTHAM PARK HOSPITAL (1777) and the ASSIZE COURTS (1773-7). Having settled in York in 1749, he served as LORD MAYOR in 1770 and 1785. In 1754 he was commissioned by the city CORPORATION to design the new grandstand for York Races at the KNAVESMIRE. He reputedly had an excellent singing voice, and in 1789 at the Races he entertained the Prince of Wales and his brother, the

"GRAND OLD" DUKE OF YORK, with a rendition of "Hearts of Oak". Carr worked with Robert Adam on Harewood House, West Yorkshire, begun in 1759, and his largest work is the Crescent in Buxton, Derbyshire (1780-90). The attention and patronage his work brought him made him an extremely rich man, leaving around £150,000 on his death in 1807. Carr founded his firm in c1750 and his assistant was Peter ATKINSON, who eventually succeeded him. J.B. & W. Atkinson were succeeded in practice by Walter BRIERLEY in 1899, and is now Brierley Groom & Associates, based in LENDAL.

CARTIMANDUA (First century AD) Queen of the BRIG-ANTES, who occupied much of Northern England at the time of the ROMAN invasions of AD43. She is believed to have signed a treaty with the Romans cAD45 although her estranged husband VENUTIUS remained fervently anti-Roman. Hostilities between the two ensued, leading to Roman intervention. At "the cost of desperate fighting", according to Tacitus, the Queen was rescued from her husband's forces in AD69. The precise location of the rescue is unknown, though Venutius is known to have had a fort at Stanwick, near Richmond, North Yorkshire.

CASTLE All that now remains of York's medieval castle is CLIFFORD'S TOWER, its "keep" (a lookout tower and place of ultimate safe retreat). The city's first castle was built in this area in 1068 by WILLIAM THE CONQUEROR, who also built a fortress on BAILE HILL. The castle was surrounded by a moat by diverting the river FOSS. The design was the customary NORMAN "motte", an artificial mound supporting a tower, and "bailey", a courtyard surrounded by a wall. The bailey would contain the buildings necessary for the administration of the area. Following the MASSACRE OF THE JEWS in 1190, the keep was rebuilt in timber on the orders of RICHARD I. Rebuilding of the whole castle in stone was ordered by HENRY III in 1244, and took around twenty years. Henry III, EDWARD I, EDWARD II and EDWARD III all stayed at the castle, and a house was built in 1333 in the bailey for Edward III's wife Queen PHILIPPA. The principal entrance to the castle was opposite FISHERGATE POSTERN, where CASTLE MILLS BRIDGE now stands. Within the bailey the DEBTORS' PRISON, the ASSIZE COURTS and the FEMALE PRISON were built in the eighteenth century. The surrounding stone wall, apart from a section still visible behind the Debtors' Prison, was removed in 1935.

CASTLE GREEN *See* EYE OF YORK

CASTLE HOWARD The great palace of the Howard family, located eleven miles (17.7km) north-east of York. Its name is developed from its location on the site of the medieval Henderskelfe Castle (rebuilt in 1683 and burnt down 1693) and a long-standing association with the family. The present palace was built between 1700 and 1726 by Charles Howard, third Earl of Carlisle, with VANBRUGH and Hawksmoor as his architects. It remains the seat of the Earl of Carlisle. Along with other country houses such as MIDDLETHORPE HALL and Bramham, Castle Howard attracted the upper classes to settle and build houses around York in the eighteenth century, leading DEFOE to describe York on his travels as a "confluence of the gentry". The Granada television adaptation of Evelyn Waugh's *Brideshead Revisited* (1981) was filmed at Castle Howard. Money from the filming helped to restore the Garden Hall, which was previously damaged by a fire in 1940.

CASTLE MILLS BRIDGE Bridge over York's river FOSS joining Tower Street to FISHERGATE, constructed in 1956. It is so-named because mills had existed in the area since the eleventh century. There was no bridge over the river on this site until the sixteenth century, when there was a small wooden footbridge. This was replaced in 1733 by a wider wooden bridge for horse-drawn traffic and pedestrians, which was destroyed by floods in January 1746. A stone bridge thus replaced the earlier wooden one.

CASTLE MUSEUM England's most popular museum of everyday life, situated at the EYE OF YORK opposite CLIFFORD'S TOWER. Its collection centres upon objects acquired by Dr John KIRK, a Pickering physician. Observing a way of life that was fast disappearing, Kirk would often accept items, many of which were thought to be worthless, in lieu of payment. In 1938 the CITY OF YORK COUNCIL opened the Museum based on Kirk's collection, housed in the old FEMALE PRISON. The reconstructed Victorian street, KIRKGATE, remains a highlight. The former DEBTORS' PRISON (built 1701-5 by William Wakefield) became part of the Museum in 1952, and HALF MOON COURT became another acclaimed addition. Among the Museum's many other attractions are the CONDEMNED CELL in which Dick

TURPIN was reputedly held prior to his execution, plus military, costume and children's galleries. New exhibitions also open frequently.

CASTLEGATE Street linking COPPERGATE to Tower Street. Castlegate was the main route to York CASTLE from the city centre, used by the vast crowds attending public EXECUTIONS. It was a major thoroughfare prior to the building of CLIFFORD STREET in 1880-81. The narrow street is the location of FAIRFAX HOUSE, CASTLEGATE HOUSE, the IMPRESSIONS GALLERY and ST MARY'S CHURCH. The notorious WATER LANES were off Castlegate and led to the river OUSE.

CASTLEGATE HOUSE Impressive Georgian house built by John CARR in 1762-3 for Peter Johnson, a Judge at the ASSIZE COURTS. It is now used as offices.

CATHEDRA in the Minster Canopied throne of the ARCHBISHOP OF YORK, located on the south side of the CHOIR in the MINSTER. The word is Greek or Latin for a seat or throne, from which the term Cathedral is derived. York Minster is thus entitled to be called a Cathedral.

CATS *See* STONE CATS

CAVALRY BARRACKS York's cavalry barracks were built in 1795 and situated on FULFORD Road. They were originally designed to accommodate 260 men and about the same number of horses. On 2 February 1829 a troop of Seventh Dragoon Guards were called out from the barracks with their fire engine to help fight the fire at York MINSTER, caused by Jonathan MARTIN. Prince "Eddy", Duke of Clarence (1864-92), a Major in the Tenth Hussars and in recent years a Jack the Ripper suspect, was stationed here while serving with the Ninth Queen's Royal Lancers, and from 1887-91 with his own regiment. The horses, having been replaced by armoured cars, finally left in 1939. York POLICE STATION, now North Yorkshire HQ, occupies part of the site. Dick TURPIN'S mare BLACK BESS is alleged to have died here.

CAVE, HENRY (1779-1836) Artist and engraver born in York. His father was an engraver who taught him print-making. In 1810 Cave published his well-known series of etchings *Picturesque Buildings in York*. He did many drawings of York and Yorkshire and published views of the city as engravings and lithographs from 1810 to 1823. He also exhibited at the Royal Academy of Arts in London. Cave taught at the BLUECOAT SCHOOL in PEASHOLME GREEN and at other York schools.

CEMETERY York's main cemetery is situated on Cemetery Road towards FULFORD. It was opened in 1837 due to pressure on burial space. James Piggot Pritchett designed the chapel and the gatehouse as a copy of the Erechtheon in Athens next to the Acropolis. The cemetery was run as a successful private company until the expanding interest in cremation during the 1940s caused the cemetery to approach bankruptcy. In 1966 liquidators closed the company, abandoning 120,000 graves. In 1987 the York Cemetery Trust bought the site from the crown and reopened the cemetery. New grave plots are available but the Trust encourages families with relatives already buried in the cemetery to enquire about family vaults in order to save space.

CENTENARY CHAPEL Methodist chapel in ST SAVIOURGATE, built in 1840 to mark a hundred years of Methodism. It can accommodate a congregation of 1500 and is currently used for social as well as religious purposes.

CENTRAL TOWER of the Minster The present tower replaced an earlier central bell tower which collapsed in 1407. The tower is 197 feet (60m) high. There are 279 steps to the top. All the windows at the top of the tower stand at a height of 150 feet (46m) and contain fifteenth-century shields with variations of the crossed keys of ST PETER on different backgrounds. The tower was built by the royal architect William of Colchester, and the key structural BOSS at its centre is the largest in the MINSTER, with a diameter of five feet (1.5m), and depicts St Peter and St Paul. The ROMAN COLUMN, located outside the SOUTH TRANSEPT, was discovered when the tower was underpinned between 1967 and 1972. This work led to the creation of the UNDERCROFT, which is open to the public.

CERIALIS *See* QUINTUS PETILLIUS CERIALIS

CHAPELS in the Minster There are ten small chapels in the MINSTER, which are occasionally used for services. They are ALL SAINTS CHAPEL, ST CUTHBERT'S CHAPEL, the OUR FATHER CHAPEL, ST JOHN'S

CHAPEL, ST NICHOLAS CHAPEL, ST STEPHEN'S
CHAPEL, the LADY CHAPEL, ST GEORGE'S CHAPEL,
ST MICHAEL'S CHAPEL and the ZOUCHE CHAPEL.

CHAPTER of the Minster Governing body of the MIN-
STER, currently comprising the DEAN as Chairman and
thirty CANONS, including the TREASURER and the
PRECENTOR.

CHAPTER HOUSE in the Minster The Chapter House
is entered via the NORTH TRANSEPT. The octagonal
building was built between 1260 and 1286. This room is
the meeting place of the DEAN and CHAPTER (the
CANONS), the governing body of the MINSTER. Each
wall contains six seats theoretically preventing anyone
from sitting centrally, emphasising the equality of the
members. Acoustically it is difficult for one person to stand
at the centre and be heard. The roof is architecturally
unique in that it has no central column supporting its vaulting. There are detailed carvings of men, women and animals at the top of the side columns and it is believed that
the stone carvers simply depicted people they knew. The
Chapter House is now rarely used for Chapter meetings
but more often for exhibitions and concerts.

CHAPTER HOUSE STREET Narrow street linking
MINSTER Yard to OGLEFORTH. It was part of the
ROMAN Via Decumana, the principal route to the north-
east. The Roman road went through the original gateway
near MONK BAR to GROVES LANE, now a narrow passageway, and out towards Malton (17miles, 27.3km from
York), crossing the river FOSS.

CHARLES I (1600-1649) King of England 1625-49. Also seventh DUKE OF YORK (1605-16), he was one of the six dukes to eventually become king. Following his succession Charles was a frequent visitor to York, including a stay at the KING'S MANOR on his way to be crowned King of Scotland in 1633. He distributed the Royal Maundy, specially minted silver pence given to the poor on the Thursday before Easter, in York MINSTER in 1639. Difficult relations with Parliament in London resulted in Charles establishing his court in York for six months in 1642, with ST WILLIAM'S COLLEGE as his printing press for Royalist propaganda. Charles and his family resided at Sir Arthur Ingram's house in DEAN'S PARK. York's CORPORATION and its clergy were keen for Charles to find a negotiated settlement with Parliament, but this proved impossible, precipitating the ENGLISH CIVIL WAR and the SIEGE OF YORK. The COUNCIL OF THE NORTH placed Charles's coat of arms above the KING'S MANOR doorway in the 1620s.

CHARLES II (1630-1685) King of England 1660-85. The citizens of York, weary of the restrictions of CROMWELL's Puritanism, greeted the Restoration of the monarchy with great public enthusiasm. However Charles II, the "Merry Monarch", made no visit to the city, an indication of the decline of York's political importance.

CHARTER Document granting or confirming rights, properties and liberties claimed by citizens. Generally granted by the monarch, York's first Charter was granted by HENRY II and signed by Thomas Beckett, the

44

subsequently martyred Archbishop of Canterbury, in c1160. Further charters were granted by JOHN and RICHARD II.

CHOCOLATE Major feature of York's economy, with a strong QUAKER connection. It was a development which began in the first half of the nineteenth century, when there were over twenty local confectioners listed. The two main producers were initially Joseph TERRY Junior and Thomas CRAVEN, before HENRY ISAAC ROWNTREE acquired fellow Quaker SAMUEL TUKE's firm in 1862. By 1908 the manufacturers of cocoa and related products were the second largest employers after the RAILWAYS in York. NESTLE ROWNTREE and TERRY'S (now Kraft Foods) remain major employers in the city. The former is perhaps best known as the manufacturer of *KitKat*, *Smarties* and *Yorkie* bars, the latter for its *Chocolate Orange*.

CHOIR of the Minster Effectively a church within a church, enclosed by wooden screens, where services normally take place. It was built in the early fifteenth century. The choir stalls (seats) and vaulting are Victorian copies of the original medieval woodwork destroyed in the MINSTER FIRE of 1829. The singers, twelve professional singers and twenty choirboys and girls, sit in the stalls. The DEAN and CANONS have their own stalls below the ORGAN. The ARCHBISHOP's seat, the CATHEDRA, is on the south side. The carved BOSS at the top of the entrance arch is of the Assumption (ascension into Heaven) of the Virgin Mary and surprisingly survived the REFORMATION.

CHOIR SCREEN in the Minster The carved stone screen depicts all the kings of England from WILLIAM THE CONQUEROR to HENRY VI. It was built in the fifteenth century to strengthen the supports for the CENTRAL TOWER. The choir of angels above the statues was added in 1805.

CHOLERA There were two outbreaks of cholera (an infectious and often fatal disease caused by water-borne bacteria) in York, in 1832 and 1849. The 1832 epidemic was the more severe, lasting from June to August, with 450 cases, 187 of which were fatal. The starting point of the disease was "Hagworm's Nest", buildings off SKELDERGATE. According to the *York Herald* NEWSPAPER, "The Pestilence silently and unobserved entered the city, and took up its deadly stand…in the dwellings of the poor." The CHOLERA BURIAL GROUND was purposely created outside the city WALLS to stop the disease spreading.

CHOLERA BURIAL GROUND Located in what is now Station Road, alongside the city WALLS. The graveyard contains twenty gravestones of those who died in the epidemic of 1832, though there are likely to be more victims buried here, the poor having unmarked graves. The first victims of the epidemic were buried in ST GEORGE'S CHURCHYARD. When bodies were being transported via North Street to the burial ground local residents, fearing infection, rioted and one coffin was thrown into the river OUSE.

CHURCHES The perhaps surprising number of churches in York has a straightforward explanation. In the 1400s the city had the second biggest POPULATION in the country, thus requiring many places of worship. Non-attendance at church was illegal. The DOMESDAY BOOK mentions eight churches in the city, though this is probably an underestimate. By 1100 there were thought to be at least fourteen. By 1200 this had risen to around thirty-seven, and thirty-nine by the fifteenth century. Around half these churches have been demolished, the most recent being St Mary's in BISHOPHILL Senior in 1963. At present there are eighteen medieval churches within the city WALLS, ten of which are currently redundant, no longer holding services and available for other purposes. The CENTENARY CHAPEL and the UNITARIAN CHAPEL are in ST SAVIOURGATE, and the FRIENDS' MEETING HOUSE is in Friargate. There are only two Catholic churches, ST WILFRID'S and ST GEORGE'S, within the Walls, as Roman Catholics were only granted full freedom of worship in 1829. Other places of worship within the Walls include the Pentecostal Church in SWINE-GATE, the Calvary Chapel in Fawcett Street, the Baptist Church, the Rock Church and the United Reformed Church, all in PRIORY STREET. The Salvation Army Citadel, erected 1882-83, is located in GILLYGATE.

CINEMAS At present, York's three cinemas are the CITY SCREEN in CONEY STREET, the ODEON in BLOSSOM STREET and the Warner Village at Clifton Moor, two and a half miles (4km) from the city centre. The first building used as a cinema in York was the Victoria Hall opposite LADY ROW in GOODRAMGATE, which may have shown films from as early as 1899. The first purpose-built cinema was the Electric in FOSSGATE, which opened in 1911. It was renamed the Scala Theatre in 1957 and remained open until 1963. It is currently a large furniture store. The Picture House in CONEY STREET closed in 1955 and is now occupied by Woolworths. Alongside FAIRFAX HOUSE was St George's Cinema, which opened in 1921 and was demolished in 1970. Other cinemas included the Tower in New Street (demolished in the 1960s), the Grand in Clarence Street (demolished in 1989), the Regent in ACOMB (closed in 1989), and the Regal (latterly the ABC), demolished as part of the COPPERGATE redevelopment of 1987. There was also the Rialto in FISHERGATE and the CLIFTON, now both bingo halls. John BARRY worked as a projectionist in the cinemas owned by his father, J.X.Prendergast.

CITY ARCHIVES Records of York's history dating back to the twelfth century, located in a small building alongside the ART GALLERY. Among the many fascinating documents are the city's first CHARTER of c1160 and the death entry of RICHARD III from 1485. There is also a copy of Francis DRAKE's *Eboracum: Or the History and Antiquities of the City of York*, dating from 1736. The City Archives are open to the public. There are also archives at the MINSTER LIBRARY and the BORTHWICK INSTITUTE, although an appointment is necessary for both.

CITY OF YORK COUNCIL York's governing body which replaced the city CORPORATION in 1835. It is the city's biggest employer with approximately 7000 people working for this local authority. Its many functions include the provision of housing, social services, education, the management of parks, libraries and other leisure services, highway maintenance and development and planning.

CITY SCREEN Award-winning CINEMA in CONEY STREET, opened in early 2000. It is part of a modern development incorporating the former *Yorkshire Herald* building, overlooking the river OUSE.

CITY WALLS *See* WALLS, CITY

CLARENCE GARDENS Small park between Haxby Road and Wigginton Road, to the north of the city centre, once the site of the principal HORSEFAIR. The park opened in May 1902, named after the Duke of Clarence who had just been given the FREEDOM OF THE CITY. It was also the site of the first municipal bowling green in York, built in 1908.

CLEMENTHORPE Suburb of York to the south of the city centre. It lies between BISHOPTHORPE Road and the river OUSE, stretching from SKELDERGATE BRIDGE to the north to Butcher Terrace and the MILLENNIUM BRIDGE to the south. Clementhorpe was the site of St Clement's Priory, which was consecrated in 1070. Much of the housing was built for Victorian workers with certain streets being designed by architects PENTY & PENTY.

CLERESTORIES in the Minster The rows of windows in the uppermost part of the archways between the aisles and the NAVE, CHOIR or TRANSEPT, above the TRI-FORIUMS.

CLIFFORD STREET Victorian street linking Nessgate to Tower Street. It was constructed in 1880-81 to connect with the new SKELDERGATE BRIDGE and to facilitate the horse-drawn TRAMS' route to and from FULFORD. It was probably also an exercise in civic pride. In the true spirit of Victorian development it rid York of its slums in the notorious WATER LANES, and created a POLICE STATION, a Fire Station, a new FRIENDS' MEETING HOUSE, a new MAGISTRATES' COURT, a Liberal Club, School Board Offices and the York Institute of Art, Science and Literature, the original York LIBRARY. Part of the old library is currently used as a nightclub and it is where the YORK DUNGEON is located.

CLIFFORD'S TOWER All that remains of York CASTLE, possibly named after Sir Roger Clifford who was hanged here in 1322, or after the powerful Clifford family who were influential throughout northern England. The name was first recorded in 1596. Locals used to refer it contemptuously as the "minced pie", seeing it as a symbol of authority, owing to its seventeenth-century status as a garrison. "To the demolition of the minced pie!" was a popular toast. In its time the tower has been a castle keep, a fort, a PRISON and a mint. The original wooden tower, built by WILLIAM THE CONQUEROR, was burned down in 1190 during the MASSACRE OF THE JEWS, and replaced in the thirteenth century. During the ENGLISH CIVIL WAR it was garrisoned on behalf of CHARLES I. The garrison remained until 1690, despite sustaining significant damage in 1684 following a bungled seven-cannon St George's Day salute. Until then it had two storeys and a wooden roof. Its quatrefoil (four-leafed clover) design is rare, the only other example being at Etampes south of Paris. Between 1727 and 1820 the tower was a folly in the garden of a private house in CASTLEGATE. DAFFODILS were planted on its ramparts in 1990. Clifford's

Tower is now run by English Heritage and is open to the public.

CLIFTON Suburb of York to the north, which was not actually recognised as part of the city until 1884 to the chagrin of some of its isolationist residents at the time. There is a DRINKING TROUGH located on Clifton Green.

CLITHEROW, MARGARET (1556-1586) Catholic martyr and saint whose shrine is in the SHAMBLES. She was baptised in ST MARTIN-LE-GRAND and brought up as a Protestant. Aged fifteen she married John Clitherow, a prosperous Protestant butcher. In 1574 she became a Catholic, attending Mass at Dorothy VAVASOUR's house. In the 1570s the first Jesuit priests arrived in York and persecution became more severe with twenty-six priests executed at TYBURN. By 1576 Margaret was sheltering priests at her house and was imprisoned several times. A prison sentence of six months was imposed for attending Mass and a 1585 Act of Parliament made sheltering priests a crime punishable by death. Margaret was arrested and tried at the GUILDHALL. She refused to enter a plea knowing that her family and friends would be forced to give evidence, putting themselves and others at risk. The penalty for not pleading was being crushed to death. Her husband could do nothing to save her and she was executed at KIDCOTES on OUSE BRIDGE. She was canonised in 1970.

COAT OF ARMS The Arms of the City of York, depicting the five lions of England upon the red cross of St George, were adopted in the early medieval period, probably granted by EDWARD III. The earliest examples of the Arms of York are found carved in stone or set in STAINED GLASS. Examples of the five lions of York may be found in the carvings in the MINSTER, on MICKLEGATE BAR, above the centre arch of FISHERGATE BAR and in the stained glass of ST MICHAEL-LE-BELFREY.

COCK AND BOTTLE Pub in SKELDERGATE. Although a relatively new building dating from 1962, the site has an interesting past. Sir THOMAS FAIRFAX built a house on this site in the early seventeenth century, replacing a demolished house dating from the 1570s. When Fairfax died in 1671, the house was inherited by his daughter Mary, and her husband George Villiers, Duke of Buckingham. The seventeenth-century building is thought to have become an inn, the Plumbers' Arms, around 1875. The present pub retains many of the original fixtures and fittings from the Plumbers' Arms. The name Cock and Bottle means "draught and bottled beers". The ghost of Buckingham, a notorious womaniser, is said to haunt the pub.

COFFEE YARD SNICKELWAY linking STONEGATE to GRAPE LANE, alongside BARLEY HALL, which was the medieval "screens passage" dividing the hall from the kitchen. It was formerly known as Langton Lane, but renamed when the first coffee house opened in the seventeenth century. The cellar of number three housed the remains of an old coffee-roasting oven. Coffee Yard was the location of Thomas GENT's printing house and of NEWSPAPERS the *YORK MERCURY* and the *YORK COURANT*.

COLLEGE OF LAW Situated in BISHOPTHORPE Road, York. The college opened in 1990, in the buildings previously occupied by KNAVESMIRE Secondary School. There are approximately 650 students.

COLLEGE STREET Street linking GOODRAMGATE and the MINSTER, the location of ST WILLIAM'S COLLEGE. In the past it was known as both Vicar Lane and Little Alice Lane. Little Alice was a local character in the 1730s, an old lady who owned an alehouse in the street. By the time Francis DRAKE published his history of York in 1736 the street had adopted her name. It became known as Vicar Lane as it was the route taken by the Minster Vicars Choral to and from their buildings in BEDERN. In medieval times the only access to Bedern was through the alley opposite College Street that remains in use today. The timber-framed entrance to MINSTER CLOSE still stands, next to the National Trust shop. The street was the first workplace of the "Railway King", George HUDSON, as an apprentice in a draper's shop.

COLLIERGATE Street linking KING'S SQUARE to WHIP-MA-WHOP-MA-GATE which takes its name from the medieval "Colyergate" meaning "the charcoal-dealer's street".

COLLINS, (WILLIAM) WILKIE (1824-89) Victorian novelist whose works include *The Moonstone* and *The Woman in White*, leading to his reputation as the father of the English detective story. He visited York on a number of occasions, setting part of his 1862 novel *No Name* in the city. At one point the villainous Captain Wragge is described taking an evening stroll on the city WALLS: "The first few lamps lit in the street below looked like faint little specks of yellow light, as the Captain started on his walk through one of the most striking scenes which England can show … all wrapped in the evening stillness, all made beautiful by the evening peace. On his left hand, the majestic west front of York Minster soared over the city and caught the last brightest light of heaven on the summits of its lofty towers."

COLONIA Civilian ROMAN York achieved the highest rank of civil settlement, a Colonia, to the south of the fortress of EBORACUM. It was common for settlements to develop around Roman military bases for the purpose of trade with the soldiers. The town grew in the first century AD with buildings to the north-east but mainly south-west of the river OUSE, becoming a thriving trading and administration centre. At its peak the Colonia covered the area within today's city WALLS to the south of the Ouse, approximately a hundred ACRES. Evidence of the settlement includes an amphitheatre and temple in MICKLEGATE, a sewerage system (near ST MARY'S in BISHOPHILL) and civilian baths in the TOFT GREEN area. Redevelopment of the former Queen's Hotel in Micklegate in the 1990s uncovered, and controversially re-encased, remains of a *Forum Basilica*, a town hall or central market.

COMMONHALL LANE Narrow passageway alongside the MANSION HOUSE leading to the GUILDHALL. It is almost certainly the route from the ROMAN fortress, the PRINCIPIA, through the Porta Praetoria to the bridge across the river OUSE, and was a continuation of STONEGATE.

CONDEMNED CELL Former cell in the DEBTOR'S PRISON of the CASTLE MUSEUM. It is believed, though not confirmed, that the notorious highwayman Dick TURPIN spent his last hours here prior to his execution at TYBURN on the KNAVESMIRE in 1739.

CONEY STREET Street joining SPURRIERGATE to ST HELEN'S SQUARE, and one of the city's principal shopping areas. Its curious name is derived from the Old Danish *Kunung* (King). Coney Street is thus "the king's street", suggesting that it was the property of a VIKING KING. It is recorded as Cuningstrete in 1150. During VIKING times the street became the city's most prosperous thoroughfare, a prime site for traders. Number seventeen was the site of the George Inn, where the BRONTË SISTERS stayed in 1849. The inn was demolished in 1869. Located on Coney Street are the church of ST MARTIN-LE-GRAND and the CITY SCREEN. Number fourteen, now a coffee shop, was designed by Walter BRIERLEY and built as a bank in 1907.

CONSTANTINE THE GREAT (AD274-337) ROMAN Emperor, born in Nis, Serbia. Constantine was with his father CONSTANTIUS CHLORUS when he died in York in AD306, and he was immediately declared Emperor by the legions. He returned to Rome via Trier in Germany, where his father's headquarters had been, to consolidate his position. In Rome he is said to have seen a vision of the cross of Jesus against the sun in c312 and converted to Christianity, prior to a crushing victory over his brother-in-law Maxentius, who also claimed to be Emperor. He was not the undisputed Emperor until AD324. While legends about his piety abound, in reality he probably only used Christianity as a practical means of unifying his supporters, allowing free religious expression throughout his empire from AD314. He was only baptised as he was dying, and probably first came into contact with Christianity through his mother Helena, later ST HELENA. In AD330 he founded the capital of the empire at Constantinople, now Istanbul. A bust of the Emperor, found in STONEGATE in the nineteenth century, is now in the YORKSHIRE MUSEUM. A bronze statue in front of the SOUTH TRANSEPT of the MINSTER, erected in 1998, symbolises York's association with this major figure in the history of European civilisation.

CONSTANTIUS CHLORUS (cAD250-306) Father of CONSTANTINE THE GREAT, Chlorus, like SEPTIMUS SEVERUS, died in York. He was himself briefly Western Emperor, from AD305-6. At the time there were three emperors, in the east, the west and an overall Caesar Augustus in Rome. He arrived in York from Asia Minor (now Turkey) in 305 to campaign in the far north of Britain. A myth grew that Chlorus had a British wife and that therefore Constantine was a Briton. This was merely medieval wishful thinking, as his wife (St) HELENA was also from Asia Minor.

COOKE, THOMAS (1807-1868) Optician and acclaimed expert in the science and production of telescopic lenses, who arrived in York from Allerthorpe, East Yorkshire, in the late 1820s. He made the telescope for the OBSER-VATORY in the MUSEUM GARDENS. His first optical shop was at 50 STONEGATE, paid for by his supporters in the YORKSHIRE PHILOSOPHICAL SOCIETY. By the 1850s he had a growing enterprise at the now demol-ished Buckingham works in BISHOPHILL, the first pur-pose-built telescope factory in the country. Cooke also invented a steam carriage that could travel at fifteen miles (24km) per hour. However, apart from having numerous crashes, the carriage was rendered useless by an im-posed speed limit of four miles per hour (6.4km) and was retired in 1872. Cooke's company continued to work in York until the 1960s as Cooke, Troughton and Simms, and went on to become part of the Vickers group.

COPPERGATE Street linking PAVEMENT to Nessgate. Possibly the medieval street of the coopers (barrel-makers), the street is clearly of VIKING origin, as "gate" derives from *gata*, the Norse word for street. Originally called "Cupergate", it refers to the trade of joinery and wood-turning, derived from the Old Scandinavian term for a joiner, *koppari*. The extensive excavations of the 1980s produced countless items from the Viking period, including houses dating from the tenth century. The work culminated in the opening of the JORVIK CENTRE in 1984. The Coppergate Centre is one of York's few modern shopping precincts.

COPPERGATE HELMET Helmet discovered in 1982, perhaps the finest individual find relating to ANGLO-SAXON York (cAD400-1066). It probably dates from the eighth century, and is only the third Anglo-Saxon helmet ever found. Although found by a workman during excavations on the site of what is now the JORVIK CENTRE, the helmet became the property of CITY OF YORK COUNCIL, who owned the land. It has been completely restored, and can currently be seen in the YORKSHIRE MUSEUM.

CORPORATION Historical governing body of York, now CITY OF YORK COUNCIL. The Corporation was a self-elected body where men kept office until their removal, death or resignation. The origins stretch back to at least 1217 when York had its first LORD MAYOR. The Corporation's main functions were to uphold justice, trade regulation, and maintenance of the city's roads, buildings, walls and bridges. York Corporation underwent major changes, including its name, in the nineteenth century due to the Municipal Corporations Act of 1835. The city was split into six wards, GUILDHALL, CASTLEGATE, WALMGATE, Monk, BOOTHAM and MICKLEGATE. Each ward elected six councillors, two of whom sought election annually. Councillors elected two ALDERMEN for each ward. The total of forty-eight men would sit in a single chamber to carry out their responsibilities, which no longer included administering justice but did include the management of their own police force from that date.

COUNCIL OF THE NORTH Yorkshire-based seat of the government of the north of England created in 1484 by RICHARD III, developed by HENRY VIII and based in the KING'S MANOR from 1539 to 1641. Richard III appointed his nephew, John De La Pole, Earl of Lincoln, as the Council's first President. De La Pole had become

Richard's heir, following the death of the king's own son EDWARD OF MIDDLEHAM in 1484. The Council would meet four times a year at Middleham Castle, North Yorkshire, and at Sandal in West Yorkshire. Following the failure of the PILGRIMAGE OF GRACE in 1536, Henry VIII reorganised the Council, the first active Lord President being Thomas Holgate, installed at the King's Manor in 1539. The authority and efficiency of the Council reached its peak during the presidency of Henry Hastings, the Puritan Earl of Huntingdon, at the time of Elizabeth I. The last Lord President (1628-41, resident until 1633) was Viscount WENTWORTH. The Council was effectively dissolved by the Long Parliament at the time of CHARLES I.

COUNTY HOSPITAL Former HOSPITAL in MONK-GATE, set back from the main road. The first County Hospital was opened in a house in Monkgate in 1740 and in 1745 a purpose-built hospital was erected next door. Each patient had to deposit twenty-five shillings to cover the cost of their funeral in case they died whilst receiving care. Due to an inadequate number of beds and poor sanitation, the hospital moved to the current building, much larger premises built by J.B. & W. ATKINSON in 1850. It is now a block of private flats.

COVERDALE, MILES (c1488-1569) York-born churchman, who as Bishop of Exeter in Devon translated and published the first complete printed English Bible in 1539. He was a key figure in the English REFORMATION, and the King JAMES I Authorised Version of the Bible of 1611 relied heavily on his work.

CRAVENS York confectioners from as early as 1803, currently based in Low Poppleton Lane, to the north-west of the city. In 1996 they were sold to Trebor Bassett, owned by Cadbury Schweppes. The original company owed its success to the efforts of Mary Ann Craven, who died in 1902, and her son Joseph William. In 1904 Joseph bought the formula for French Sugared Almonds, which became an internationally popular confection. Cravens were based in COPPERGATE until 1966, the eventual demolition of the site revealing the VIKING settlement which was to become the JORVIK CENTRE. There were additional premises on Foss Islands Road, also closing in the 1960s. The present site was acquired in 1964.

CRICHTON, EDNA ANNIE (1887-1970) The first woman Lord Mayor of York (1941-2). A QUAKER from Gloucestershire who settled in York in 1901, Edna Crichton served the city CORPORATION as an independent for over thirty years, becoming an ALDERMAN and Honorary Freeman of the City. There have since been a further seven women Mayors.

CROMWELL, OLIVER (1599-1658) Leading Parliamentarian or "Roundhead" in the ENGLISH CIVIL WAR, who later became Lord Protector of England from 1649-58. Cromwell participated in the SIEGE OF YORK, he and his forces being led by Lord FERDINANDO FAIRFAX, who subsequently became Governor of the city. He also fought at the battle of MARSTON MOOR in 1644. Dispute over Cromwell's role in the Siege of York is resolved by the existence of a surviving letter to a friend in which he describes himself as "a beleaguer of York". He may have been involved in the attack on ST MARY'S TOWER and the sortie into the orchard of the KING'S MANOR. The restoration of CHARLES II in 1660 was greeted with delight by many York citizens, some of whom burnt an effigy of Cromwell in PAVEMENT.

CROSS KEYS Pub in GOODRAMGATE, situated opposite the East End of York MINSTER. When the building became an inn is unclear, though an earlier Cross Keys is known to have stood on the same site. The pub was completely rebuilt in 1904. The sign of the Cross Keys is associated with the apostle ST PETER, who holds the keys to the Gates of Heaven.

CROWN COURT *See* ASSIZE COURTS

CRYPT of the Minster The chamber beneath the east end of a church, containing an altar, once used for burials and still used for occasional services. Its name derives from the Latin *crypta*, meaning a secret or hidden place. Contained in the MINSTER Crypt is a font commemorating the baptism of King EDWIN in AD627, and a shrine containing the remains of ST WILLIAM OF YORK. There is also evidence of the NORMAN Minster built by ARCHBISHOP OF YORK Thomas of BAYEUX and of a ROMAN pillar from the PRINCIPIA. The discovery of the pillar in 1931 indicated that the Roman building was fourteen feet (4.2m) below the present ground level of the Minster. The Crypt, along with the Treasury, is now incorporated into the UNDERCROFT.

CUMBERLAND HOUSE Largest house on KING'S STAITH. It was built c1710 by William Cornwell, LORD MAYOR of York in 1712 and 1725. It appears to have derived its present name from the second son of George II, the Duke of Cumberland (1721-65). The Duke's treatment of the JACOBITES three months prior to his visit in July 1746 led to his becoming known as the "Butcher of Culloden", a battle near Inverness in the Scottish Highlands. Despite his visit lasting a mere three hours and his making no visit to the premises, such was local enthusiasm for royal visits that the house and the adjoining street were named after him. The house now contains offices.

CURRY, WILLIAM "MUTTON" (c1765-1841) York's most notorious hangman. He owed his nickname to being a sheep-stealer. The holder of the hangman's post was generally a convicted villain under sentence of death, who received a pardon if he accepted the job. Curry had twice been sentenced to death, later commuted to transportation. He was imprisoned in York CASTLE awaiting transportation to Australia when the job of hangman came up, which he accepted in 1802. He served his profession for over thirty years, dispatching dozens at the NEW DROP at the Castle or at BAILE HILL. His fondness for gin, however, resulted in many of his hangings being shockingly bungled. On one occasion in 1821 his intoxication led to him being unable to locate his victim's head with the noose. On another occasion in the same year, he managed to fall through the trap door along with the five men he was executing, sustaining, luckily for him, nothing worse than a few bruises.

D

DAFFODILS Yellow flowers (narcissus) which cover the ramparts of the city WALLS and of CLIFFORD'S TOWER every spring. In the early twentieth century the first daffodils were donated to the CITY OF YORK COUNCIL by the former Backhouse Nursery. They were planted along the section of walls across the road from the RAILWAY STATION at first, for the benefit of visitors arriving in the city. From the late 1960s onwards they were planted around all the ramparts and in 1990 they were first planted around Clifford's Tower.

DAVID I (c1084-1153) King of Scotland 1124-1153. Scottish ruler who unsuccessfully laid siege to York in 1138. His intervention in the civil wars between the warring NORMAN cousins Stephen and Matilda (1130s-50s) nonetheless enabled him to acquire significant portions of NORTHUMBRIA. David was finally defeated at the Battle of the Standard, near Northallerton (32miles/51.5km north of York) on 22 August 1138. The victorious English army was led by THURSTAN, ARCHBISHOP OF YORK. He marched under the banners, or standards, of a number of saints, including that of ST PETER, thus giving the battle its name.

DAVY TOWER Medieval stone tower located on the corner of TOWER PLACE and South Esplanade alongside the river OUSE. It is named after a medieval tenant. A brick summerhouse was added on top of the tower in 1750. In the early medieval period a chain could be stretched across the river from Davy Tower to its counterpart, the vanished Hyngbrig Tower, in order to protect the city from invading ships. By 1553 the chain was regarded as redundant and sold off. The tower was allegedly a brothel in the seventeenth century catering for sailors from nearby KING'S STAITH. The Franciscan Friary was near here and part of its boundary wall dating from c1290 is still visible.

DAVYGATE Street linking ST HELEN'S SQUARE and ST SAMPSON'S SQUARE, site of one of the ancient PRISONS of the city, the Forest Prison, used to imprison poachers. The street is named after Davy Hall, the home of the Larderers, the gamekeepers of the FOREST OF GALTRES, until the 1500s when it passed to the FAIR-FAX family. Later the area contained tenements for impoverished cobblers notorious for selling ill-fitting shoes. The city CORPORATION purchased Davy Hall and its grounds in 1744, demolishing the Hall. New Street and the relocated graveyard for ST HELEN'S CHURCH were created, and the latter is now a seating area.

DE GRAY or **DE GREY, WALTER** (c1175-1255) ARCH-BISHOP OF YORK (1215-1255), who resolved to build the present MINSTER as the greatest church in the kingdom. He ordered the building of the SOUTH TRANSEPT, which was completed in his lifetime. Walter de Gray was originally King JOHN's Chancellor and later a senior minister of HENRY III. In 1241 he bought the village of Thorpe St Andrew (known as BISHOPTHORPE by 1316) and began building a residence with a chapel, which was completed c1250 and was to become the present ARCH-BISHOP'S PALACE. De Gray donated the land and the house to the Minster for future Archbishops. His tomb is in ST MICHAEL'S CHAPEL in the South Transept of the Minster.

DE GREY ROOMS Large building situated in EXHIBITION SQUARE, built in 1841 by George Townsend ANDREWS. Originally designed to serve as the officers' mess for the Yorkshire Hussars (the building took its name from the regiment's colonel, Earl de Grey), the De Grey Rooms opened in 1842, quickly becoming a venue for balls, concerts and parties. The building now houses York's principal Tourist Information Office.

DEAN *Churchman and head of a CHAPTER of CANONS and the chief administrator of a cathedral or church.*

DEAN COURT HOTEL Located in DUNCOMBE PLACE, in the shadow of the MINSTER, alongside ST WILFRID'S CHURCH, this hotel was originally three separate houses, built by J.B. & W. ATKINSON in 1865.

DEANERY Residence of the DEAN of York, situated alongside GRAY'S COURT in MINSTER Yard. The house and gardens viewed from the BOOTHAM BAR to MONK BAR stretch of the city WALLS are those of the Dean. It was built in 1939 replacing the previous Deanery, built between 1827 and 1830, which stood on the site of the MINSTER SCHOOL.

DEAN'S PARK Small park situated behind the MINSTER. It was once the site of part of York's ROMAN legionary fortress, the PRINCIPIA, and later the original ARCHBISHOP'S PALACE. The palace has long since disappeared but its chapel building remains and currently houses the MINSTER LIBRARY, which is open to the public. All that remains of the original palace is a row of arches, now a WAR MEMORIAL to the Second Division of the British Army 1809-1945. In the seventeenth century, Dean's Park was the garden of Sir Arthur Ingram's house, a great mansion built in 1616, which included elegant walkways, statues, fish ponds, a tennis court and a bowling green. In 1642 this mansion became the temporary home of CHARLES I. By 1792 the main house was in ruins. The land was purchased by the DEAN and CHAPTER of the MINSTER in 1814, and the remains of the mansion were demolished. The PUREY-CUST HOSPITAL was built in the grounds in 1915 and the present DEANERY in 1939. Dean Purey-Cust is buried alongside the Minster in Dean's Park at the angle of the NAVE and the NORTH TRANSEPT.

DEBTORS' PRISON Situated on the EYE OF YORK and part of the CASTLE MUSEUM. It was designed by William Wakefield, influenced by VANBRUGH and Hawksmoor, and built between 1701 and 1705 from stone taken from the ruins of York CASTLE. As its name suggests, it once housed York's debtors, unfortunates who, until the latter half of the nineteenth century, were imprisoned until such time as they were able to pay off their creditors. Prison conditions for debtors were somewhat better than those for common criminals and their washing was done by the women of the adjacent FEMALE PRISON. They were allowed any luxury, provided they could pay the going price, and were allowed to sell their handiwork in the prison courtyard, once a favourite promenade for the city's general public.

DEFOE, DANIEL (1660-1733) Author of *Moll Flanders* (1722) and *Robinson Crusoe* (1719). Born in London, he was a frequent visitor to York. He described the city as a place catering for "the confluence of the gentry" because of the building of stately homes, manors and granges around York at the end of the seventeenth and beginning of the eighteenth centuries. The gentry were attracted to York for a number of reasons. Prosperous farming families were attracted by the fertile land around the city, the RACECOURSE and the ASSIZE COURTS. Defoe made his journey through Great Britain between 1722 and 1724 and his observations on York gave the clearest picture available of the city at that time. In *A Tour through the Whole Island of Great Britain* (1724-6), Defoe said "The antiquity of York showed itself so visibly at a distance, that we could not but observe it before we came quite up to the city…" The first line of *Robinson Crusoe* is: "I was born in the year 1632, in the city of York, of a good family…"

DENCH, JUDITH OLIVIA (1934-) Oscar-winning actress born in York. Her family lived in HEWORTH Green and her father was a GP and the doctor for the THEATRE ROYAL. Judi attended the MOUNT SCHOOL. In 1951 she played an angel in the MYSTERY PLAYS at ST MARY'S ABBEY and in 1957 played Mary to great acclaim. In 1953 she enrolled at York School of Art but, unhappy, she decided to go to drama school, attending the Central School of Speech and Drama in London for three years. She subsequently acted at the Old Vic in London, the RSC and the National Theatre in SHAKE-SPEARE plays among other works. Her most successful television programmes are *As Time Goes By* and *A*

Fine Romance. Her films include *A Room with a View*, *Mrs Brown*, and *Shakespeare in Love*, for which she received an Oscar for Best Supporting Actress playing Queen Elizabeth I. She played Iris Murdoch in *Iris* (2001) and currently plays M in the James Bond films. She was married to the actor Michael Williams, who died in 2001. She was created Dame of the British Empire in 1988. DAME JUDI DENCH WALK alongside LENDAL TOWER was named after her in 2000 and she received the FREE-DOM OF THE CITY in 2002.

DERWENT VALLEY LIGHT RAILWAY The railway was built in 1912 to bring agricultural produce to market in York from Cliffe Common, fourteen miles (22.5km) to the south-east. Passenger trains also ran daily except Sundays, until 1926. The line was used for goods traffic, particularly heavy during WORLD WAR TWO. There were eleven stations and the main one was in Layerthorpe, near York city centre. A spur line ran parallel with Dodsworth Avenue to the factory of ROWNTREE & CO., now a cycle track and public footpath which opened in 1992. After the Beeching Report of 1963, which recommended closure of minor routes, the line went into decline and trains only ran between Layerthorpe and Dunnington. The last train ran in 1981. On Sundays DVLR trains run at the YORKSHIRE MUSEUM OF FARMING on the last section of line, a length of half a mile (0.8km).

DICKENS, CHARLES (1812-1870) Novelist who visited York many times to give readings. His most famous works include *Oliver Twist*, *Great Expectations* and *David Copperfield*. Fond of the city, particularly the MINSTER, the FIVE SISTERS WINDOW inspired him to tell the fictitious story of the five sisters in *Nicholas Nickleby*. In 1858 he gave his first reading in York, at the now vanished Festival Concert Rooms on the corner of BLAKE STREET and Museum Street. Tickets cost between one and five shillings. According to the *Yorkshire Gazette* NEWSPAPER, he "elicited unbounded applause, and sent his audience home delighted with their evening's amusement".

DIJON Twin city of York in eastern France. Civic links were established between York and Dijon in 1953, at a time when WORLD WAR TWO was still a recent memory and twinning was seen as a way of developing international relationships. Through the York-Dijon Association, set up in 1976, companies in York have twinned with similar companies in Dijon, such as NESTLÉ ROWNTREE. York is also twinned with MUNSTER in Germany and the FANTEAKWA district in Ghana, West Africa.

DISSOLUTION OF THE MONASTERIES (1536-40) Closure of over 800 religious institutions all over the country following HENRY VIII's break from papal authority in 1529. The Act of Supremacy of 1534 placed Henry at the head of the Church in England. His motive was perhaps more financial than spiritual. Many of the properties were sold off to speculators who sold the treasures, the lead from the roofs, the timber and the glass. The aristocracy then bought the land and remaining ruins and the stone was used for other projects. Other properties, including ST MARY'S ABBEY and the ARCHBISHOP'S PALACE alongside the MINSTER, were simply closed and not destroyed, as is often believed.

DOBSON, FRANK (1940-) Labour MP for Holborn & St Pancras in London since 1979, who was born in York and attended ARCHBISHOP HOLGATE'S SCHOOL. He was in the Cabinet as Health Secretary from 1997 to 1999 and ran unsuccessfully against Ken Livingstone in the election to be Mayor of London in 1999.

DOMESDAY BOOK WILLIAM THE CONQUEROR'S survey of England, commissioned in 1086, which includes a number of references to York. The only street recorded is the SHAMBLES and eight churches are mentioned including ALL SAINTS (PAVEMENT), HOLY TRINITY (GOODRAMGATE), and ST MARTIN-CUM-GREGORY. Key landowners in the area were William Malet, governor of York CASTLE, and Odo the Crossbowman, a military chief. William's monumental survey showed that over half the country was under the direct control of 170 individuals, only two of whom were English, thus conveying the extent of NORMAN power a mere twenty years after their victory at Hastings. To the subjugated English, the *Domesday Book* carried the authority of the Biblical Last Day of Judgement, hence the book's name. The Conqueror ordered that a record be made of his new lands, tenants and possessions. According to the *Anglo-Saxon Chronicle,* it was Christmas 1085 when "the King had much thought and very deep discussion with his council about this country – how it was held and with what sort of people. Then he sent his men over all England into every shire and had them find out … how much money it was worth."

DRAGON in the Minster Gilded dragon, dating from the fifteenth or sixteenth century, situated high on the north side of the TRIFORIUM above the NAVE. The exact purpose of this object is a mystery but the hole in its neck suggests that it was once used to lift a heavy object, possibly the lid of a font. The hole may have held a chain.

DRAKE, FRANCIS (1696-1771) Historian of York, not to be confused with his more famous namesake, the Elizabethan explorer (c1545-1596). Drake was the author of *Eboracum: Or the History and Antiquities of the City of York,* published in 1736, in which the city is described as "a labyrinth of imperfect mazes and obscurities". A copy of the book can be seen in the CITY ARCHIVES, and Drake's history remains the basis of many subsequent histories of York. He came to York from Hemsworth, West Yorkshire, as a young man and began to practice as a surgeon in 1717. So successful was he that, in 1727, the city CORPORATION appointed him City Surgeon. Indulging his passion for history, Drake began work on *Eboracum* two years later and, receiving the full support of the city authorities, was granted access to all available civic records. His book, the first detailed history of York, appeared to great acclaim, receiving over 500 subscriptions from the local gentry.

DRINKING FOUNTAIN The city's only drinking fountain is situated near the entrance to the MUSEUM GARDENS in Museum Street. It was built by local sculptor and mason, Job Cole of 26b LORD MAYOR'S WALK, and was presented as a gift to the city by local solicitor Henry Cowling in 1880.

DRINKING TROUGHS Animal drinking troughs were plentiful in York early in the last century. Many watering places were built by the York Tram Company to ensure the horse-drawn TRAMS functioned efficiently. The most elaborate surviving trough, built in 1883, can be seen on CLIFTON Green. It has two drinking levels, for creatures great and small. Another trough, erected in 1905, is located near SKELDERGATE BRIDGE opposite BAILE HILL, and dedicated to Henry Richardson of Cherry Hill, York. He and his wife were both committee members of York RSPCA (Royal Society for the Prevention of Cruelty to Animals). The trough contains the inscription "A Righteous Man Regardeth the Life of his Beast". Further troughs can be viewed on Lawrence Street (near WALM-GATE BAR), near ACOMB Green (erected by the Metropolitan Drinking Trough & Cattle Trough Association) and in CLIFTON outside the former home of Faith Rowntree, a member of York RSPCA Lost Dogs Home Branch committee from 1957 to 1965.

DUCHESS OF KENT (1933-) Katharine Worsley of Hovingham, North Yorkshire, married the Duke of Kent, first cousin of ELIZABETH II, in the MINSTER in 1961. It was the first ROYAL WEDDING in the Minster since 1327, when EDWARD III married PHILIPPA of HAINAULT.

DUCKING STOOL York's ducking stool was situated either at TOWER PLACE or at nearby ST GEORGE'S FIELD, on the banks of the river OUSE, close to the spot where SKELDERGATE BRIDGE now stands. This medieval punishment for so-called nagging females involved the poor woman, or "common scold", being tied to a stool and "ducked" three times in a pond or river. Interestingly, many women preferred to brave the punishment rather than be denied the right to speak their mind.

DUKE OF YORK This fourteenth-century title was created by RICHARD II for his uncle, EDMUND OF LANGLEY. Together with Gloucester, created on the same day, York is the oldest surviving dukedom. Prior to 1474, the title, like any other peerage, passed to the nearest male relative, usually the eldest son. However, in 1474 it became a royal dukedom, when EDWARD IV, proud of his ancestral title, made his second son, RICHARD OF SHREWSBURY, fifth Duke of York. The title is now reserved for the second in line to the throne, the first son being traditionally Prince of Wales. When no candidate exists for the dukedom of York, or when a monarch, as was the case with Queen VICTORIA, chooses not to revive the title, it remains in abeyance. To date six Dukes of York, including HENRY VIII, CHARLES I, and GEORGE VI, have become king. The Duke's estates are the property of the crown, and he has no specific estates or ownership over the city. Prince ANDREW is the current holder of the title.

DUNCOMBE, AUGUSTUS WILLIAM (c1815-1880) DEAN of York (1858-80) who instigated the creation of DUNCOMBE PLACE. The narrow Lop Lane was acquired and demolished between 1859 and 1864, with the exception of the RED HOUSE. Duncombe wanted to create an open space so there would be a fine view of the West End of the MINSTER when approached from the river OUSE. The son of Lord Feversham of Duncombe Park in Helmsley, North Yorkshire, he was buried at his ancestral home. There is a memorial to him in the SOUTH TRANSEPT of the Minster.

DUNCOMBE PLACE Street between the ASSEMBLY ROOMS and the west door of the MINSTER, on which ST WILFRID'S CHURCH, the BOER WAR MEMORIAL and the RED HOUSE can be found. It was created at the instigation of DEAN DUNCOMBE between 1859 and 1864.

DUNGEON *See* YORK DUNGEON

DUTCH HOUSE Distinctive house in OGLEFORTH, dating from 1660. It was owned by the Gossip family from 1733 to 1808, William Gossip being the director and treasurer of the ASSEMBLY ROOMS. Under his ownership the house was much altered. Today it is considerably smaller compared to its size in the eighteenth century when it probably backed on to ST WILLIAM'S COLLEGE. Given the high cost of bricks in the seventeenth century, it was probably one of the first brick houses in York.

E

EADRED (d.AD955) King of the English (AD946-55). He was the son of Edward the Elder and the half-brother of ATHELSTAN. He fought against the VIKING settlers of JORVIK eventually expelling the last VIKING KING of York, ERIC BLOODAXE, in 954. He was then elected King of York. Eadred left money in his will to Viking leaders to bribe them to stay away from the city.

EAGLE LECTERN in the Minster Brass lectern situated in the NAVE close to the ALTAR, given to the MINSTER in 1686. An eagle is used perhaps because it is St John's traditional emblem, or it may be a welcoming design, with its open wings, which has been much copied. The oak plinth of the pulpit behind the lectern was made by Robert "Mousey" THOMPSON in 1948.

EARLY MUSIC FESTIVAL *See* YORK EARLY MUSIC FESTIVAL

EAST WINDOW in the Minster *See* GREAT EAST WINDOW

EBENEZER CHAPEL Redundant chapel built in 1851 in Little STONEGATE for Primitive Methodists. The chapel closed in 1900 when they moved to MONKGATE. It is now part of a large bookshop in DAVYGATE and the former gallery of the chapel is the café.

EBOR DAY Most prestigious meeting at York RACE-COURSE, held annually in August at the KNAVESMIRE. Ebor Day is the second of the three days of the meeting.

EBORACUM ROMAN name for York, following their foundation of the city in AD71. The name probably means "the place of the yew trees". The Roman NINTH LEGION had left its base in Lincoln and moved north to campaign against the BRIGANTES. Under the command of the Governor of Britannia, QUINTUS PETILIUS CERIALIS, they built their PRINCIPIA or military headquarters on the site where the MINSTER now stands. The fortress was initially a wooden construction, before being rebuilt in stone cAD107. It was surrounded by a wall enclosing around fifty ACRES. Evidence of the Principia can be seen in the UNDERCROFT of the Minster. Eboracum was made the capital of Lower Britannia (furthest from Rome) in cAD213. Two Roman Emperors, SEVERUS (AD211) and CONSTANTIUS CHLORUS (AD306), died in Eboracum, and CONSTANTINE THE GREAT was declared Emperor in the city in AD306. A COLONIA, or civilian settlement, developed on the southern side of the river OUSE, in the area which is now BISHOPHILL.

EBORIUS The first mentioned Bishop, rather than ARCH-BISHOP, of York. He was one of three Romano-British Bishops to attend a meeting in Arles, southern France, in AD314, signing himself as Eborius Episcopus. He is evidence of a Christian community at the time of CON-STANTINE and he is represented in a STAINED GLASS window in HOLY TRINITY CHURCH, MICKLEGATE.

EBRAUK or EBRAUCUS Mythical founder of York at the time of the Biblical King David (1010BC). Ebrauk is said to have been once commemorated by a statue in BOOTHAM BAR, which disappeared in the nineteenth century. There are records of a statue at the junction of ST SAVIOURGATE and COLLIERGATE, where the mythical king is supposed to have laid the first stone of the city. It is likely that Ebrauk was a medieval creation, perhaps based on the finding of an unidentifiable statue. During HENRY VII's reign in 1486, he was greeted at MICKLEGATE BAR by a local dressed as Ebrauk who handed the king his "city, key and crown to rule and redress".

EDMUND OF LANGLEY (1341-1402) First DUKE OF YORK, created as such by RICHARD II, thus giving the HOUSE OF YORK its name. Edmund of Langley was one of EDWARD III's many sons, and the great-grandfather of RICHARD III.

EDWARD I (1239-1307) King of England 1272-1307. A tall and imposing warrior king, "Longshanks" or "The Hammer of the SCOTS" is best remembered for his role in the Scottish Wars of Independence (1290s-1314). It was during this period that York for seven years effectively became the CAPITAL OF ENGLAND. Edward transferred the Treasury, the Courts of Justice, and Parliament to York from Westminster, seeing the city as a convenient base for his campaigns against the Scots. Valuable documents were also transferred, including the DOMESDAY BOOK.

EDWARD II (1284-1327) King of England 1308-1327. Edward fled to York CASTLE to avoid his disgruntled barons in 1310, re-fortifying it by constructing an outer ditch and a wooden fence. He also built a moat to divide the stone keep from the rest of the Castle. The ill-fated son of EDWARD I, Edward II was decisively defeated at Bannockburn in 1314 by Scottish king Robert Bruce. In 1319 his forces were again defeated by the SCOTS at the Battle of MYTON, fourteen miles (22.5km) north-west of York. Despite regaining some credibility with his army's victory over opposition leader Thomas of Lancaster at Boroughbridge in North Yorkshire in 1322, Edward's reign continued to be largely disastrous. He was eventually deposed by his French wife Isabella and her lover Roger

Mortimer, and brutally murdered. His life and death were dramatised by SHAKESPEARE's contemporary Christopher Marlowe.

EDWARD III (1312-1377) King of England 1327-1377, who married PHILIPPA of HAINAULT in the MINSTER in 1327. Edward's eight sons and the minority of his ten-year-old grandson, who became RICHARD II, precipitated the WARS OF THE ROSES (1455-87), a significant chapter in York's history.

EDWARD IV (1442-1483) King of England 1461-1483. Son of RICHARD DUKE OF YORK and a major figure in the WARS OF THE ROSES. Edward was the first king of the HOUSE OF YORK and the elder brother of RICHARD III. A tall, strikingly handsome "warrior-king" in his younger days, Edward's compulsive womanising and overeating, plus a tendency towards indecision and melancholy, led to a premature death. His chief association with York is his famous victory at TOWTON in 1461, securing him the throne. He also ascended MICKLEGATE BAR the same year to remove the HEADS of both his father and his brother Edmund, which had been displayed on spikes following the Yorkist defeat at Wakefield in 1460. He replaced them with a clutch of fresh Lancastrian heads from Towton. Edward appeared several times in York, but given the city's support for the Lancastrian cause understandably had little affection for the city. In 1471, during HENRY VI's brief restoration, the CORPORATION was reluctant to admit him, fearing he may lose the Wars of the Roses. In 1478, when he was well established as king, a civic deputation had to be sent to persuade him to come to York.

EDWARD V (1470-unknown) One of the so-called "Princes in the Tower", Edward was never crowned. His mysterious fate, and that of his younger brother RICHARD OF SHREWSBURY, is perhaps best explored in York's RICHARD III MUSEUM.

EDWARD OF YORK (1373-1415) The second DUKE OF YORK, Edward was the only English nobleman to be slain at the great battle of Agincourt in France. Edward probably suffocated inside his heavy armour. His corpulent frame was deemed too substantial to transport home, so he was boiled all night in a cauldron and his bones taken to the church at Fotheringhay in Northamptonshire, which he had founded in 1411. The son of EDMUND OF LANGLEY, he was much in favour with RICHARD II, though in and out of favour with Richard's successor HENRY IV. As the Duke of Aumerle in SHAKESPEARE's *Richard II*, he is discovered to be plotting against King Henry by his own father ("Treason! Foul treason! Villain! Traitor! Slave! Act V, Scene II), though he manages to save himself by abject confession.

EDWARD AUGUSTUS (1739-1767) Tenth DUKE OF YORK 1760-1767. The charming, popular and pleasure-seeking younger brother of GEORGE III was the first Duke to receive the FREEDOM OF THE CITY in 1761. He made a whistle-stop tour of North Yorkshire in that year, breakfasting at the BLACK SWAN and staying briefly at the then relatively new MANSION HOUSE. Though apparently by no means good-looking, Edward was nonetheless extremely successful with the ladies, having numerous notorious affairs to the annoyance of his brother the king. His visit to York RACECOURSE in 1766 was to prove his last, as he died of a fever in Monaco the following year, aged just twenty-eight. He is buried in Westminster Abbey, London.

EDWARD OF MIDDLEHAM (1473-84) Only child of RICHARD III and Anne NEVILLE. Born at Middleham Castle, North Yorkshire, and invested as Prince of Wales at the now demolished ARCHBISHOP'S PALACE in DEAN'S PARK in September 1483. A tomb at Sheriff Hutton church (12miles/19km north of York) is tradition-ally said to contain his remains, thought it is also thought they could be those of a son of Richard Neville, Earl of Salisbury. Another theory is that he was buried in the MIN-STER, although no tomb is marked.

EDWIN (AD585-633) King of NORTHUMBRIA, the ANGLO-SAXON kingdom incorporating York. Edwin was named by the scholar-monk BEDE as *bretwalda*, a king over other kings. His reign of AD616-633 saw the origins of the MINSTER and the rebirth of Christianity in York. His wife was Queen ETHELBURGA, sister to the Christian king of Kent. She brought PAULINUS to York and he became Edwin's Bishop. The city's first Minster, constructed out of wood, was built in the courtyard of the old Roman PRINCIPIA for Edwin's baptism on Easter Day AD627. Edwin died in battle at Hatfield, South Yorkshire.

EGBERT (d.AD766) The first ARCHBISHOP OF YORK (AD735-66) to be recognised by Rome following his cam-paign to secure the title for the city. While PAULINUS is often thought of as the first Archbishop, York was not officially an Archbishopric until AD735. Egbert was a pupil of the scholar BEDE, and set up the MINSTER LIBRARY and a school, attended by ALCUIN. York thus became famous across the Christian world as a centre of learning. His brother Eadbert became king of NORTHUMBRIA in 738, though later gave up his throne to enter a monastery. Both Egbert and Eadbert are buried in York MINSTER, though the site of the graves is unknown.

ELIZABETH II (1926-) The present Queen has been a frequent visitor to York. In June 1971 she visited the city to celebrate its 1900th anniversary. The Queen and Duke of Edinburgh entered through the traditional royal gateway, MICKLEGATE BAR. They had lunch at the ASSEMBLY ROOMS and hosted a garden party for 2000 guests in the MUSEUM GARDENS. There was a flypast of twenty-one aircraft. The Queen's Path near the East End of the MINSTER was so-named following her distribution of the Royal Maundy (specially minted coins) on Maundy Thursday, the day before Good Friday, in 1972. The last monarch to distribute it in York had been CHARLES I in 1639.

ELIZABETH OF YORK (1466-1503) HENRY TUDOR'S queen 1487-1503, following the end of the WARS OF THE ROSES. The eldest daughter of the Yorkist EDWARD IV and Elizabeth Woodville, her 1487 marriage to Henry Tudor (HENRY VII) is commemorated by the ROSE WINDOW in the MINSTER. Tudor, an exiled Lancastrian earl, had vowed on Christmas Day 1483 in Rennes Cathedral in western France to marry her, as a means of uniting the warring HOUSE OF YORK and the

House of Lancaster. Tudor initially proposed a joint rule, but rejected this following the defeat of RICHARD III at Bosworth Field in 1485. After the death of Richard's wife Anne Neville in 1484, Elizabeth, his niece, was seriously proposed as Richard's future wife (See Act IV, Scene IV in SHAKESPEARE's *Richard III*). Richard was forced to issue a public denial of any marriage plans, yet nonetheless Elizabeth was still rumoured to be his mistress.

ELM BANK HOTEL Large hotel situated on THE MOUNT, built around 1870 by J.B. & W. ATKINSON as a private house for Sidney Leetham. The interiors were completed in around 1898 by PENTY & PENTY and George Walton, a follower of the Scottish architect and designer Charles Rennie Mackintosh. The STAINED GLASS is art nouveau and the wall paintings by Walton are of a late pre-Raphaelite style.

ENGLISH CIVIL WAR (1642-51) Conflict between Parliament (Roundheads) and Royalists (Cavaliers) resulting in England becoming a republic for eleven years. The country came to be governed by the Protectorship of Oliver CROMWELL (1649-58) and briefly his son Richard (1658-60). King CHARLES I was executed in 1649. Charles established his court in York for six months in 1642, and the city became a Royalist stronghold, resulting in the SIEGE OF YORK in 1644. "If York be lost, I shall esteem my crown little less" wrote Charles in a letter to his nephew and General of Horse, Prince RUPERT. York indeed fell, to Parliamentary forces led by FERDINANDO FAIRFAX and his son SIR THOMAS FAIRFAX. Despite Parliamentary successes at York and MARSTON MOOR, the conflict continued for a further seven years.

EOFORWIC Name given to York (cAD650-c866) by ANGLO-SAXONS. It is pronounced "everwick" and is derived from the word for Boar, *eofor*, after the Roman boar badge of Eboracum, and the word *wic*, meaning fortified dwelling. It is not known exactly when York fell into Anglo-Saxon hands. What is certain is that when the VIKINGS captured York in 866 they found a centre of church power, learning and trade. The great scholar ALCUIN referred to York in 793 as "the chief of the kingdom", meaning that it was the ecclesiastical centre of the north.

ERIC BLOODAXE (cAD885-954) Last VIKING KING of York, a Norwegian who had two reigns in the city. The first lasted just over a year from 947 to 948 before he was deposed by the Dublin Viking Anlaf, supported by EADRED, king of the ANGLO-SAXONS. In 952 he was reinstated and ruled until 954 when he is thought to have been betrayed and murdered. KING'S SQUARE is named after the palace of the Danish kings that once stood in the vicinity. It seems likely that this is where Bloodaxe had his court, perhaps in one of the remaining ROMAN gatehouses. He appears in the thirteenth-century saga, *Egil's Saga*. Egil, the warrior-poet hero of the tale has been wrecked off the Yorkshire coast and finds himself at the court of his old enemy Bloodaxe. To save his head he recites a poem in praise of the king. It portrays him as a mighty warrior: "As edges swing, Blades cut men down, Eric the king earns his renown." The scene takes place in the royal hall of the palace.

ERNEST AUGUSTUS OF HANOVER (1674-1728) Ninth DUKE OF YORK. George I, perhaps unfamiliar with

English traditions, created his brother Ernest Duke of York in 1716, despite him not being second in line to the throne. It mattered little, as the pious and virtuous Ernest spent most of his time in his native Osnabruck in north Germany, scarcely visiting England.

ESHER, LORD (1913-) Lionel Brett, Lord Esher, an architect, published his groundbreaking report, *York: A Study in Conservation*, in 1968. He highlighted many of the city's problems including traffic congestion, depopulation of the city centre, and poor conservation of historical buildings. His report put forward a bold plan for York. This included the strengthening of its commercial centre and the elimination of noise, pollution and congestion from traffic, by the PEDESTRIANISATION of almost the whole of the city within the WALLS. The historic character of buildings was to be preserved and only new buildings of high architectural standards were to be permitted in future. The report recommended that the city centre should be turned into a major residential area once more, with development within the Walls in areas such as BEDERN and ALDWARK.

ETHELBURGA, QUEEN (d.AD647) Queen of NORTHUMBRIA who brought the bishop PAULINUS to York, resulting in the conversion and baptism of her husband EDWIN.

ETTY, WILLIAM (c1675-1734) York-born architect, carpenter and carver. He built the RED HOUSE in c1704. He also designed the façade of the MANSION HOUSE (1725-30), the stone bridge at STAMFORD BRIDGE (1727) and CUMBERLAND HOUSE (1710). He was Clerk of Works to VANBRUGH at CASTLE HOWARD.

ETTY, WILLIAM (1787-1849) York-born painter. One of the few English artists to paint the nude almost exclusively, influenced by Titian and Rubens. He travelled widely in Europe where he met the artist Delacroix in 1825. In 1828 he defeated the painter Constable in the elections to become a Royal Academician. His 1840 oil painting *Mlle Rachel* is in the ART GALLERY, as is *Benaiah*, dating from 1829. The statue to Etty outside the gallery is by George Walker Milburn and dates from 1910. Etty is buried in ST OLAVE'S churchyard. He campaigned to save the city WALLS from demolition in the 1830s.

EVENING PRESS York's main NEWSPAPER launched as an evening daily in 1882. Until 1996 it was known as the *Yorkshire Evening Press*. The paper's offices and printing works were based in CONEY STREET before moving to WALMGATE in 1989. The Coney Street offices currently house a record store, while the CITY SCREEN cinema, originally the *YORK HERALD* printing works, was where the paper was printed. The paper has a circulation of approximately 42,000.

EXECUTIONS Records show that between 1370 and 1879 at least 564 people were executed at York, either beheaded or hanged. Various sites were used for executions, but it was decided in 1379 to erect a GALLOWS on KNAVESMIRE, to be called the TYBURN of York, after its London counterpart. The gallows or THREE-LEGGED MARE was built by Joseph Penny, a joiner based in BLAKE STREET. The crowds flocked to the ensuing executions in their thousands, a public hanging being a day of festivity with a carnival atmosphere. Executions were carried out at the NEW DROP at York CASTLE from 1801. Public executions ceased in Britain in 1868.

EXHIBITION SQUARE Small square outside the ART GALLERY opposite BOOTHAM BAR, the location of the statue of William ETTY. The square was created for the 1879 Yorkshire Fine Art and Industrial Exhibition. The first exhibition was held in the grounds of BOOTHAM PARK HOSPITAL in 1866, inspired by the Great Exhibition of 1851 in London. The FOUNTAINS were a gift to the citizens of York from the YORK CIVIC TRUST in 1971, to commemorate the 1900th anniversary of the ROMAN foundation of the city.

EYE OF YORK Also known as Castle Green, this is a circular grassed area around which are situated the ASSIZE COURTS, the CASTLE MUSEUM and CLIFFORD'S TOWER. It was once part of the county PRISON. The green was created in the eighteenth century and has had several uses, including declarations of war and peace, county elections and public hangings from 1801 to 1868. The name signifies that it is the centre of the YORKSHIRE RIDINGS.

F

FAIRFAX, FERDINANDO (1584-1648) Yorkshire-born General of northern Parliamentarian (Roundhead) forces during the ENGLISH CIVIL WAR. He commanded the attacking forces during the SIEGE OF YORK with his son THOMAS FAIRFAX. After the surrender of the city's garrison on 16 July 1644 he became York's Governor. It is largely thanks to Lord Fairfax that the MINSTER and many of York's CHURCHES and medieval treasures survived the wrath of the victorious soldiers. He is buried at Bolton Percy, eight miles (13km) from York.

FAIRFAX, **THOMAS** (1612-1671) General Thomas Fairfax was a Parliamentarian (Roundhead) and army leader, who played a crucial part in the ENGLISH CIVIL WAR of 1642-51. He became Lord Fairfax on his father FERDINANDO FAIRFAX's death in 1648. He was a charismatic military leader who first served under CHARLES I, though he was opposed to the so-called royal prerogative. In June 1642 Charles I held a meeting of freeholders and farmers at HEWORTH Moor, to form the beginnings of an army. Fairfax, in favour of a negotiated settlement, presented him with a petition asking him to cease raising troops. He was allegedly struck from his horse, and subsequently became Commander-in-Chief of the Parliamentary forces. He did not participate in the trial of Charles I in December 1648, and led a commission to visit CHARLES II in The Hague, the Netherlands, in 1660 to urge his speedy return. He was elected MP for Yorkshire in Charles II's "free" Parliament. He spent the last eleven years of his life in retirement at Nun Appleton, North Yorkshire, where he died. He is buried at Bilbrough, six miles (9.7km) from York.

FAIRFAX HOUSE Georgian house in CASTLEGATE. It was built in 1762 and designed by John CARR for the ninth Viscount Fairfax. It now houses the Noel TERRY collection of Georgian furniture, donated in 1980, one of the finest collections in England and valued at over £4 million. The house fell into disrepair and was renovated between 1982 and 1984 by YORK CIVIC TRUST. During renovation, the Trust discovered that the house contained original features by well-known craftsmen, which have been restored. Part of the building was used as a CINEMA between 1921 and 1970. The house is open to the public.

FALCON Pub in MICKLEGATE, renamed Rumours in 2002. In 1736 historian Francis DRAKE recorded it as "one of the two inns of good resort in the street". One of York's early newspapers, the *YORK COURANT*, records the pub being auctioned in 1743, when the licensee was one Joseph Anderea.

FANTEAKWA District in Ghana, West Africa, twinned with York. The link was initiated by the York Local Agenda 21 Citizens' Forum in 1998. The Forum was interested in linking with a town or district in a developing country. Fanteakwa was chosen because of its involvement in cocoa-growing, providing a common interest due to York's CHOCOLATE industry. York is also twinned with DIJON in France and MUNSTER in Germany.

FAWKES, GUY OR GUIDO (1570-1606) York-born religious extremist, known for the Catholic GUNPOWDER PLOT of 1605. The plot was an attempt to blow up the Houses of Parliament and the Protestant king JAMES I. Guy Fawkes was born to a family of Protestant lawyers but converted to Catholicism when his father died and his mother married a Catholic. There remains controversy over his precise birthplace, though it was probably a building between STONEGATE and HIGH PETERGATE (behind YOUNG'S HOTEL). Fawkes was baptised at ST MICHAEL-LE-BELFREY CHURCH on 16 April 1570. Following the failure of the plot he was tortured in the Tower of London and executed at Westminster on 31 January 1606. He attended ST PETER'S SCHOOL, where the pupils do not participate in the traditionally English custom of burning his effigy each 5 November.

FEASEGATE Street linking ST SAMPSON'S SQUARE and Market Street. The name derives from the old Scandinavian for "cowhouse lane", suggesting that it was one of the many areas of York where cattle were sold. This was also the site of a second MULTANGULAR TOWER from the ROMAN defences. The only remaining tower can still be seen in the MUSEUM GARDENS.

FEMALE PRISON Situated on the EYE OF YORK and, since 1938, part of the CASTLE MUSEUM. The PRISON was built in 1780 by Thomas Wilkinson and John Prince as a mirror image of John CARR's ASSIZE COURTS. It replaced the Court Sessions House of 1675, from which, along with the Grand Jury House opposite dating from 1668, justice was generally administered. The Female Prison closed in 1929.

FERRIES The locations of the nineteenth-century LENDAL BRIDGE and SKELDERGATE BRIDGE were determined by ferry services which ran in these exact positions. There was also periodically a ferry across the river OUSE where the MILLENNIUM BRIDGE now stands.

FESTIVAL OF CORPUS CHRISTI *See* MYSTERY PLAYS

FESTIVAL OF FOOD AND DRINK Annual ten-day festival in the city, which began in 1997 and is usually held in September. The festival incorporates many different events, from demonstrations and specialist markets in PARLIAMENT STREET, to food samplings and an ale trail.

FIRE MARKS Examples of private fire insurance, these are small metal discs with insurers' names and designs upon them. Some are still visible on buildings in York, noticeably in GOODRAMGATE, BOOTHAM and LOW PETERGATE, around the former YORK COLLEGE FOR GIRLS. It was only following the Metropolitan Fire Brigade Act of 1865 that a general fire-fighting force came into being. Prior to this, from the Great Fire of London of 1666 onwards, properties would take out private insurance. Companies were said to be reluctant to fight fires in buildings not insured by them.

FISHERGATE Street linking Tower Street to FULFORD Road. The area was believed to be an ANGLO-SAXON trading settlement in EOFORWIC, abandoned around the time of the VIKING invasions in the AD860s. The Priory of St Andrew's stood near BLUE BRIDGE and an archaelogical dig in 2001 revealed evidence of the site's use from Anglo-Saxon times, and kilns dating from the medieval period. There is evidence of a timber church dating from cAD1000.

FISHERGATE BAR Gateway in the section of city WALLS bordering the WALMGATE area. It was built in the early fifteenth century on the site of an earlier gate, but is not one of the city's main BARS despite its name. It was damaged in 1489 following a rebellion against taxes imposed by HENRY TUDOR, and consequently bricked up until its restoration in 1827. The gateway was reopened in 1834 to accommodate farmers using the Cattle Market in PARAGON STREET. It was used as a PRISON for supposed lunatics and Catholics in the sixteenth century, at the time of Queen Elizabeth I.

FISHERGATE POSTERN Gateway in the city WALLS next to FISHERGATE POSTERN TOWER.

FISHERGATE POSTERN TOWER Tower on the city WALLS at the end of PICCADILLY, built in 1505 in place of an earlier structure known as Talkan Tower after Robert de Talkan, LORD MAYOR in 1399. It was built at the end of the Walls by the river FOSS, when the water lapped at its foundations creating a natural defence, and it replaced the blocked FISHERGATE BAR. It was known as Edward's Tower in the seventeenth century and consists of three storeys linked by a spiral staircase. The roof was added in 1740. It is currently an artist's studio.

FITZBALDRICK, HUGH (eleventh century) Landowner in NORMAN times after whom HEWORTH is named. The suburb's name means "Hugh's homestead" or "Hugh's farm". Fitzbaldrick may have been of German origin and he provided WILLIAM THE CONQUEROR with a company of archers. As a consequence he was rewarded with land, the DOMESDAY BOOK recording him as being the owner of "Hewarde" or Heworth. Fitzbaldrick appears to have become SHERIFF of York after the HARRYING OF THE NORTH. However, in the 1080s he sided with the eldest son of William the Conqueror, Robert Curthose, against the king, losing his lands as a result.

FITZHERBERT, WILLIAM *See* ST WILLIAM OF YORK

FIVE LIONS Pub in WALMGATE. Along with the Spread Eagle, the inn is one of only two remaining on Walmgate. In 1800 the street had no fewer than twenty-six pubs. An earlier building on the site was known as the City Arms. At the turn of the eighteenth century the pub was rebuilt to cater for the expanding coaching trade, and evidence of considerable stabling can be seen in its rear yard. The name comes from the five lions on the city's COAT OF ARMS.

FIVE SISTERS WINDOW in the Minster Largest window of its type in the world. Located in the NORTH TRANSEPT, each of the five lancets is fifty-three feet (16.2m) by five feet (1.5m) and the window contains over 100,000 pieces of glass. It was completed in 1250 in *grisaille*, mosaic grey glass. The name could be a corruption of "five Cistercians" as g*risaille* glass is often found in Cistercian monasteries. The window features in DICKENS's novel, *Nicholas Nickleby*, when the boys of Dotheboys Hall are stranded at an inn. An old man recounts the fictional story of five York sisters who worked on tapestries, which the others had copied into STAINED GLASS when the youngest sister died. The window has been referred to as the Jewish Window as it contains geometrical designs consistent with the Old Testament prohibition of images. Another theory is that for the first time Englishmen fighting the Crusades in the Holy Land became aware of Islamic art based on pattern. The window must be restored every hundred years, most recently in 1924, having been removed for safety during WORLD WAR ONE. It is now dedicated to the women of the British Commonwealth who died in the war, their names recorded in the ST NICHOLAS CHAPEL.

FLAXMAN, JOHN (1755-1826) Neoclassical sculptor and illustrator born in York. From 1775 he worked for Wedgwood as a designer. His public works include monuments to Admiral Nelson and Joshua Reynolds in St Paul's, London, and to Robert Burns in Westminster Abbey. In 1810 he became the Royal Academy's first Professor of Sculpture.

FLOODS The most devastating York floods to date were in November 2000. Surrounding areas such as Selby, Barlby, Cawood, Malton, Norton and Stamford Bridge were also severely affected. The river OUSE rose to seventeen feet ten inches (5.43m) above its normal level. The FOSS BARRIER, built after the 1982 floods, was employed to prevent even more severe flooding to the north of the city. Previously the worst levels were recorded in 1625 and 1636, when in each case the Ouse rose to seventeen feet and seven inches (5.36m) above normal. The floods of 1564 destroyed the medieval OUSE BRIDGE. High levels of the Ouse were also recorded in 1982 (seventeen feet (5m) above normal) and in 1947 (sixteen feet seven inches (5m)). Although the flood level was not as high in 1947 as in 2000, the water took two weeks to subside, rather than four days. Given the lack of flood barriers in that year, the damage was more extensive. Other serious flooding occurred in 1892, 1931, 1939 and 1968. Following the 1982 floods defence barriers were constructed, but these could not prevent all the disastrous consequences of 2000. Both Prime Minister Tony Blair and the Prince of Wales visited York to view the scenes and the government subsequently pledged an extra £51m over four years to the city's flood defence budget.

FOREST OF GALTRES Medieval forest to the north of York which extended to the city WALLS between BOOTHAM BAR and MONK BAR. It was probably "forested" (made the property of the king, giving restricted hunting rights) by HENRY II. The lantern tower at ALL SAINTS CHURCH in PAVEMENT was illuminated to guide travellers through the treacherous forest, which by night was said to be rife with wolves and robbers. The source of much of the city's oak, the forest was not cleared until the latter half of the eighteenth century, although in reality little of it remained by then. In Tudor times the timber was used to build ships for the Royal Navy. The names of villages outside York such as Sutton-on-the-Forest and Stockton-on-the-Forest are an indication of the vast area covered. The first three scenes of Act IV of SHAKESPEARE's *Henry IV part II* take place in the Forest of Galtres. The ARCHBISHOP OF YORK (Richard SCROPE at the time) asks: "What is this forest called?" Hastings replies: "Tis Gaultree forest…"

FOSS York's second river, the Foss is one of the reasons the ROMANS chose to locate their military headquarters in the area. The confluence of two rivers was seen as easy to defend. Both the ROMANS and the VIKINGS built quays in the area of Foss Islands Road, as the area offered a sheltered harbour free from tides. The Foss was diverted by the NORMANS to create both a moat for York CASTLE and the KING'S FISHPOOL. Canalisation of the Foss by the Foss Navigation Company took place in 1792. The river is still navigable, joining the river OUSE at what is now the BLUE BRIDGE, near FISHERGATE. The FOSS BARRIER protects the north of the city against FLOODS.

FOSS BARRIER Barrier erected across the river FOSS following the FLOODS of 1982, between the BLUE BRIDGE and CASTLE MILLS BRIDGE. During flooding it pumps water back into the river OUSE, preventing it from entering the Foss Basin, thus protecting areas including FOSSGATE, WALMGATE and Huntington Road. During the floods of November 2000 the barrier was raised for a record seventeen days.

FOSS BRIDGE Narrow bridge crossing the river FOSS where FOSSGATE joins WALMGATE. It is believed that there has been a bridge on this site since the VIKING period. The current bridge was built in 1811, designed by Peter ATKINSON Junior who was also responsible for OUSE BRIDGE. It replaced an earlier wooden bridge at the same location. During the fifteenth century Foss Bridge was the site of one of the city's fish markets.

FOSSGATE Street running from PAVEMENT to FOSS BRIDGE, where there is an entrance to the MERCHANT ADVENTURERS' HALL. Alongside FOSS BRIDGE, Dorothy Wilson's ALMSHOUSES are visible. They were endowed in 1717 for the maintenance of ten poor women and to teach twenty poor boys reading and writing. There is a monument to Dorothy Wilson in ST DENYS' CHURCH.

FOUNTAIN Located at the centre of PARLIAMENT STREET. It was installed in 1992 and redesigned in 2002.

FOUNTAINS Situated in EXHIBITION SQUARE in front of the ART GALLERY, overlooked by the statue of William ETTY. The fountains were a gift to the citizens of York from YORK CIVIC TRUST in 1971, commemorating the 1900th anniversary of the ROMAN foundation of the city. They were refurbished in 1991 and redesigned in 1998, when they were reopened.

FOX Victorian pub in Holgate Road, built in 1878 to serve the workers from the nearby RAILWAY yards.

FOX TALBOT, WILLIAM HENRY (1800-77) Pioneering photographer who was born in Melbury, Dorset. He took some of the earliest known photographs of York, including of the MINSTER, ST MARY'S ABBEY and KING'S STAITH, in July 1845.

FREEDOM OF THE CITY The highest honour York can give to an individual, granted by the LORD MAYOR. The word "freeman" first came into use in the fourteenth century, when a man had to be a freeman before he could trade or become a master craftsman and join one of the GUILDS. A freeman also had the right to graze two cows on one of York's STRAYS. There were traditionally three ways to become a freeman: birthright, apprenticeship or purchase. Today freedom can be claimed via ancestry or through apprenticeship. The Guild of Freemen was formed in 1835 to protect the traditions of freemen. Honorary Freedom, a different title, is given to people who have served the city or to citizens who have made significant achievements. The first Honorary Freedom was given to Lord BURLINGTON in 1731. In 2002 actress Judi DENCH and composer John BARRY were given Honorary Freedom of the city. Nowadays, to be given the Honorary Freedom of York is purely symbolic.

FRIENDS' MEETING HOUSE QUAKER place of worship, situated in Friargate between CASTLEGATE and CLIFFORD STREET. The original house was built in 1673 and the building was also the location of a Quaker school which eventually became the MOUNT SCHOOL. The present building was constructed in 1981, replacing a meeting house of 1817, and incorporates a small meeting room dating from 1884.

FRIENDS OF RICHARD III York-based society founded in 1978. Their aim is to promote the reputation of RICHARD III in the north, and especially in York. Their achievements to date include presentations to the MINSTER, plaques in the GUILDHALL and outside the MINSTER LIBRARY, and the spectacular Richard III window in the Minster's ALL SAINTS CHAPEL, installed in 1997 and depicting his Coat of Arms.

FULFORD Suburb to the south of the city. Unfortunately Fulford means "foul or dirty ford" in Old English. In 2001 it was linked to the South Bank area of York via the MILLENNIUM BRIDGE. Fulford Road joins FISHERGATE to the village, and is the location of the former CAVALRY BARRACKS, now the POLICE STATION, and IMPHAL BARRACKS.

FULFORD, BATTLE OF Battle which took place on 20 September 1066 near York. The king of Norway, Harald Hardradi, whose name is often rendered as Hardrada or Hardraada, roughly translating as "drives a hard bargain", was attempting to snatch the English throne from Harold GODWINSON. He attacked the country from the south, sailing 200 long ships down the river OUSE and disembarking 10,000 warriors at Riccall, ten miles (16km) from York. He was aided by Harold Godwinson's younger brother, the treacherous Earl TOSTIG. The northern ANGLO-SAXON Earls Edwin and Morcar proceeded from York to meet the Norwegian king at FULFORD. The result was a Norwegian victory, and a contemporary Norwegian poet wrote of "the hardy Men of Norway" being able to "cross the marsh on a causeway of corpses." However, Hardradi was defeated and killed five days later by Godwinson's army at the battle of STAMFORD BRIDGE. The two battles served to weaken Godwinson's army prior to their defeat by WILLIAM THE CONQUEROR at Hastings on 14 October 1066.

FULFORD CROSS The preserved base of a stone cross on FULFORD Road, located alongside what is now a supermarket car park. The cross was established in 1484 as a boundary between Fulford, then owned by ST MARY'S ABBEY, and the city after many disputes over animal grazing rights. It was known as the Franchise Cross after this agreement. It is not known if the existing monument is the original. It was on this site that in 1541 the citizens of York met HENRY VIII following the PILGRIMAGE OF GRACE.

G

GALLOWS York had numerous gallows situated throughout the city. Imprisonment was generally not used as a punishment option, but more for those awaiting trial. The usual punishments were branding or public hanging. The right to hand out justice was given to York's most influential groups. Even the DEAN and CHAPTER of the MINSTER maintained their own gallows, though not on consecrated land. York's most famous site of EXECUTION was the THREE-LEGGED MARE at TYBURN although there were other sites including BAILE HILL and the NEW DROP at the CASTLE.

GALTRES FOREST *See* FOREST OF GALTRES

GAS LIGHTING York's streets were first lit by gas on 22 March 1824. Evidence of the city's gas lighting can still be seen by two lamps outside the SOUTH TRANSEPT of the Minster, and two outside its WEST FRONT. These lamps are still powered by gas today. Other examples of gas lighting exist in ST HELEN'S SQUARE. The original York Gas Light Company was based off MONKGATE, with QUAKER Samuel TUKE on the Management Committee.

GENT, THOMAS (1691-1778) Dublin-born collector of antiquities who moved to York, where he printed a number of historical works and a NEWSPAPER, the *York Journal*. He is known to have died in PETERGATE.

GEORGE FREDERICK ERNEST ALBERT (1865-1936) Twelfth DUKE OF YORK 1892-1901, who became King George V. Created Duke of York in May 1892, he made a tour of the city with his bride May (Mary) of Teck the following year, receiving the FREEDOM OF THE CITY. Vowing never to forget York, he presented a new CAP OF MAINTENANCE to the City CORPORATION in 1915, which is still worn by the city Swordbearer.

GEORGE HUDSON STREET Street linking MICKLE-GATE to ROUGIER STREET. The street was named after the "Railway King" in 1843, when his power and influence was at its peak. Following his disgrace in 1849 it was renamed Railway Street and did not revert to its original name until 1971, when York celebrated the 1900th anniversary of its foundation.

GEORGE IV (1762-1830) King of England 1820-1830. As Prince of Wales, he visited York Races with his brother the "GRAND OLD" DUKE OF YORK in 1789 and was enthusiastically received.

GEORGE VI *See* ALBERT GEORGE

GERT & HENRY'S Current name of the timber-framed building at the centre of NEWGATE MARKET, close to the SHAMBLES. It was known as Lawrie's delicatessen in the 1990s. The building dates from the fourteenth century with early seventeenth-century additions, and was extensively restored by Walter BRIERLEY. The original name and purpose of the building is unknown.

GHOSTS York has a reputation as the most haunted city in Europe, with a rumoured 140 ghosts. The most well-known sightings include the ROMAN soldiers seen by Harry MARTINDALE at the TREASURER'S HOUSE, and the Earl of NORTHUMBERLAND's headless corpse at HOLY TRINITY CHURCH in GOODRAMGATE. The voices of children who died at BEDERN'S Ragged School in the nineteenth century are also still to be heard, while the Grey Lady of the THEATRE ROYAL and the Tudor Lady of KING'S MANOR make occasional appearances. The SNICKLEWAY INN, in Goodramgate, claims to be York's most haunted pub. There are a number of ghost-walks available in the city.

GILLYGATE Street running alongside the city WALLS from BOOTHAM to LORD MAYOR'S WALK. Its name is pronounced "jillygate". Gillygate gets its name from St Giles's Church which was declared redundant in 1547. The church has long since disappeared, but it stood near where the Salvation Army building is now. Close to the great FOREST OF GALTRES, it was an expansive rural area and there was a farm and market gardens near Lord Mayor's Walk. In the 1960s there were plans to demolish the street in order to build a new inner ring road, but local people protested and eventually Gillygate was saved.

GODWINSON, HAROLD (c1022-66) King of England 1066. ANGLO-SAXON king who defeated Harald Hardradi at the battle of STAMFORD BRIDGE, eight miles (14km) east of York in September 1066. His treacherous brother TOSTIG was slain in the battle. His weakened forces were defeated by WILLIAM THE CONQUEROR at Hastings three weeks later.

GOLDEN BALL Victorian pub in BISHOPHILL, situated on the corner of Victor Street (formerly St Mary's Row) and Cromwell Road (formerly Jail Lane). Its history has proved difficult to trace accurately, owing to the name changes of the two roads, and the one-time existence of another Golden Ball on nearby Fetter Lane. Jail Lane was so named because it linked the city with the PRISON alongside BAILE HILL.

GOLDEN BIBLE Sign above a shop at 35 STONEGATE, where York's premier bookshop of the eighteenth and nineteenth centuries was located. The "Sign of the Bible" also had a printing press, and in 1759 John Hinxman published the first two volumes of Laurence STERNE's *Tristram Shandy*. The volumes sold rapidly and London publishers soon took on Sterne's masterpiece. In 1766 John Todd began a commercial circulating library here, which continued until 1794 when it was replaced by the Book Society. The building is currently used by an astrologer.

GOLDEN FLEECE Pub in PAVEMENT, known to have been an inn since at least 1656. Both the Fleece and YE OLDE STARRE in STONEGATE may well be York's oldest pub although others including the RED LION, the OLD WHITE SWAN and the THREE TUNS could make a similar claim. The Fleece was one of the ancient "high class" inns, and was once owned by John Peckett, LORD MAYOR of York in 1702. It became a major coaching inn with stables at the rear known as LADY PECKETT'S YARD, named after the Mayor's wife. The distinctive sign and the pub's name are a reference to the commercial importance of the WOOL TRADE in medieval York. The GHOST of Lady Peckett is said to haunt the pub.

GOLDEN LION Pub in Church Street, the licence of which can be traced back to 1711. Due to the poor state of the original building, the pub was demolished and rebuilt completely in 1971. It then took the name The Nineteen Hundred, to mark the founding of York (EBORACUM) in AD71. It reverted to its original name in the 1980s.

GOLDEN SLIPPER Pub in GOODRAMGATE, situated next door to the ROYAL OAK. Although only traceable back to 1821, the section adjoining the Royal Oak pub is clearly a great deal older, and was the original bar of the Golden Slipper. The rooms to the left on entering the pub were a separate house or shop until the late nineteenth century. Unusually for a small pub there are extensive cellars, which are thought to extend as far back as ST WILLIAM'S COLLEGE. It is thought that the pub was originally called The Shou. Perhaps the current name was intended to create a more upmarket image. An old shoe, found during refurbishments, is displayed in the bar. Another theory is that Golden Slipper was originally the name of a greyhound.

GOODRAMGATE Street linking KING'S SQUARE and MONK BAR. It was originally known as Gutherumgate possibly after the VIKING KING Guthrum, who was defeated and christianised by King Alfred in the late ninth century. It is more likely to be named after an unknown local man, as King Guthrum was based in East Anglia. Situated on Goodramgate are LADY ROW, the medieval entrance to BEDERN, HOLY TRINITY CHURCH, the RICHARD III MUSEUM and pubs including the ROYAL OAK and the CROSS KEYS.

GOODRICKE, JOHN (1764-1786) Dutch astronomer who lived in York from 1782 to 1786. Goodricke was on his way to becoming one of the greatest astronomers of his age when he died tragically early. His talent was especially remarkable considering that he was deaf and mute after a childhood illness. Goodricke first noticed the variability of starlight and won acclaim for his work from the Royal Society just two weeks before he died of pneumonia in York. Goodricke carried out his observations from the TREASURER'S HOUSE. A college at the UNIVERSITY OF YORK is named after him.

GRAND OLD DUKE OF YORK "The Grand Old Duke of York/ He had ten thousand men/ He marched them up to the top of the hill/ And he marched them down again". The nursery rhyme refers to Frederick (1763-1827), second son of George III and eleventh DUKE OF YORK (1784-1827). The rhyme recounts his alleged incompetence leading British forces against Revolutionary France in 1793. In reality, the British army was in a pitiful state, and Frederick was probably no worse a military leader than many of the time. Indeed, his experiences led to major reforms in the British army, for which he became known as the "Soldiers' Friend". His work contributed to the victories at Trafalgar in 1805 and Waterloo in 1815. Frederick was briefly forced to resign as commander-in-chief in 1809, following a "cash for promotions" scandal, run by his scheming mistress, Anne Clarke. He and his elder brother George (later GEORGE IV) were enthusiastically received at York Races in 1789. Frederick, however, saw little of York during his stay, being indisposed with measles.

GRAND OPERA HOUSE Theatre and music venue in CLIFFORD STREET which celebrated its centenary in January 2002. It has had a chequered history and several name changes. The venue has seen performances by many celebrities over the years, including Charlie Chaplin in 1904, Gracie Fields in 1927 and Laurel and Hardy in the 1950s. The building's first role was as the Corn Exchange, providing a covered area for trade, from 1868 to 1901. Prior to this, corn had been traded on PAVEMENT. By the main entrance to the theatre is a plaque commemorating Frankie HOWERD, who was born in York.

GRANGE, THE Large Victorian building in Huntington Road overlooking the river FOSS. It was formerly the York Workhouse, a workhouse being an an institution for the poor in the eighteenth and nineteenth centuries. It opened in 1848 and was designed to hold 300 people, kept busy by an assortment of manual tasks. It later became a HOS-PITAL and is currently used as accommodation for the students of YORK ST JOHN COLLEGE.

GRAPE LANE Cobbled street linking LOW PETERGATE to SWINEGATE. The name has nothing to do with vine-yards but everything to do with medieval prostitution, being originally called "Gropec**tlane". Ironically the medieval "stews" (brothels) were situated on church property.

GRAYS Firm of solicitors whose practice goes back to 1695 and possibly earlier. The first Gray to be associated with the firm was William Gray (1751-1845) who, in 1788, bought the "Great House" behind the MINSTER, later called GRAY'S COURT. Gray's original offices were located in PETERGATE and STONEGATE. The firm's current offices are in the redbrick building in DUNCOMBE PLACE, dating from 1897 and the work of Edmund Kirby of Liverpool, the architect who also designed Barclays Bank in PARLIAMENT STREET. Part of the building was the former York Dispensary.

GRAY'S COURT Medieval buildings surrounding a court-yard alongside the TREASURER'S HOUSE in MINSTER Yard. Gray's Court was part of the original TREA-SURER'S HOUSE from the eleventh century until the time of HENRY VIII, when the post of TREASURER was suppressed during the DISSOLUTION OF THE MONAS-TERIES in 1547. The building was bought in 1788 by William Gray of GRAYS Solicitors and was the Gray family home until 1962. Part of the building was leased to St John's College, now YORK ST JOHN COLLEGE, as the

Department of History in 1949, and in 1969 the Departments of English and Theology relocated there. A plaque on the city WALLS opposite Gray's Court commemorates the contribution of Edwin Gray, LORD MAYOR of York in 1898, to the restoration of that section of the walls.

GREAT EAST WINDOW of the Minster Largest STAINED GLASS window in the world, created between 1405 and 1408 by John Thornton of Coventry. It is located above the LADY CHAPEL in the East End of the MINSTER. The window measures seventy-six feet (23m) by thirty-two feet (9.7m), which is roughly the size of a tennis court. The theme is the beginning and end of the world, taken from the Old Testament. The easiest stories to see with the naked eye are Jacob's Ladder and the creation of the sea. To the right of the Lady Chapel is a pictorial guide to all 117 panels.

GREAT FIRE OF YORK Fire of 1137 which caused great destruction in the city. While not on the scale of London's Great Fire of 1666, ARCHBISHOP Thomas of BAYEUX's MINSTER and ST LEONARD'S HOSPITAL were both seriously damaged, while a number of parish CHURCHES were said to have been destroyed. The fire was largely confined to the area now enclosed by the Minster, DUNCOMBE PLACE and EXHIBITION SQUARE. The historian Francis DRAKE suggests that thirty-nine churches were destroyed, but this is undoubtedly an exaggeration.

GREAT WEST WINDOW of the Minster Created in 1338-9, this window measures fifty-four feet (16.5m) high by twenty-five feet (7.6m) wide. The window is above the WEST DOORS in the NAVE of the MINSTER. The lowest row of figures in the window depicts eight ARCHBISH-OPS OF YORK. The original faces were lost and replacements painted by William PECKITT in the late 1700s. In the next row up there are some of the apostles and above that are scenes from the life of Christ. The top row shows Mary being crowned Queen of Heaven. The heart-shaped top section of the window is known as the "Heart of Yorkshire".

GREAT YORKSHIRE TRAIN ROBBERY Unsolved crime which took place in October 1867. A train left the RAILWAY STATION with the pay for the North Eastern Railway officials in the guard's van at the rear of the train. It made two stops just outside the city yet when it reached Strensall (8 miles/13km away) the guard's van was no longer attached. It was found down the line though the confused guard had no idea what had happened. The money was never recovered and no one was ever apprehended

GREEN, FRANK (1861-1954) Businessman who restored and lived in the TREASURER'S HOUSE. His wealth supported an eccentric bachelor lifestyle. He restored the Treasurer's House to what he thought was its original seventeenth-century appearance, as a show-case for his vast collection of antiques, many positioned by fixed floor studs in recreated period settings. He was a fastidious man, impeccably dressed and very particular in his personal requirements, ensuring that his French chef, M. Viande ("Mr Meat"), came up from London for his stays in York and that his own laundry was sent down to the capital. After donating the house and its contents to the National Trust in 1930 he died penniless in Somerset aged ninety-three. It was from Somerset that he is said to have issued threats to return to York to haunt anyone who dared to move any piece of furniture from the places he had so carefully marked.

GREY COAT SCHOOL Residential school for poor girls, often orphans, which opened in York in 1705. It was initially based at 60-62 MARYGATE before moving in 1784 to 33 MONKGATE, currently a health centre. The pupils wore grey, the name probably being derived from the Gray Coat Hospital in Westminster, London. Like the BLUE COAT SCHOOL for boys, it was closed in 1947.

GROVES LANE Narrow lane which continues the route outside the city WALLS of the ROMAN Via Decumana or CHAPTER HOUSE STREET. This route originally ran through a north-eastern gateway in the Walls near MONK BAR. The former road is now a passageway which leads to the Groves area of York.

GUILDHALL Civic building located down a narrow passage, COMMONHALL LANE, behind the MANSION HOUSE opposite ST HELEN'S SQUARE. The building overlooks the river OUSE. The construction of the original Guildhall was begun in 1446, intended as a meeting hall for York's GUILDS. In reality, the guilds rarely met in the building, and it became a meeting place for the city CORPORATION whose first meeting was held here in 1459. The newly crowned king RICHARD III was entertained in the Guildhall at a feast in 1483. Among the more important events to take place in the building was the Court of Enquiry to investigate the charges against Mary Queen of Scots (Queen of Scotland 1542-67) and the trial of Margaret CLITHEROW. Following the ENGLISH CIVIL WAR, the SCOTS were promised £500,000 by Parliament in gratitude for their support. In 1648 the first instalment of £200,000 was paid in the Guildhall and the Scots took twelve days to count it. Additional chambers were built adjoining the Great Hall in the early nineteenth century after the council chambers on OUSE BRIDGE were demolished. The building that exists today is partly a reconstruction, made necessary by the extensive damage suffered during the BAEDEKER BLITZ in 1942.

GUILDS or GILDS Powerful organisations that dominated York's trades in medieval times. The term "guild" is derived from the German *geld* (money). The guilds set rules to regulate trades in the city, handled tradesmen's disputes, upheld standards of workmanship and guarded against competition. Guilds also had a charitable and social function, often of a religious nature, most visible in their productions of the MYSTERY PLAYS. They also cared for old or invalided "guild brothers". A list on the 1415 copy of the Mystery Plays contains fifty-seven different trade guilds. It is likely guilds existed in some form well before that of the Middle Ages, as laws passed in ATHELSTAN's reign in the 940s refer to "gild men". The peak of the guilds' influence was in the fifteenth century, but changing patterns in the economy meant that they were in sharp decline by the end of the sixteenth century. Most guilds used ST ANTHONY'S HALL on ALDWARK for meetings. Some had their own halls, the

110

only remaining examples being the MERCHANT TAY-LORS' HALL and the MERCHANT ADVENTURERS' HALL. BEDERN Hall has been renovated to serve as the guildhall for the Master Builders, the Freemen and the Company of Cordwainers. The few guilds which still operate in York have been re-established as charitable and fundraising bodies.

GUNPOWDER PLOT Catholic plot by York-born Guy FAWKES, with Robert Catesby, Thomas Tresham, Thomas PERCY and others to blow up JAMES I and Parliament during the State Opening on 5 November 1605. The plot is commemorated annually as part of Bonfire Night celebrations.

GYLES, HENRY (1645-1709) York-born glass painter. His work includes a window depicting the royal arms of CHARLES II in St Stephen's Church in ACOMB, painted in 1663. Gyles also painted glass for the GUILDHALL in 1684, and for the MERCHANT TAYLORS' HALL between 1700 and 1702.

H

HAINAULT RIOTS Fourteenth-century conflicts on the streets of York. In 1327 some 60,000 troops were billeted around York to prepare for war against the SCOTS. Tensions rose between the English and their allies from Hainault (Holland and Zealand) and many of the Hainaulters were slain. Ironically, in the midst of all the internal fighting, Scottish ambassadors arrived to sue for

peace. Two years later, following the marriage of
EDWARD III and PHILIPPA of Hainault in York MINSTER,
a three-week celebration of feasting, jousting and revelry
took place. However, old tensions resurfaced between
the citizens and their foreign visitors, resulting in a formal
challenge being issued by the English. A pitched battle
ensued, ending up on the banks of the river OUSE, where
347 Hainaulters and 242 English drowned.

HALF MOON COURT Recreated Edwardian street in the
CASTLE MUSEUM, added in 1963. The other street in
the Museum is KIRKGATE, located in the DEBTORS'
PRISON part of the museum, which opened in 1952.

HANSOM, JOSEPH ALOYSIUS (1803-1882) York-born
inventor of the Hansom Cab, who was baptised at the
BAR CONVENT. Although an award-winning architect,
Hansom is primarily known for designing the "Patent
Safety Cab" or "Hansom Cab" as it became known. So
common a sight did it eventually become, that Prime
Minister Disraeli called it "the gondola of London". A fully
restored Hansom Cab can be seen in KIRKGATE in the
CASTLE MUSEUM. Hansom's premises were at 114
MICKLEGATE. Among the 200 buildings he designed,
both at home and abroad, is ST GEORGE'S CHURCH
off WALMGATE.

HANSOM CAB Pub in Market Street. In 1836 PARLIA-
MENT STREET was built to connect the two markets in
ST SAMPSON'S SQUARE and PAVEMENT, to create
more space. Around 1840 the Burns Hotel opened in
JUBBERGATE. In 1852 Jubbergate was renamed Market

Street, and in 1870 the City and County Bank (currently the HSBC bank) was enlarged, taking the Burns Hotel with it. The new Burns Hotel, now next door to the bank, was renamed the Hansom Cab after extensive refurbishment.

HARDRADI, HARALD *See* FULFORD, BATTLE OF

HARRYING OF THE NORTH Also known as the "Wasting" or "Destruction" of the North, which took place in 1070. In 1069 a force of Danes and English under Earl Waltheof retook York from its NORMAN occupiers, slaying the garrison and organising a popular revolt against WILLIAM THE CONQUEROR's rule. William reacted swiftly. He despatched troops to York and bribed the Danes to abandon their English allies. William intended to have every Englishman, soldier, and SCOT put to the sword. Once York was secure, William's men then set about destroying the whole district, every living thing between York and Durham allegedly being slaughtered. According to Peter Langstaff's *Chronicle*, "William turned again and held what he had sworn/ All made he wasteyn, Pasture, Medow, Korne…". The DOMESDAY BOOK records that sixteen years later, land was still only worth a fraction of what it had been worth before William's brand of Norman "ethnic cleansing". It also records that 940 of York's 1400 houses were so derelict as to be liable for either no tax or one penny in tax.

HAXBY ROAD SCHOOL Primary school, one of the first council-built schools in York, designed by Walter BRIERLEY and completed in 1904.

HEADS The heads of executed traitors were displayed on spikes on York's BARS, facing outwards as a deterrent, from the fourteenth century to 1746, principally on MICKLEGATE BAR. The most famous of these were Harry HOTSPUR (1403), ARCHBISHOP OF YORK Richard SCROPE (1405), RICHARD DUKE OF YORK and his son Edmund of Rutland (1461). This gruesome practice finally ceased in 1746 with the last heads being those of two unfortunate JACOBITES.

HELEN or HELENA, ST (cAD250-330) Mother of the ROMAN Emperor CONSTANTINE THE GREAT, who was declared Emperor in York. She was born in Asia Minor, now Turkey, and at the age of twenty married CONSTANTIUS CHLORUS. Constantius later separated from Helen to make a more politically advantageous marriage, and by AD306 had become Emperor of Rome's western empire. He died that year in York, and was immediately replaced by Constantine. As a devoted son Constantine proclaimed his mother Empress. When, in 312, she embraced the newly emerging religion of Christianity, her son followed, establishing it as the official religion of Rome. Aged almost eighty, she went on a pilgrimage to the Holy Land, where according to tradition she discovered the remains of the True Cross, buried below the surface of Mount Calvary. She died in the Holy Land, and her body was taken back to Rome, where the remains of her tomb may still be seen. ST HELEN'S CHURCH and ST HELEN'S SQUARE are named after her.

HENRY I (1068-1135) King of England 1100-1135. The country's only Yorkshire-born monarch, born in Selby fourteen miles (22.5km) south of York. However, there is no record of him having visited the city. The younger son of WILLIAM THE CONQUEROR and Matilda of Flanders, Henry was a well-educated and capable ruler. In 1120 his life was blighted by the White Ship Tragedy, when both his sons were drowned in the Channel.

HENRY II (1133-1189) King of England 1154-1189. Henry granted York its first CHARTER (c1160) and visited York at least three times. Henry was a great reformer, founding English common law and establishing the jury system. His reign was marred by the rebellions of his four quarrelsome sons, Henry, Geoffrey, RICHARD (I) and JOHN. The latter two would eventually become kings of England themselves. On each visit to York, Henry was asked to repair the CASTLE, at that time made of wood, and in 1172 he duly paid £15 for the repair of the castle keep.

HENRY III (1207-1272) King of England 1216-1272. Both the construction of the MINSTER (1220-1472) and the city WALLS (1240s-1340s) began during Henry's reign. Henry once spent Christmas at York CASTLE when the building was damaged by a storm, and it was subsequently left to deteriorate. In 1244, however, the threat of war with the SCOTS brought the king back to York and he ordered the rebuilding of the castle in stone. In 1251 Henry held a spectacular Christmas extravaganza in York, when ten-year-old Alexander III of Scotland was knighted and then married, in the Minster, to Henry's eleven-year-old daughter Margaret.

HENRY IV (1366-1413) King of England 1399-1413. Henry "Bolingbroke", Duke of Lancaster, overthrew his cousin RICHARD II, who was popular in York, in 1399. After ARCHBISHOP SCROPE's rebellion in 1405 Henry marched to York vowing to "wipe it off the face of the earth" if the city resisted. At BISHOPTHORPE he was met by a crowd of "barefoot and ungirt" (without belts) citizens with nooses around their necks as a sign of submission, who fell to their knees and begged for mercy. The furious king sent them home and for a year he saw that York was ruled directly by royal governors. He personally oversaw Scrope's trial in BISHOPTHORPE PALACE, eager for the death sentence to be imposed. Scrope was duly executed and when miracles were reported at the Archbishop's tomb in the MINSTER, Henry banned people from praying there. It was shortly after Scrope's execution that Henry began showing signs of the illness, possibly leprosy, which later killed him. Many saw this as divine retribution for executing an Archbishop.

HENRY V (1387-1422) Great warrior king whose most celebrated victory was at Agincourt in France in 1415. Harry HOTSPUR dies heroically in Act V Scene IV of SHAKESPEARE's *Henry IV Part I*, killed in a fight with Prince Henry, later Henry V. He is known to have visited York, though only briefly.

HENRY VI (1421-1471) King of England 1422-1471. Henry became king when just nine months old. During the period of his youth the seeds of the WARS OF THE ROSES were sown as rivals attempted to gain power. Henry and Queen Margaret held their court in York prior to the Battle of TOWTON in 1461 and participated in the battle.

HENRY VII (1457-1509) *See* HENRY TUDOR

HENRY VIII (1491-1547) King of England 1509-1547. He is best remembered for his collection of six wives and for his placing of himself at the head of the Church in England. Henry visited York in 1541, accompanied by his fifth wife Catherine HOWARD. Given York's significant role in the PILGRIMAGE OF GRACE of 1536-37, the CORPORATION, not for the first time, decided to grovel. Falling to their knees at FULFORD CROSS, they apologised for "grievously and traitorously offending" the king and swore eternal loyalty. As a token of this, they gave Henry a goblet containing £100, and to his "most gracious and virtuous" Queen, who was at the time already having an affair with courtier Thomas Culpepper, one containing £40. Henry was the first royal visitor for over half a century, and broke with tradition, entering the city via WALMGATE BAR rather than MICKLEGATE BAR.

HENRY TUDOR (HENRY VII) (1457-1509) King of England 1485-1509. Henry Tudor's accession effectively ended the WARS OF THE ROSES. Victorious over the Yorkist RICHARD III at the Battle of Bosworth Field in 1485, Tudor claimed the throne by right of conquest. Although technically Lancastrian, and distantly descended from EDWARD III, he had no real claim, being an estimated twenty-ninth in line at the time of Bosworth. Tudor thus married ELIZABETH OF YORK, daughter of EDWARD IV, in 1487 for political reasons, in an attempt to unite the HOUSE OF YORK and the House of Lancaster. The marriage is commemorated by the ROSE WINDOW in the MINSTER. However York's affection for RICHARD III presented an initial problem for Tudor and he received only a lukewarm welcome when he visited the city in 1486. He therefore pardoned the eighty or so men of York who fought at Bosworth Field. However, his sending of the Earl of Northumberland to Yorkshire to collect taxes in 1489 resulted in the Earl being dragged from his hunting lodge near Thirsk (20 miles/32km from York), and hanged from an oak tree. The Yorkshire people had not forgotten Northumberland's lack of participation at Bosworth, where he and his thousand or so troops failed to come to King Richard's aid.

HERBERT, SIR THOMAS (1606-1681) Friend of King CHARLES I and a strong supporter of the king during the ENGLISH CIVIL WAR. He was born in HERBERT HOUSE in PAVEMENT. Herbert accompanied the king to his execution on 30 January 1649 at Whitehall, London. Charles requested two shirts for his execution, in order not to shiver in the cold and appear to be fearful. As the person responsible for the King's wardrobe, it must be assumed that they were provided by Thomas Herbert. Herbert was at first a negotiator for Parliament but later became an ardent Royalist. He returned to York from London in 1665 and bought a house in HIGH PETER-GATE where he lived until his death.

HERBERT HOUSE Timber-framed house, built in 1557 in PAVEMENT. It is opposite the entrance to the SHAM-BLES. It was once the home of Christopher Herbert,

LORD MAYOR of York in 1573, though his great-grand-son Sir Thomas HERBERT was perhaps a more cele-brated occupant. CHARLES I dined with him in the house in 1639. The building is currently a shop, with LADY PECKETT'S YARD at its rear.

HESLINGTON Village to the south-east of the city, the location of HESLINGTON HALL and the UNIVERSITY OF YORK. Heslington means "farmstead by the hazel wood" in Old English.

HESLINGTON HALL. Large brick mansion with a court-yard which is now used as the administrative headquar-ters of the UNIVERSITY OF YORK in HESLINGTON. The building is mostly Victorian with alterations made in 1903 by Walter BRIERLEY. The old hall dates from 1565 and was built by Sir Thomas Eynns, Secretary to the COUN-CIL OF THE NORTH. The interior is mostly Brierley's work but the ceiling of the entrance hall is Elizabethan. In the garden are ancient yews and there is an early eigh-teenth-century gazebo or summerhouse. It is believed that the building was used as the headquarters of FER-DINANDO FAIRFAX during the SIEGE OF YORK. The Hall was used as a base by Bomber Command, part of the Royal Air Force, in WORLD WAR TWO.

HEWORTH Suburb of York a mile (1.7km) to the north-east of the MINSTER. In the DOMESDAY BOOK "Hewarde" is owned by Hugh FITZBALDRICK. "Worth" comes from the Old English "warde", thus Heworth means "Hugh's land". Following the HARRYING OF THE NORTH Hugh Fitzbaldrick became a substantial landowner in the area.

HEWORTH MOOR, **SKIRMISH OF** Fight seen by many as a catalyst for the WARS OF THE ROSES conflict, despite there being no fatalities. In August 1453, at HEWORTH, an armed party of NEVILLES were making their way to a wedding at Sheriff Hutton, twelve miles (19km) north of York. They were ambushed by a group led by their bitter rivals, the PERCYS.

HIGH ALTAR of the Minster The present altar is twentieth-century and the High Altar Cross is from Aguilar in southern Spain, dating from c1570. It was bought for the MINSTER in 1949.

HIGH PETERGATE Street linking BOOTHAM BAR to LOW PETERGATE. The street was the ROMAN Via Principalis, the main entrance to the fortress of EBORACUM from the north. It once included one of the four entrances into the MINSTER precinct, the Peter Gate, which spanned the road linking the corner of High Petergate with what is now DUNCOMBE PLACE.

HINDLEY CLOCK in the Minster Located in the NORTH TRANSEPT between the CHOIR SCREEN and the ST NICHOLAS CHAPEL. The clock was made by Henry Hindley in 1749. The two oak figures date from the sixteenth century and are known as "quarter jacks", striking the hour and each quarter of the hour. The clock has to be wound every two days by Geoff Newey, who maintains all the MINSTER clocks as his father did before him.

HOB MOOR Part of the STRAY of MICKLEGATE, located on the boundary with ACOMB, so-named since at least

1413. The name probably means "Goblin Moor", "Hob" being "goblin" in Old English. Ridges in part of the moor are the remains of medieval field systems. There is a PLAGUE STONE, as victims of the PLAGUE were housed in huts on the moor. There is also a stone knight dating from the 1720s, placed there by the Pasture Master who stole it from the CASTLE MILLS. Due to his light-hearted inscription, "This statue long Hob's name has bore, Who was a knight in days of yore, And gave this common to the poor", it is often thought that the stone refers to an ancient knight.

HOLE IN THE WALL Pub in High PETERGATE, near BOOTHAM BAR. Its history is unclear, though in the eighteenth century it was known as The Board. The pub, due to fear of collapse, was rebuilt completely in 1979. Several theories exist regarding the pub's name, including the possibility that the hole was an escape route for churchmen following a crafty drink. PRECENTOR'S COURT can be reached via a SNICKELWAY alongside the pub.

HOLGATE, ROBERT (1481-1555) First Protestant ARCHBISHOP OF YORK (1545-1554), and the first to be married. He was born in Hemsworth, West Yorkshire. While still a relatively obscure bishop (of Llandaff, South Wales) he was appointed as the first active Lord President of the York-based COUNCIL OF THE NORTH in 1538. Following the death of HENRY VIII (1547) and the accession of the Catholic Mary Tudor (1553), Holgate shed his religion and deserted his wife to save his skin. He founded ARCHBISHOP HOLGATE'S SCHOOL, initially in MINSTER CLOSE, in 1546, and a suburb to the south-west of York is named after him.

HOLGATE BRIDGE Iron bridge opened in 1911, the third bridge to be built on Holgate Road crossing the RAILWAY to the west of the city centre. It was designed to link the village of ACOMB with York via the new electric TRAM service.

HOLY TRINITY CHURCH Situated in GOODRAMGATE behind LADY ROW, first recorded in the eleventh century. The church stands in a small churchyard, reached through an eighteenth-century archway in Goodramgate or via HORNPOT LANE. The STAINED GLASS in the church dates from 1471 and the East Window was donated by Reverend John Walker, who is depicted at Christ's feet. The church has no electricity so the three annual services are conducted by candlelight. The rare box pews date from the seventeenth and eighteenth centuries. There is a squint, or gap in the wall, between the side chapel and the main altar, so that the priest saying Mass in the smaller chapel could see what the priest at the High Altar was doing. The church is occasionally used for concerts.

HOLY TRINITY CHURCH Situated in MICKLEGATE, comprising the last remnants of a Benedictine Priory. Until 1855 it had a gateway which was used by the medieval GUILDS to stage the opening performances of the MYSTERY PLAYS. Only the nave survives from Holy Trinity Priory. A church mentioned in the DOMESDAY BOOK was given to French Benedictine monks c1090, who established the Priory in York. The church had many alterations made between the twelfth and fifteenth centuries. The Priory closed in 1538 after the DISSOLUTION OF THE MONASTERIES and the church fell into ruins. During a storm in 1551 the NORMAN tower collapsed, severely damaging the church. Restoration began in 1850 when the ATKINSONS rebuilt the south aisle. The GHOSTS of a young woman, a nurse and a child are said to have haunted the churchyard for the last 400 years. The origin of the story is that the child and the nurse died of the PLAGUE and were buried outside the city WALLS. The woman died later and was buried at Holy Trinity. The ghosts are seen through the STAINED GLASS emotionally reuniting. York's only surviving STOCKS can be seen in the churchyard.

HORNPOT LANE SNICKELWAY giving access to HOLY TRINITY CHURCH in GOODRAMGATE from LOW PETERGATE. It once accommodated medieval craftsmen known as horners, who made cups, pots and book coverings from animal horn.

HORSEFAIR Fairs situated throughout the city for the sale of horses and cattle. The fairs were controlled by the ARCHBISHOP OF YORK, rather than by the SHERIFF. A special Horsefair court was empowered to deal out suitable punishments for misdemeanours. In 1218 the three fairs were divided, two going under the jurisdiction of the LORD MAYOR and one remaining with the Archbishop. Control of the fair was a lucrative business as there were certain tolls to be paid by both the buyer and the seller. The principal Horsefair was located where CLARENCE GARDENS now stands.

HOSPITALS Prior to the opening of YORK DISTRICT HOSPITAL in 1976, York's main hospitals were the COUNTY HOSPITAL in MONKGATE, the City Hospital (between Haxby Road and Huntington Road), and the FULFORD Maternity Hospital. There were also hospitals at Naburn (alongside the Fulford Hospital), with Yearsley Bridge Hospital (the "fever hospital"), the Grange Hospital and the Bungalow Hospital situated on Huntington Road. Other hospitals were at CLIFTON, a Maternity Hospital in ACOMB, and the Military Hospital Civilian Wing opposite the POLICE STATION. Although two of these are still used as community units, the remainder have been closed and redeveloped. Other hospitals remaining in the city are psychiatric hospitals BOOTHAM PARK and THE RETREAT, and the PUREY-CUST private hospital.

HOSPITIUM Timber-framed medieval building situated in the MUSEUM GARDENS, once used as the guesthouse for ST MARY'S ABBEY. The ground floor was built in 1310, the first floor in 1420 and a new roof added in 1930. The Hospitium is used as a café and occasionally for exhibitions and events.

HOTSPUR, HARRY (1364-1403) Nickname of Sir Henry PERCY, a noted soldier who helped HENRY IV to the throne in 1399. He later rebelled against the king and was defeated and killed at Shrewsbury. He dies heroically in Act V Scene IV of SHAKESPEARE's *Henry IV Part One*, killed in a fight with Prince Henry (HENRY V). The latter nonetheless pays tribute to him, "…brave Percy… Fare thee well, great heart!" His HEAD was placed on a spike above MICKLEGATE BAR.

HOUSE OF YORK The collective name of the descendants of EDMUND OF LANGLEY, the fifth son of EDWARD III and the first DUKE OF YORK. His grandson, RICHARD DUKE OF YORK, having become dissatisfied with the rule of the pious but feeble HENRY VI of the House of Lancaster, descendants of John of Gaunt, decided to lay claim to the throne. The bloody conflict which ensued thus became known as the WARS OF THE ROSES. The city of York, entirely different from the House of York, had sympathies with the Lancastrian Henry VI.

HOWARD, CATHERINE (1520-42) Queen of England 1540-42. The fifth wife of HENRY VIII, and the only one known to have visited York. The king brought his new bride to the city in 1541, the year prior to her execution. The queen is said to have consummated her affair with Thomas Culpepper in the rose garden of the house of the Abbot of ST MARY'S, now the KING'S MANOR.

HOWERD, FRANKIE (1917-1992) Comedian born at 53 Hartoft Street, off FULFORD Road. Christened Francis Alick Howard, he changed the spelling of his surname to Howerd saying later that, "there were so many funny Howards around". His father was a sergeant in the Royal Artillery and his mother worked at TERRY'S. His professional career started as a radio performer in 1946 with *Variety Bandbox*. However it is for his role as Lurcio in the television comedy *Up Pompeii* (also a film in 1971), and as the serf Lurkalot in *Up the Chastity Belt*, that he is perhaps best remembered. He was awarded an OBE in 1977 and continued to work until his death. There is a commemorative plaque to him outside the GRAND OPERA HOUSE.

HUDSON, GEORGE (1800-1871) RAILWAY speculator whose determination to "mak all t'railways cum to York" saved the city from economic stagnation. He was born in Howsham, nine miles (14.5km) north-east of York. He was originally employed at a linen draper's in COLLEGE STREET. In 1828, having inherited the then vast sum of £30,000, Hudson invested heavily in the North Midland Railway, creating an empire from a chaotic rail network and becoming a millionaire by 1848. Controlling a third of Britain's railways, the "Railway King" could do no wrong. He bought a house at 44 MONKGATE, was instrumental in the construction of LENDAL BRIDGE and became LORD MAYOR on three occasions (1837-38, 1838-39 and 1846-47). However, his business practices involved a scam which is not unfamiliar. He floated new railway companies to placate shareholders of previous companies until he was unable to create any more. By 1849 the "Magnate of Monkgate", as Hudson was called by his arch-enemy George LEEMAN, was sunk. Revealed as a fraud and publicly accused of bribery, Hudson fled to France. He died, penniless, on his return to London to see a doctor. Nonetheless, despite his flaws, Hudson is owed a great debt by York. A street in the city is named after him.

HUNGATE Area of central York originally bordered by ALDWARK, ST SAVIOURGATE, part of FOSSGATE and the river FOSS. Between the thirteenth century and 1539 a large Carmelite friary was here, with its main entrance in FOSSGATE. Hungate was one of the city's poorest

126

areas in the nineteenth and early twentieth centuries, and a Victorian red-light district. With dozens of houses packed into a small area, slaughterhouses added to the dirt and grime. The skyline was dominated by LEETHAM'S MILL, the warehouse of which still survives as ROWNTREE WHARF. Most of the houses were demolished in the 1930s, with residents relocated in council houses in CLIFTON, Tang Hall and ACOMB. Final demolition occurred in the early 1960s. A short street off STONEBOW still bears the Hungate name. Archaeological excavations in 2002 have revealed a ROMAN road and cemetery, and remains from the ANGLO-SAXON and VIKING periods. The precise location of a medieval church, St John in the Marsh, has also been discovered.

HUTTON, MARY (d.1587) Prominent woman of the sixteenth-century Catholic resistance, a friend and contemporary of Margaret CLITHEROW and Dorothy VAVASOUR. She was the wife of William Hutton, a draper, and they lived in the parish of the now demolished Holy Trinity, KING'S SQUARE. Much of the information about the conditions in which Catholics were held is based on the writings of her husband, who was imprisoned in York CASTLE. She was convicted of not attending the Anglican church and imprisoned in the KIDCOTES in 1579. It was here that she died, probably from disease.

I

ICE HOUSE Red brick, igloo-like structure situated alongside the city WALLS near MONK BAR. It was constructed around 1800 for the purpose of storing ice as a form of refrigeration for food.

IMPHAL BARRACKS Located in FULFORD Road, alongside the POLICE STATION. After a longstanding association with the PRINCE OF WALES OWN REGIMENT OF YORKSHIRE, the barracks are now used as a Ministry of Defence vetting agency. They are also used by York's Territorial Army.

IMPRESSIONS GALLERY Pioneering photographic gallery located near CLIFFORD'S TOWER, in the COPPERGATE Centre. When it opened in 1972 it was at the cutting edge of art in Europe, and has kept its reputation with exhibitions of contemporary digital art and photography.

INGRAM'S ALMSHOUSES Buildings located in BOOTHAM halfway between BOOTHAM BAR and CLIFTON. Sir Arthur Ingram's ALMSHOUSES were built in 1640 for the purpose of housing York's widows. As they could only accommodate ten people, however, they would have had little impact upon the city's growing number of poor and needy. The decorative central arch came from St Giles's church which used to stand in GILLYGATE. The almshouses are currently private flats.

INL CLUB Situated in Speculation Street off WALMGATE from 1890 until its closure in February 2002. The Irish National League Club was York's oldest surviving club, set up by migrant Irish workers. Its eventual closure was perhaps symbolic of Walmgate having ceased to be perceived as the city's "Irish Quarter".

IVAR THE BONELESS (d.c873) Semi-legendary VIKING warrior who was the first to capture York after a ferocious battle with the ANGLO-SAXONS in 866. He was known as "the Boneless" on account of his remarkably chubby face. He was the son of Ragnar Lothbrok, the most famous Viking of the ninth century. It is conceivable that Ivar and Imhar, king of Norsemen of all Ireland and Britain, were one and the same. The Viking occupation of York lasted until 954.

J

JACOB'S WELL Fifteenth-century timber-framed house in Trinity Lane off MICKLEGATE. The name is biblical in origin, referring to baptism (John 4). It was originally built to house the priest of HOLY TRINITY Priory, which occupied a large area around Holy Trinity church and was closed in 1539 during the DISSOLUTION OF THE MONASTERIES. From 1750 to 1903 it was a pub. The Edwardian stonework dates from 1905. The finely carved porch came from another inn, the Wheatsheaf in DAVY-GATE, once the residence of the Bishops of Durham, which was demolished in 1905. In 1992 the Butchers' Company, one of the ancient GUILDS dating back to the fourteenth century, made this their guildhall and it is sometimes used as a church hall.

JACOBITES Supporters of the deposed Catholic king JAMES II, his son James (the "Old Pretender"), and his grandson Charles Edward ("Bonnie Prince Charlie", the "Young Pretender"). Their support was largely centred in the north-east lowlands of Scotland. The last two HEADS to be displayed on spikes above York's MICKLEGATE BAR were those of Jacobites James Mayne and William Connolly. They were captured at the Battle of Culloden (1746), in the Scottish Highlands, effectively the last major conflict of the cause. They were imprisoned, tried in York and condemned to death. Their heads were not removed from the BAR until 1754.

JAMES I (1566-1625) James VI of Scotland (1567-1625), King of Great Britain (1603-25). On his way from Edinburgh to London to be crowned, James visited York in July 1603. ALDERMAN Robert Asquith (later LORD MAYOR of York 1606 and 1617) was despatched north with a loan of £1000 towards royal expenses, though under instructions to allege that the city was "very poor". In Asquith's absence the city CORPORATION were informed that the king had a morbid fear of assassination, resulting in the impounding of all firearms. The visit, however, was such a resounding success that the following day James chose to walk, rather than take a carriage, from his lodgings at the KING'S MANOR to the MINSTER, so his subjects could see "his body as well as his face". The next day he summoned Lord Mayor Robert Watter to Grimston, near Tadcaster, and knighted him.

JAMES II (1633-1701) King of England 1685-88. Deposed Catholic king, having adopted the faith in 1668, and the eighth DUKE OF YORK. The womanising brother of CHARLES II, he had a long-standing feud with the city of York, perhaps dating back to 1665, when he and his first duchess, Anne Hyde, stayed in the city for seven weeks. Attending a large banquet at the LORD MAYOR's house, James tactlessly ordered the city CORPORATION to hand over to him the right to issue licences to retail wine, which he was busy enjoying. Aware that the Corporation would lose considerable profits as a result, he reluctantly agreed to pay £50 a year to the city's poor. York's opposition to a Catholic successor was considerable, and James generally received a cold reception in the city. His major contribution to world history is having NEW YORK named after him, following the English capture of New Amsterdam in 1664. He was deposed in favour of the Protestant William of Orange.

JAMES IV (1478-1513) King of Scotland 1488-1513. James's 1503 marriage to Margaret Tudor, sister of HENRY VIII, is commemorated by PRINCESS MARGARET'S ARCH in BOOTHAM. Local enthusiasm for the attractive and energetic young king did not last, however. Following his rebellion against the English and defeat at Flodden, Northumberland, in 1513, his body was carried on a cart through BOOTHAM BAR to much cheering. His marriage to a Tudor nonetheless changed the course of history, resulting in the accession of his great-grandson (JAMES VI & I) to the English throne.

JAMES, ERIC (1909-1992) Lord James of Rusholme (Manchester) was the founding Vice-Chancellor (1962-1973) of the new UNIVERSITY OF YORK. He studied Chemistry at Oxford, taught Science at Winchester (establishing a well-earned reputation as a mimic), and was appointed High Master of Manchester Grammar School at the age of thirty-six. On appointment to the new

University he chose all the founding staff, who made a vital contribution to the current excellent reputation of the University. He also wrote the institution's *Development Plan* of 1962, which laid down the academic and social qualities to be achieved. A college of the University, built between 1991 and 1997, is named after him.

JENKINS, HENRY (1500-1669) Labourer born in Ellerton-on-Swale, near Catterick, forty miles (64.3km) north-west of York. While no church records existed in 1500, his reputed great age was legendary. In the seventeenth century he recalled being sent to Northallerton, near Catterick, with a horse-load of arrows prior to the Battle of Flodden, Northumberland, in 1513. Even in his mid-140s, Henry would apparently think nothing of walking from Catterick to York. He was called to give evidence at the ASSIZE COURTS several times in the 1660s, showing a remarkable memory of ancient rights of way over property and tithes (taxes). His great age was never disputed and the testimonies of his contemporaries are all in favour of his claim. Yorkshire writer William Grainge, who paid considerable attention to the matter, concluded that Jenkins' remarkable longevity was "established beyond the reach of reasonable doubt".

JESSE WINDOW in the Minster STAINED GLASS window dating from c1310, located in bay three of the SOUTH NAVE AISLE. The window shows Christ's family tree, a popular theme for medieval glass painters, taken from the Book of Isaiah in the Old Testament. A green stem rises from the recumbent figure of Jesse with the prophets and kings of Judah seated on the branches.

JEWBURY Street just outside the city WALLS near PEASHOLME GREEN, the location of the medieval Jewish cemetery as Jews were not permitted to be buried within the city Walls. The street's name means "the Jews' quarter". In the early 1980s an archaeological dig was carried out and the remains found were reburied in 1984 in the presence of the Chief Rabbi. A supermarket car park is now on the site. The finds suggested that in the thirteenth century there was a Jewish community of around 300 people. In c1230 the Jews wanted to extend their cemetery by buying a garden next to it, owned by John ROMANUS. An agreement for the transfer of land was made. His copy of the agreement survives in the MIN-STER archives, witnessed by the highest authorities of church and state in York, suggesting that there must have been a good relationship between Jews and Gentiles.

JEWS OF YORK In the mid-1100s Jews began to settle in York. Christians were forbidden to lend money so the Jews traditionally took on this service, known as usury. In 1190 the MASSACRE OF THE JEWS took place at CLIFFORD'S TOWER. It has been alleged that afterwards there were no more Jews in the city, but in 1195 two Jews were wealthy enough to be listed on the York PIPE ROLL. In 1200 York was named as an official centre for the registration of Jewish debts. The growing size and wealth of the community suggests new arrivals, but there were also survivors of the massacre. From c1220 to 1250 was the Jews' most prosperous period. In 1218 York was listed as one of the places with Jews under government protection and a document exists from 1221 referring to a bailiff for "our Jews of York". They lived all over the city, but particularly in JEWBURY, CONEY STREET and JUB-BERGATE. By the 1250s their wealth was in decline, the king was no longer prepared to protect them and their position in England was becoming very insecure. They began to emigrate and by 1290 there were only six Jewish households left in York. That year all Jews were expelled from England by EDWARD II.

JOHN (1166-1216) King of England 1199-1216. John was the brother of RICHARD I (the "Lionheart"). He is said to have much favoured York, visiting some sixteen times during his reign. However, of the fifteen signatories of the Magna Carta (a document outlining people's rights and effectively curbing a monarch's power), six were Yorkshire barons, and John later fined York for siding with the rebels. ARCHBISHOP OF YORK Walter DE GRAY was King John's Chancellor and was with him when he signed the document at Runnymede, five miles (8km) from Windsor, near London.

JOLABLOT Annual VIKING festival held in February. The name comes from *jola* (midwinter festival of yule) and *blot* (blood or blood sacrifice). Historically during February the Danes of JORVIK celebrated the end of another winter and the coming of spring. Each year the Vikings again "invade" York, this time in a celebration of the city's heritage. Throughout the week there are longships, craft fairs, food markets and people dressed as Vikings marching through the streets.

JORVIK VIKING name for York in the ninth century. Jorvik is a direct corruption of the ANGLO-SAXON name

EOFORWIC, as the Viking dialect replaced the F with a V. York was invaded by a Viking army in AD866 led by IVAR THE BONELESS and his two brothers, Halfdene and Hubba. The kingdom of Jorvik occupied the area of the old ANGLO-SAXON kingdom of Deira in NORTHUMBRIA. The word Jorvik outlived the Viking occupation, remaining in use until medieval times when it was again corrupted into the word York. Viking York is recreated in accurate detail at the JORVIK CENTRE.

JORVIK CENTRE One of York's most popular attractions, situated in the COPPERGATE Centre, next to ST MARY'S CHURCH, which opened in 1984. It accurately recreates, in great detail, the buildings of the tenth-century VIKING city, found by the YORK ARCHAEOLOGICAL TRUST on that precise site during the excavation of 1976-1982, following the demolition of CRAVENS' sweet factory. The original timbers of the houses were preserved, together with thousands of artefacts and vegetable and animal remains, by the waterlogged state of the ground near the river FOSS. It was necessary to rebuild the attraction in 2000, in order to represent more accurately the information arising from the archaeological research of the intervening years. Jorvik is internationally renowned and has changed the nature of archaeological presentation and of TOURISM in York. Over thirteen million people have visited the Jorvik Centre so far.

JOSCE THE JEW (d.1190) Josce died in the MASSACRE of the JEWS at CLIFFORD'S TOWER. He had taken most of the Jews to York CASTLE for refuge after his house and that of BENEDICT were attacked. When they realised the hopelessness of their situation, Rabbi YOMTOB OF JOIGNY called for the men to kill their wives and children before killing themselves. Josce allegedly set an example to the other men by cutting the throats of his wife and children first. Many of the Jews were in favour of suicide. It is believed that Yomtob killed Josce before killing himself. Some Jews may have been hidden by local people. The first indication of a Jewish community in York appears in 1175 in a record of land being leased from ST MARY'S ABBEY by Josce, son of David.

JOSEPH ROWNTREE FOUNDATION Founded by JOSEPH ROWNTREE as a Village Trust in 1904 to administer his model village, NEW EARSWICK, created in 1902 just outside York. Its headquarters, along with those of the Joseph Rowntree Housing Trust, are based in Water End, CLIFTON. In 1959 the organisation widened its objectives to include research and development, and adopted its new name in 1990. The Foundation shares the aspirations of its founder to "seek out the underlying causes of weakness and evil" in order to "change the face of England". Its work now covers the whole of the UK, concentrating on housing, social care and social policy.

JOSEPH ROWNTREE SCHOOL Secondary School in Haxby Road, NEW EARSWICK, two miles (3.2km) north of York. It was officially opened in 1942 by Conservative MP Rab Butler and it became a comprehensive school in 1976.

JOSEPH ROWNTREE THEATRE Theatre in Haxby Road, opposite the NESTLE ROWNTREE factory, one mile (1.6km) from the city centre. It was opened in 1935 and has capacity for four hundred people.

JUBBERGATE Short street off PARLIAMENT STREET leading to NEWGATE MARKET. York's POLICE STATION was situated here until 1880 when the CLIFFORD STREET Station was built. Originally the street ran from the SHAMBLES to CONEY STREET but was cut in half by the creation of PARLIAMENT STREET in 1836. Its southern half was renamed Market Street. Its original Scandinavian name was Bretgate, meaning "street of the Britons", who may have been the servants or slaves of the dominant VIKING community. Later the JEWS OF YORK lived here, and by the fourteenth century the street had become Jubretgate. Over the years the modern form of Jubbergate developed. It is probable that the medieval Jewish synagogue was situated on this street or on Coney Street.

JUDGES' COURT Early eighteenth-century house in a small courtyard off 28-30 CONEY STREET. It was used as a residence by judges when they attended the ASSIZE COURTS in York from the mid-eighteenth century until 1806, when they began to use the JUDGES' LODGINGS. The house now contains offices.

JUDGES' LODGINGS Large house with gardens and a courtyard, situated in LENDAL. It was built between 1715 and 1725, on the site of the churchyard of the original St Wilfrid's Church, by Dr Clifton Wintringham. From 1806 until 1979 the building was the official residence of the Judges of Assize who sat at the ASSIZE COURTS. The Judges' Lodgings is currently a hotel.

K

KALER, BERWICK (1946-) York's premier "pantomime dame". An actor born in Sunderland in the north-east of England, he has appeared in the city's annual Christmas production at the THEATRE ROYAL for over a quarter of a century. Despite television and theatre work, Kaler remains a celebrity perhaps only in York, which adds to the enormous success of his performances. He received an Honorary Degree from the UNIVERSITY OF YORK in 2002.

KIDCOTES PRISON situated on OUSE BRIDGE until the nineteenth century. Kidcotes was the colloquial name for a PRISON in the north of England in the Middle Ages. The Kidcotes existed from as early as 1278. York prisoners would be held here while offenders from other parts of Yorkshire would be held at the CASTLE. Eventually Ouse Bridge housed two Kidcotes, one run by the SHERIFF for felons and one by the LORD MAYOR for drunks and prostitutes. At the time of Queen Elizabeth I, a Protestant, the anti-Catholic SHERIFFS would put Catholics who refused to take the Oath of Allegiance in the disease-ridden and flood-prone Lower Kidcote. Margaret CLITHEROW spent her last days here prior to her execution in 1586. Both Mary HUTTON and Dorothy VAVASOUR died here in 1587. The prison was abandoned in 1807 when the jail opened at BAILE HILL.

KING'S ARMS Pub on KING'S STAITH, overlooking the river next to OUSE BRIDGE. It has been an inn since at least 1783. The pub's name changed to the Ouse Bridge Inn in 1867, before reverting to the King's Arms in 1974. The king whose painting and coat of arms are displayed is RICHARD III. The pub is the oldest remaining building on King's Staith, once York's busiest quay when the city was a thriving port in medieval times. Regularly one of the most flooded pubs, its cellars are housed upstairs. The annual levels of FLOODS are recorded just inside the front door, with the year 2000 the worst to date.

KING'S FISHPOOL Lake which once lay between LAYERTHORPE BRIDGE and the RED TOWER. It was effectively created in c1068 when the NORMANS dammed the river FOSS. The lake became well stocked with fish and was maintained by local families. Eventually, the Fishpool began to silt up and by the late 1700s it was described as "the disgrace of York, being little better than a stinking morass". The historian Francis DRAKE wrote of repeated proclamations to prevent people "throwing into this great fish-pond any dung of beasts or other nastinesses". Canalisation of the Foss by the Foss Navigation Company took place in 1792. The City CORPORATION gained control in 1854, drained the lake and created Foss Islands Road.

KING'S MANOR Located alongside EXHIBITION SQUARE. Originally the Abbot's house, part of ST MARY'S ABBEY, its earliest remains date from the thirteenth century. After the DISSOLUTION OF THE MONASTERIES the COUNCIL OF THE NORTH was held there until 1642. HENRY VIII built the wine cellars using stone from the ruined Abbey. The principal entrance bears the coat of arms of CHARLES I and also of JAMES I (James VI of Scotland) to mark his stay on his way south to assume the crown of England in 1603. WENTWORTH, Earl of Strafford, resided here as Lord President of Charles I's Council of the North. The building suffered minor damage during the SIEGE OF YORK in 1644. From 1688 onwards it became the residence of military governors of York and in the early eighteenth century a private boarding school for girls was established there. A School for the Blind opened in 1833 and the Principal's House, built by Walter BRIERLEY, was added in 1902. The Blind School moved to Tadcaster Road in 1956 and the CITY OF YORK COUNCIL bought the Manor. In 1963 the new UNIVERSITY leased the buildings and restored them to use for half the University until 1967. The Departments of Archaeology, Eighteenth-Century Studies and Medieval Studies are currently housed in the Manor.

KING'S SQUARE Small square between PETERGATE and the SHAMBLES which reputedly contained the palace of the VIKING KINGS who ruled York in the ninth and tenth centuries. Its name is recorded as "Kuningesgard" in the thirteenth century, meaning the King's Court, and it is likely the palace was built on the site of a ROMAN gatehouse. This was the Porta Principalis Sinistra, the eastern gateway in the walls of the Roman fortress of EBORACUM. The church of Holy Trinity stood in King's Square until 1937 and the outline of the building can still be seen in the shape of the paved Square, as can gravestones. King's Square hosts some of York's many street entertainers in the summer.

KING'S STAITH Quay situated on the north bank of the river by OUSE BRIDGE. It stretches from what is now the KING'S ARMS pub to Friargate. Along with QUEEN'S STAITH, King's Staith was one of the city's landing areas where ships would unload their goods. The area was notorious for pressgangs (naval and military gangs empowered to seize men for service) in the late eighteenth century. King's Staith is often affected by FLOODS.

KIRK, JOHN LAMPLUGH (1867-1940) Dr Kirk of Pickering in North Yorkshire was a collector of antiquities and his collection, donated to the city of York in 1935, formed the basis of what was to become the CASTLE MUSEUM.

KIRKGATE Street in the CASTLE MUSEUM, named after Dr John Lamplugh KIRK. It is a recreated Victorian street containing shopfronts and a HANSOM CAB.

KNAVESMIRE One of the ancient STRAYS, a vast area of land to the south of the city centre, largely occupied by the RACECOURSE. The name derives not from the executions of "knaves" or criminals but from the ANGLO-SAXON "knab" meaning a servant or serf. Thus the Knavesmire was land set aside for the poorer citizens of York as grazing ground for their cattle. Part of the Knavesmire was known as TYBURN, where public EXECUTIONS were held, the most notorious being that of Dick TURPIN in 1739. The Knavesmire played a role in both World Wars, being the location of a huge military encampment and the Red Cross hospital in WORLD WAR ONE, bombed during the ZEPPELIN RAIDS, and housing Prisoners of War in WORLD WAR TWO.

L

LADY ANNE MIDDLETON'S HALL House dating from the 1650s, located in SKELDERGATE. It was built for Anne Middleton, wife of the SHERIFF of York, Peter Middleton. It has had many uses including as a hospice for the widows of freemen and is now a hotel. In its grounds is the YORVIK BRASS RUBBING CENTRE in two converted ALMSHOUSES.

LADY CHAPEL of the Minster Largest of the three chapels at the East End of the MINSTER. It is dedicated to the Virgin Mary and occasionally used for services for up to fifty people. The chapel was created during the late fourteenth century. The chapel contains the GREAT EAST WINDOW, completed in 1408, and the tomb of ARCHBISHOP OF YORK Richard SCROPE, who was executed in 1405. There is new seating carved by Robert "Mousey" THOMPSON.

LADY HEWLEY'S ALMSHOUSES Houses located in ST SAVIOURGATE, built in 1840. The original hospital was founded by Lady Hewley in 1700 in TANNER ROW, where it remained until the construction of the first RAILWAY STATION in 1840. Lady Sarah Hewley (1627-1710) was the wife of John Hewley, MP for York, and is buried in ST SAVIOUR'S CHURCH. In her will she left money providing for the ALMSHOUSES, as well as contributing to the UNITARIAN CHAPEL. The houses are still used as accommodation for the elderly.

LADY PECKETT'S YARD Medieval alleyway which runs alongside HERBERT HOUSE from PAVEMENT to FOSSGATE. In 1312 it was known as "Bakehouse Lane". The alley has been known by its current name since the eighteenth century. John Peckett was LORD MAYOR in 1702 and occupied a house on this site. Following his death in 1707 his widow, Lady Peckett, continued to live here and gave her name to this ancient thoroughfare. In 1857 JOSEPH SEEBOHM ROWNTREE and JOHN STEPHENSON ROWNTREE founded an Adult School to teach reading and writing behind Rowntree's grocers' shop in Lady Peckett's Yard.

LADY ROW Oldest houses in York, dating from 1316, located in GOODRAMGATE. The houses were originally occupied by priests associated with HOLY TRINITY CHURCH. Originally known as Our Lady's Row, they are the earliest surviving example in England of houses with overhanging jetties, an upper floor projecting over the lower. This style of house was common in medieval times, owing to the fact that tax was only paid on the ground area occupied. The city CORPORATION bought the houses after the DISSOLUTION OF THE MONASTER-IES and let them to tenants, but by the late seventeenth century some of them were privately owned. In 1766 the house at the southern end of the row was demolished to make way for a new arched gateway to Holy Trinity Church. Between 1825 and 1850 major rebuilding work took place when the northern house was heightened and the original entrance to the churchyard disappeared. In the nineteenth and twentieth centuries two of the houses were used as pubs. The row currently contains shops and a café.

LADY WELL Well-house designed by John CARR in 1752, located towards the end of the NEW WALK near the BLUE BRIDGE. In 1749 it was decided by the city CORPORATION to make a decorative feature of the well, and "to contract with proper workmen for making a hansoom fountain at the pikeing well". The path alongside the well was originally known as the Pye Kell and the well waters were said to be good for sore eyes. Work is currently being undertaken by the CITY OF YORK COUNCIL to restore the building, including the careful removal of silt which covered the flight of steps leading down to the well. The stonework is to be repointed, a new roof will be provided and the iron gates restored.

LAMEL HILL Hill to the south-east of the city, where The RETREAT hospital is situated. Previously referred to as HESLINGTON Hill and standing some ninety feet (27.4m) above the level of the OUSE, in 1644 it was the site of a gun-emplacement erected by Parliamentarian forces during the SIEGE OF YORK. Significant damage to WALMGATE BAR was inflicted from here. Lamel Hill was also the site of York's first formal archaeological dig in 1849. Apart from debris from the ENGLISH CIVIL WAR, such as coins and cannon balls, hundreds of human bones were discovered suggesting the existence of a large ANGLO-SAXON grave.

LAYERTHORPE BRIDGE Road bridge over the river FOSS linking Layerthorpe and PEASHOLME GREEN. The first bridge here was built in the early 1300s. It was destroyed during the SIEGE OF YORK in 1644 and not replaced for over a decade. In the early 1800s there was a notorious dunghill near the bridge, where the city's sewage was collected. A new bridge was built in 1829, designed by Peter ATKINSON the younger. Layerthorpe POSTERN, a fourteenth-century rectangular tower with an archway which was part of the city WALLS, was located here and demolished in 1829. Until 1850 the KING'S FISHPOOL was still visible. The bridge was again rebuilt and widened in 1998.

LEEMAN, GEORGE (1809-1882) Chairman of the North Eastern RAILWAY (formed 1854) and arch-rival of York's "Railway King" George HUDSON. He was said to be the second most important York citizen after Hudson in the nineteenth century, and was chiefly responsible for the latter's exposure and downfall. A statue of Leeman can be seen on Station Road, near the RAILWAY STATION. A solicitor, he was MP for York as an Independent (elected 1865, 1871 and 1874), and served the city as LORD MAYOR three times (1853-4, 1860-1 and 1870-1). His work improving York's drainage systems, streets and burial grounds made him very popular, and the money for the statue was raised by public subscription. Some say that the statue was originally intended to be of Hudson, but Leeman's head was grafted onto it. He gives his name to Leeman Road, the site of the NATIONAL RAILWAY MUSEUM.

LEETHAM, HENRY (d.1896) Owner of LEETHAM'S MILL, a flour mill once situated in the HUNGATE area, on the banks of the river FOSS. He became a major employer and by 1888 was a wealthy man. Grain became the main cargo carried along the river OUSE. In 1895-6 Leetham built a huge warehouse on WORMALD'S CUT by the Foss consisting of five storeys plus a nine-storey water tower. This building later became a warehouse for cocoa beans for ROWNTREE & CO, now ROWNTREE WHARF.

LEETHAM'S MILL Imposing building once situated by WORMALD'S CUT on the river FOSS. It was built by Henry LEETHAM and was part of the largest flour mill in Europe. Designed by Walter PENTY, it opened in 1861 and quickly expanded until by 1911 it employed around 600 workers. It was supplied with grain by barge. ROWN-TREE & CO took over the warehouse in 1937 and NESTLÉ ROWNTREE turned down the idea of a £500,000 "Chocolate Experience" there in 1989. Cadbury's then pre-empted this with the opening of the hugely successful "Cadbury World" in Bournville, Birmingham, in 1990. Despite the potential financial rewards, Rowntree's board maintained their skills were in confectionery, rather than in entertainment. The warehouse is now Rowntree Wharf containing flats and offices. It has been described as "York's best industrial building".

LENDAL Street linking ST HELEN'S SQUARE and Museum Street. The name is derived from the landing stage for ST LEONARD'S HOSPITAL. York's principal POST OFFICE has been located here since 1703. It was the site of the Augustinian friary where RICHARD III (as Duke of Gloucester) stayed on his visits to the city. The JUDGES' LODGINGS is located on this street.

LENDAL BRIDGE One of two Victorian bridges over the river OUSE, which opened in 1863. It was built by Thomas

Page who also designed SKELDERGATE BRIDGE and Westminster Bridge in London. The designs on the parapet feature the lions of England, the WHITE ROSE OF YORK and the crossed keys of the Diocese of York. Below, on the bridge itself, further ironwork features York's COAT OF ARMS and also the intertwined letters V and A, standing for VICTORIA and Albert, the Prince Consort. In 1860 a toll bridge was begun on this site, which collapsed during construction killing five men. In 1861, at a cost of over £35,000, a second bridge was begun. The first one was dredged from the river and sold to Scarborough Council to form a part of Valley Bridge. In 1863 the ferryman, put out of business by the new bridge, was given compensation of a horse and cart and £15 in cash. The toll houses are still visible on Lendal Bridge and are used as a shop and a café. Tolls were abolished in 1894. The bridge was strengthened in 1910 to accommodate electric TRAMS.

LENDAL TOWER Stone tower situated on the north bank of the river OUSE next to LENDAL BRIDGE. It was built in the fourteenth century. Initially used for defensive purposes, it became York's first waterworks in 1682. Water was pumped directly from the Ouse, through the tower and into the city by the use of pipes made of tree trunks. This system of providing water for the city was deemed sufficient until new waterworks were built in 1846 at CLIFTON. In 1677 the tower was leased from the city to York Waterworks for five hundred years at a yearly rent of two peppercorns. A peppercorn rent is a nominal rent reserved for the purpose of having a tenancy acknowledged by the tenant. The peppercorn ceremony is still held today and will continue until the year 2177 when the lease expires. During the medieval period a chain was hung from here to BARKER TOWER across the river theoretically to prevent ships leaving the city without paying their due taxes. Another chain ran between the DAVY TOWER and the now demolished Hyngbrig Tower, near BAILE HILL.

LIBRARY York's main library is located in Museum Street next to the remains of ST LEONARD'S HOSPITAL. It was designed by Walter BRIERLEY and opened in 1927. The city CORPORATION first discussed the building of a public library in 1851. The idea remained in discussion until 1887 when celebrations were planned for Queen VICTORIA's Golden Jubilee. Like forty-nine other cities, York chose to commemorate the Jubilee by creating a public library. The first public library was on CLIFFORD STREET, in the Literary Institute building, and was officially opened in 1893 by the then DUKE OF YORK (later George V). By the end of WORLD WAR ONE the library was outgrowing its premises and the current library was built in Museum Street. It houses not only York's main lending library but also the reference library. The CITY ARCHIVES, which contain material dating back to the twelfth century, are situated alongside the ART GALLERY.

LITTLE ADMIRAL Small figure on top of the clock on ST MARTIN-LE-GRAND in CONEY STREET. The Little Admiral, complete with navigation instrument, is actually an eighteenth-century addition to the seventeenth-century clock. The Admiral came through the BAEDEKER BLITZ of April 1942 unscathed, although the church was severely damaged and the clock face needed replacing.

LITTLE EASE Prison cell in MONK BAR, which claims to be the world's smallest. It measures just five feet three inches (1.6m) in diameter, and housed recusant Catholic Alice BOWMAN at the time of Queen Elizabeth I.

LITTLE JOHN Pub in CASTLEGATE near CLIFFORD'S TOWER. Formerly the ROBIN HOOD, although the legendary outlaw has only a tenuous York connection. The present building was built around 1730 and, like the majority of the older York inns, was originally a coaching house. Prior to the construction of CLIFFORD STREET in 1881, Castlegate, though narrow, was a major thoroughfare, leading to the CASTLE and the road to Selby.

LLOYD-JONES, DAVID (1928-1994) Potter who worked in a studio in FULFORD from 1962 until his death. Born in London, he attended Guildford Art School. He worked for his father-in-law Jack Prendergast in his York CINEMA business for ten years from 1952 until he set up his studio. Influenced by Bernard Leach in his style, he exhibited regularly as part of the York Four, the other members being the painters John Langton, Russell Platt and Reg Williams. His pots are in many public collections including the Victoria & Albert Museum in London and in Norway, Belgium, Germany, York ART GALLERY and the Ismay Collection in the YORKSHIRE MUSEUM. He took part in exhibitions at galleries all over the country. In 1989 he was awarded an Honorary Doctorate by the UNIVERSITY OF YORK.

LORD MAYOR OF YORK Initially known simply as the Mayor of York, the first Mayor was appointed c1213. Hugh de Selby is recorded as Mayor in 1217. In 1387 RICHARD II gave the sword from his side to be borne as SWORD OF STATE before the Mayor, who was to be known thenceforth as the Lord Mayor of York. The Mayor's job description, as devised in the Middle Ages, is to "keep and guard the city for our Lord the King" and to "maintain and advance the City's rights and jurisdictions". He is also expected to "do right by rich and poor". The post is currently held for one year. Among the most famous mayors were George HUDSON (1837-8, 1838-9 and 1846-7), George LEEMAN (1853-4, 1860-1 and 1870-1) and John Bowes MORRELL (1914-15 and 1949-50).

LORD MAYOR'S WALK Street running from St Maurice's Road to GILLYGATE, alongside the city WALLS. The wealthy of the city, needing an outside area in which to promenade owing to the filth and the foul SMELLS within the city Walls, initiated the planting of trees on this street in 1718. Previously they had strolled around the MINSTER to avoid the stench outside. Newbigging Street was thus renamed the gentrified Lord Mayor's Walk. Civil engineers may be interested to learn that in 1825 it was the first street in the city to be surfaced with Tarmacadam. In 1846 St John's Training College, now YORK ST JOHN COLLEGE, moved to the street. ARCHBISHOP HOLGATE'S SCHOOL occupied part of the college between 1858 and 1963.

LOW PETERGATE Originally part of the Via Principalis (or main street) of ROMAN York, the street links KING'S SQUARE to the top of STONEGATE near the MINSTER. The present Petergate is so-called because of its proximity to the Minster, the cathedral church of ST PETER.

LOWRY, LAURENCE STEPHEN (1887-1976) Artist born in Lancashire, best known for his paintings of urban landscapes. Lowry's depiction of CLIFFORD'S TOWER can be seen in the ART GALLERY.

LOWTHER Victorian pub in KING'S STAITH, overlooking the river OUSE. The construction of CLIFFORD STREET and the Lowther Hotel were part of the city CORPORATION's determination to rid the city of its notorious WATER LANES, streets leading to the river which were rife with slum-dwellings, poverty, crime and prostitution. The hotel, like Clifford Street, was completed in 1881. Like its neighbour, the KING'S ARMS, the pub can be severely affected by the FLOODS.

M

MACE Silver gilt, ornate rod representing the monarch which is carried with the SWORD OF STATE in York's civic processions. As with the sword, the mace is carried upright and turned downwards in the presence of the monarch. The tradition dates from RICHARD II who gave York its first mace in 1396. The present mace was made in 1647 with the arms of CHARLES I depicted on its top, but it now bears the arms of CHARLES II. The mace is normally kept in the MANSION HOUSE.

MAD ALICE LANE. SNICKELWAY linking SWINEGATE and LOW PETERGATE. The name is derived from Alice Smith, who was hanged in the 1820s for the "offence" of insanity.

MAGISTRATES' COURT Imposing courthouse in CLIF-FORD STREET, built between 1890 and 1892. The centre bay has a carved stone scene of RICHARD II presenting the first SWORD OF STATE to the LORD MAYOR of York.

MALEBYSSE, RICHARD (d.1209) One of the leaders of the mob responsible for the MASSACRE OF THE JEWS. A landowner who owned Acaster Malbis near York, he was out of favour with RICHARD I and feared he would lose his post of Keeper of the FOREST OF GALTRES. He supported the king's brother JOHN, and was later involved in John's plots against Richard I. Malebysse was in debt to Jewish moneylenders. In 1190 King Richard was away on crusade and Malebysse saw his chance to orchestrate anti-Jewish riots. In March 1190, during rioting, JOSCE led the other JEWS OF YORK to CLIF-FORD'S TOWER to take refuge, where they were trapped. Rabbi YOMTOB called upon them to commit sui-cide and he killed about sixty men, including Josce, after they had first killed their wives and children. After Yomtob took his own life, a fire raged, endangering the few sur-vivors. They pleaded for mercy, agreeing to leave the Tower and accept baptism. Malebysse and his men then massacred them. He and the mob rushed to the MIN-STER, demanded the Jewish bonds which were deposited there and burnt them in the NAVE. Afterwards Malebysse's lands were seized and only recovered years later on payment of a fine. His name is derived from *mala bestia* which, ironically, means "evil beast" in Latin.

MALLARD Locomotive which can now be seen at the NATIONAL RAILWAY MUSEUM. The Mallard is the holder of the world record for steam traction on rail, reaching 126mph (203kph) on 3 July 1938. The Mallard, an A4 4-6-2 class locomotive, was built in 1938 at a cost of £8500. It remained in service until 1963.

MANCHESTER, EARL OF (1602-71) Major-general of the Parliamentarian forces of the eastern counties of England during the ENGLISH CIVIL WAR. He arrived at York on 2 June 1644 to assist in the SIEGE OF YORK and due to his arrival the city became completely surrounded. He was in supreme command at the Battle of MARSTON MOOR on 1 July 1644. Like many Parliamentarians, such as Sir THOMAS FAIRFAX, he was opposed to the trial and subsequent execution of CHARLES I, and played an active role in the Restoration of CHARLES II in 1660.

MANSION HOUSE Official residence of the LORD MAYOR during his or her year of office. It is situated on the south side of ST HELEN'S SQUARE. When the building was completed in 1730, York preceded London in having a building specifically for the Mayor to live in. London's equivalent was completed in 1753. The Mansion House was only built because Sir William Robinson, Lord Mayor in 1700, refused to give up the RED HOUSE. In 1761 EDWARD AUGUSTUS, tenth DUKE OF YORK, was the first royal visitor to the Mansion House. Restored by YORK CIVIC TRUST in 1999, the building is occasionally open to the public and pre-booked groups can also arrange tours.

MARSTON MOOR Major battle of the ENGLISH CIVIL WAR which took place eight miles (13km) south-west of

York on 2 July 1644. The Parliamentary forces, led by Lord FERDINANDO FAIRFAX, Sir THOMAS FAIRFAX and the Earl of MANCHESTER, defeated the Royalist army led by Prince RUPERT. Oliver CROMWELL participated in the battle, sustaining a head wound early on and only returning (with bandaged head) as the tide turned in the Parliamentarians' favour. The Royalists suffered heavy losses, with 4000 men killed and 1500 captured. The Royalist Duke of NEWCASTLE, defender of the city of York, did not arrive on the field of battle until 5pm, his men being too busy looting the abandoned positions of the Parliamentarians, where they found, among other things, 4000 pairs of boots.

MARTIN, JONATHAN (1782-1838) Religious fanatic responsible for the MINSTER FIRE of 1829. He was the brother of the painter, John Martin, whose work can be seen in the ART GALLERY. Jonathan Martin had written a threatening letter saying "You blind hypocrites, you Serpents and Vipers of Hell ... Your gret Church and Minsters will come rattling down upon your Giltey Heads". On Saturday 1 February, after a service, he hid in the MINSTER, and during the night started a fire with pages from prayerbooks and old sheets of music, before escaping by a rope from a window. Next morning a choirboy called Swinbank fell on the ice outside the Minster and, looking up, noticed smoke billowing out of a window and raised the alarm. It was too late to save many treasures including the ORGAN, supposedly the finest in England. In all there was £50,000 of damage and the roof of the NAVE was destroyed. Martin was apprehended on 6 February and first examined at the Peter PRISON. He was tried at York CASTLE on 31 March, and found not guilty due to insanity, he spent the rest of his life in Bedlam Hospital in London.

MARTINDALE, HARRY (1935-) York man who witnessed the city's most famous GHOSTS. In 1953 during alterations to the TREASURER'S HOUSE, he was a young apprentice, working in the cellar installing pipes for central heating. While standing on a ladder, he heard the sound of a trumpet and a horse lumbered through the wall, causing him to fall off the ladder in shock. On the horse was a ROMAN soldier, followed by unkempt troops shuffling along with heads downcast. The figures appeared to have no lower legs but when they reached the trench for the pipes (the original Roman ground level) Harry could see their whole legs. When the phantoms disappeared through the opposite wall, he rushed upstairs and was met by the Curator who asked him if he'd "seen the Romans". Apparently, this was not the first sighting of the soldiers who were apparently heading for the MINSTER where the NINTH LEGION, who supposedly disappeared, had its headquarters in Roman times. Despite the story originally being mocked, his detailed description of the unusual type of armour worn led to local historians giving his tale credibility.

MARYGATE Street joining BOOTHAM to the river OUSE, on which is situated ST OLAVE'S CHURCH, some of the walls of ST MARY'S ABBEY, and ST MARY'S TOWER. During the ENGLISH CIVIL WAR (1642-51), St Mary's Tower was used to store almost all the records of medieval religious houses in Yorkshire for safekeeping under the orders of Sir THOMAS FAIRFAX. Marygate was originally known as Galmanho and was the site of Earlsborough, the palace of the Earls of NORTHUMBRIA. After the establishment of St Mary's Abbey, the street was renamed.

MASON'S ARMS Pub in FiISHERGATE built in 1935 on the site of a previous inn. It contains the oak panelling from York CASTLE and the fireplace from the main gate-house of the Castle.

MASSACRE OF THE JEWS One of the darkest episodes in York's history. In 1190 there were riots against the JEWS OF YORK, BENEDICT'S house was looted and his widow killed. Some Jews were forcibly baptised. Over 150 Jews were taken for refuge to CLIFFORD'S TOWER by JOSCE and Rabbi YOMTOB. The SHERIFF of York decided that the Jews must be driven out of the Tower and organised a siege with landowner Richard MALE-BYSSE. The Jews held out for several days, but it was soon clear that they could not survive. On the night of Friday 16 March 1190, they chose to die rather than renounce their faith. It was agreed that the men would kill their wives and children then themselves, and they set fire to Clifford's Tower. The few survivors who surrendered to the mob were immediately massacred. When the news reached King RICHARD I, who was on Crusade in the Holy Land, he sent the Chancellor, William de Longchamp, to investigate and to punish the perpetra-tors. However, by the time he reached York most of the ringleaders had fled. Few of the mob could be identified or punished, but the city had to pay a fine by Michaelmas 1193. When the king returned, much stricter controls over the recording of Jewish bonds and property were introduced and Jews were given greater protection.

MATTHEWS, FRANCIS (1931-) York-born actor, best-known as the voice of marionette *Captain Scarlet* in Gerry Anderson's cult television series, first shown in 1967. Anderson chose Matthews after hearing his Cary Grant impersonation. He also starred in fifty-two episodes of *Paul Temple* between 1969 and 1971 on the BBC, and in several Hammer Horror films.

MEMORIAL GARDENS Situated at the junction of Station Avenue and Leeman Road, containing the city WAR MEMORIAL, with the inscription "To the citizens of York 1914-1918 and 1939-1945". The memorial was designed by the architect Sir Edwin Lutyens, who was responsible for the Cenotaph in Whitehall, London. The unveiling ceremony in June 1925 was performed by the DUKE OF YORK, later GEORGE VI, and his Duchess, Elizabeth Bowes-Lyon, the late Queen Mother, who died in 2002. Also within the gardens is a small memorial to those killed in the Korean War (1950-53), when British forces lost over a thousand men following communist North Korea's invasion of South Korea. Opposite are the "Bed of Peace" roses, commemorating the International Year of Peace of 1986, and the "Reconciliation Roses" presented by the Royal British Legion in 1995 to both York and its German twin city MUNSTER, marking the fiftieth anniversary of WORLD WAR TWO.

MERCHANT ADVENTURERS The Mercers' GUILD was renamed the Merchant Adventurers' Company in a royal charter of 1581. The Mercers' (dealers in textiles) Guild was created in 1357, becoming the Fellowship of Mercers in 1430. Its main imports were iron, hemp and flax from northern Germany and the Baltic. WOOL was transported to the quay outside the MERCHANT ADVENTURERS' HALL on the river FOSS for loading onto ships travelling to the Low Countries. Most went to Ghent in Belgium and the Customs House where it arrived is still there. The Merchant Adventurers controlled York's trade, the guild being the only one to maintain a continuous existence in the city for nearly 600 years. No one was permitted to run a shop unless they were members of the guild. For seven years MARY TUKE fought the Merchant Adventurers who wanted to prevent her from running a grocery shop in WALMGATE. Considered ineligible for membership of the guild as she was not the widow or daughter of a member, she was fined several times, but eventually given permission to trade in 1732. In 1835 the guilds' restrictive rights were abolished by an Act of Parliament.

MERCHANT ADVENTURERS' HALL Possibly the finest remaining guildhall in the country, situated in FOSSGATE but also accessible from PICCADILLY. It was built between 1357 and 1368 as a hospital dedicated to the Blessed Virgin but in 1430 it became the meeting place of the Fellowship of Mercers, who dealt mainly in WOOL, and the GUILD of the MERCHANT ADVENTURERS. The control of trade for the entire city was carried out from within this building. The hall is framed in oak cut from the FOREST OF GALTRES. The building is open to the public.

MERCHANT TAYLORS' HALL One of the two surviving halls used by York's GUILDS, the other one being the MERCHANT ADVENTURERS' HALL. The Hall was built by the Guild of Merchant Taylors and first recorded in 1380. The brick exterior dates from the late seventeenth century. There are two STAINED GLASS windows of c1700 by Henry GYLES, both with arms of the guild and one with a portrait of Queen Anne. The hall is not usually open to the public.

METCALFE, MILES (1428-86) Friend of RICHARD III, born in Wensleydale, North Yorkshire, who died in the uppermost room of MONK BAR. Metcalfe was a talented lawyer and politician, and was made MP for York in 1477. He was a member of the COUNCIL OF THE NORTH from its inception in 1483. All his appointments ceased on the accession of HENRY TUDOR (HENRY VII).

MICKLEGATE Principal street into York from the south, linking MICKLEGATE BAR to OUSE BRIDGE. The earliest recording of its name is as *Myglagata* ("the great street") in 1161. By 1180 it had become Mykelgate. The *Forum Basilica* or administrative centre of the ROMANS almost certainly stood between Micklegate and Fetter Lane. Micklegate probably became a main thoroughfare in VIKING times, created to skirt around the ruins of Roman buildings of the COLONIA. Eighteenth-century excavations suggest that a Roman temple to the god Mithras, as well as an amphitheatre, stood alongside Trinity Lane off Micklegate. The street is the location of the churches of HOLY TRINITY and ST MARTIN-CUM-GREGORY.

MICKLEGATE BAR Effectively the city's "front door", joining BLOSSOM STREET to MICKLEGATE. A gateway is known to have stood on this site since VIKING times. The present BAR dates from the twelfth century, the top two storeys from the fourteenth. The shields on its front are the arms of England and France, and those of Sir John Lister Kaye, LORD MAYOR in 1737 when the Bar was renovated. The BARBICAN was removed in 1826. In the nineteenth century it was threatened, like all the Bars, with destruction by the city CORPORATION. The novelist Sir Walter Scott (1771-1832), whose novel *Ivanhoe* is partly set in York, offered to walk to the city from Edinburgh (193 miles/310km from York) to save the barbican, but to no avail. The displaying of traitors' HEADS on the Bar continued until 1746. It was inhabited from 1196 and used as a policeman's house from 1838 to 1918. The victorious Parliamentarians entered the city through Micklegate Bar following the SIEGE OF YORK during the ENGLISH CIVIL WAR.

MICKLEGATE BAR MUSEUM Small museum housed in MICKLEGATE BAR itself. The Museum offers a fascinating insight into the history of York, including exhibits about the traitors whose HEADS were stuck on spikes above the BAR.

MICKLEGATE HOUSE Georgian house situated at 88-90 MICKLEGATE. It was originally the townhouse of the Bourchiers of BENINGBROUGH, built for John Bourchier in 1752 by John CARR. His ancestor Sir John Bourchier was one of the signatories to the warrant for the execution of CHARLES I. In 1897 the pharmaceutical company

Raimes & Co. took over the house and used it as a warehouse and factory. In 1960 the building was bought by the UNIVERSITY OF YORK, which used it as offices until 1995. It is currently a Youth Hostel.

MIDDLEHAM JEWEL Large jewel which can be seen in the YORKSHIRE MUSEUM. It is thought to be one of the finest examples of medieval jewellery in Europe. It was discovered in 1985 in the grounds of Middleham Castle, Wensleydale, the home of RICHARD III before he became king, and purchased for the nation. It was originally auctioned to a foreign buyer for £1.3m, but due to its importance it was denied an export licence. The Yorkshire Museum started a fund to purchase it and raised £2.42m. The National Heritage Memorial Fund gave £1.77m and John Paul Getty Junior gave £350,000. There were also many smaller private donations. The Jewel, which opens like a locket, is made of engraved gold with a large sapphire mounted on the front, and was originally surrounded with pearls and decorated with black enamel. Experts have suggested it was made in London between the years 1450-75 and it was probably worn by a wealthy noblewoman. It may have been worn by Richard III's mother-in-law, Anne Beauchamp, and has an inscription warding off epilepsy, from which she was known to suffer.

MIDDLETHORPE HALL Large country house built between 1699 and 1701 on the road to BISHOPTHORPE, near York RACECOURSE. It was built for Thomas Barlow of Leeds and is now a hotel. During the SIEGE OF YORK the SCOTS contingent of besiegers led by Lord Leven, was based in the village of Middlethorpe.

MILLENNIUM BRIDGE Striking modern pedestrian and cycle bridge over the river OUSE between the FULFORD and CLEMENTHORPE areas of York. The bridge was the idea of a small group of local people who proposed to unite the two areas divided by the river. Until then they had to use the busy SKELDERGATE BRIDGE to the north. There had been earlier FERRIES, and a temporary bridge built on the present site by the army. The new bridge was paid for with lottery funding from the Millennium Commission, equally matched by resources from the CITY OF YORK COUNCIL, the JOSEPH ROWNTREE FOUNDATION and three of York's major employers. The total cost of the project, including work on the riverside walks like the NEW WALK, was £4.22m. The revolutionary design in stainless steel created an outstanding landmark, completed in April 2001, a few months late owing to the FLOODS of 2000. The DUKE OF YORK, Prince ANDREW, opened the bridge. It is now used for thousands of cycle journeys annually and has revitalised the area.

MINERVA, STATUE OF Distinctive statue of the goddess of wisdom and drama which can be seen above a shopfront on the corner of MINSTER GATES and HIGH PETERGATE. The sign indicates that the premises were once a bookshop, owned by John Foster who had a stock, impressive for the time, of 3000 books. His shop stood here between 1580 and 1607. A sign that served a similar purpose is the GOLDEN BIBLE.

MINSTER York Minster is the fifth or perhaps the sixth to stand on this site, and was built between 1220 and 1472.

It is the Cathedral Church of ST PETER, the largest medieval building in England and the largest Gothic cathedral north of the Alps. The name Minster is derived from the Latin *monasterium* (place of learning), generally used to refer to an adjacent monastery although York Minster was never a monastic site. The Old English *mynster* developed from *monasterium*. The Minster is built in the shape of a cross, facing east towards Jerusalem. The first Minster was a small wooden construction built on the site of the ruined ROMAN fortress, the PRINCIPIA, in AD627 for the baptism of the newly Christianised king EDWIN of NORTHUMBRIA. It was soon developed into a stone Minster, built in 633. Thereafter there were a further two ANGLO-SAXON stone churches (built in 741 and from 767 to 781) and a NORMAN Minster (built between 1080 and 1100). Since HENRY VIII's sixteenth-century REFORMATION it has been an Anglican church. The historian Francis DRAKE wrote in *Eboracum* that the Minster was "not only a singular ornament to the city and these northern parts, but to the whole kingdom". No one has been buried in the Minster since 1836, and in 1854 there was an order from the Crown to prevent anyone else from being buried in a church.

MINSTER CLOSE Walled area surrounding the MINSTER from 1285 to 1550. The Close had four guarded gates, one opposite DUNCOMBE PLACE (the Peter Gate), one opposite STONEGATE (MINSTER GATES), one at the entrance to College Street near ST WILLIAM'S COLLEGE (the remains of which are still visible) and one on OGLEFORTH. With the city WALLS stretching from BOOTHAM BAR to MONK BAR, the Minster was effectively enclosed. As well as the Minster, the Close contained ST WILLIAM'S COLLEGE, the CANONS' houses, the TREASURER'S HOUSE, the DEAN's house, the MINSTER LIBRARY, the Peter PRISON and ST MICHAEL-LE-BELFREY CHURCH. Until the nineteenth century Minster Close was known as the Liberty of ST PETER, and was under the jurisdiction of the Dean and CHAPTER, rather than the city.

MINSTER FIRES York MINSTER has suffered some seven fires since its creation in AD627. In 741 the ANGLO-SAXON stone Minster was accidentally burned down and in 1069 its replacement was torched by the NORMANS during the HARRYING OF THE NORTH. During the GREAT FIRE OF YORK in 1137 the East End was all but destroyed and not repaired until 1154. In 1753 fire destroyed the roof of the SOUTH TRANSEPT. The religious fanatic Jonathan MARTIN burnt down the CHOIR and the ORGAN in 1829 and in 1840 a workman's candle started an accidental fire which damaged the south-west tower and the NAVE roof. The most recent fire, of 1984, was allegedly caused by lightning and destroyed the roof of the SOUTH TRANSEPT.

MINSTER GATES Short street linking HIGH PETER-GATE to Deangate opposite the South Door of the MIN-STER. Its name is derived from the existence of the main gates to MINSTER CLOSE. It was formerly known as Bookbinders Alley and the statue of MINERVA is on the corner above a former bookshop.

MINSTER LIBRARY Thirteenth-century building in DEAN'S PARK, close to the MINSTER. Apart from the arches in the Park, it is all that remains of the medieval ARCHBISHOP'S PALACE. The first Minster Library was created by ARCHBISHOP EGBERT in the AD750s. The present building dates from around 1230, and was extended in 1998 to provide reading rooms. Closely linked to the UNIVERSITY OF YORK, it is now the largest cathedral library in Britain with over 120,000 items, specialising in theology and local history. ALCUIN, the greatest scholar of the age, was Librarian in the late 770s. The early collections were plundered by the VIKINGS in the 860s and what remained was destroyed by the forces of WILLIAM THE CONQUEROR in 1069. York was thus deprived of what may have provided illuminating knowledge on the city during the so-called Dark Ages (c410-c650). Following the NORMAN invasion, no library existed until 1414. From that date until 1810 the Library was housed in the Minster itself, alongside the SOUTH TRANSEPT, in what is now part of the Minster shop. It is open to the public.

MINSTER POLICE The title of MINSTER Policeman is first recorded in 1855 but the office is closely linked to the post of Constable of the Liberty, which dates back to at least 1285 when MINSTER CLOSE was enclosed by a twelve-foot-high (3.6m) stone wall. Until 1839 the DEAN and CHAPTER, having their own constables, magistrates and bailiffs, had jurisdiction within this boundary, known as the Liberty of ST PETER. The Peter PRISON, a small prison with a court on the upper storey, was situated in Minster Close until its demolition in 1838. The arsonist Jonathan MARTIN was examined at the Peter Prison before being committed for trial at the ASSIZE COURTS. The nine Minster Policemen continue to keep order in the

MINSTER and the surrounding area. Their office in the NORTH CHOIR AISLE can be identified by the two old truncheons hanging by the door.

MINSTER SCHOOL Independent preparatory school in Deangate. It was built in 1830-33 as ST PETER'S SCHOOL, which moved to CLIFTON in 1844. The building was used as York School of Art until 1903 when it became the Minster Song School.

MINSTER SERVICES Although York MINSTER is ecumenical, welcoming all Christian faiths, the majority of services held are Anglican. On Sundays the services are Holy Communion, Sung Eucharist, Choral Matins and Choral Evensong. On weekdays the services are Matins, Holy Communion and Choral Evensong. All are welcome to attend and full details are posted outside the Minster. On Sundays sightseeing is not permitted before 12.30pm.

MODEL RAILWAY MUSEUM Situated next to the RAILWAY STATION in Tea Room Square, York Model Railway has up to fourteen trains running at any one time on a third of a mile of "OO" gauge track. This is the equivalent of twenty-five miles (40km) through dockland, town and country scenery. The attraction took over 10,000 hours to build and has entertained over 250,000 visitors. It opened in 1984.

MONK or MONCK, GEORGE (1608-1670) General and statesman who fought for CHARLES I during the ENGLISH CIVIL WAR. Following Charles' defeat the Parliamentarians (Roundheads) recognised Monk's abilities and gave him command in Ireland. He subsequently became Commander-in-Chief during CROMWELL's Scottish campaign (1650-51). Following Cromwell's death in 1658 Monk became an advocate of the restoration of the monarchy, arriving in York in 1660 "to liberate the city" from the Parliamentarians. The theory that MONK BAR was named after him is erroneous.

MONK BAR One of York's four main gateways, situated between GOODRAMGATE and MONKGATE. The building dates from c1300, and is the tallest (63ft/19.2m) of the four BARS. Monk Bar was a guardhouse in the Middle Ages, a policeman's house until the twentieth century and inhabited until 1914. The top storey was added in 1484 by RICHARD III, and the Bar now houses the RICHARD III MUSEUM. Monk Bar has the city's only working PORTCULLIS, said to be largely original, last lowered in 1953 for the coronation of Queen ELIZABETH II. The Bar includes the LITTLE EASE prison, used during the reign of the Protestant Elizabeth I (Queen of England 1558-1603) to incarcerate recusant Catholics. The blocked archway once led to a guardhouse alongside the Bar. The BARBICAN was removed in 1826, the side arches added in the 1820s and the larger arch widened for traffic in 1861. The coats of arms are those of the Plantagenet kings. The original ROMAN GATEWAY was further west with CHAPTER HOUSE STREET (the Via Decumana) running through it. Monk Bar was probably built where it is so that the road did not run through MINSTER CLOSE.

MONKGATE Street leading from MONK BAR towards HEWORTH, on which are situated many Georgian houses. York's GREY COAT SCHOOL was in the building now used as a medical centre. In 1070 the street was known as Munecagate and by 1154 as Munkgate. Remains of a monastery exist on Heworth Golf Course, perhaps suggesting the origin of the street's name.

MOORE, ALBERT JOSEPH (1841-1893) York-born artist, an important figure in the Aesthetic Movement, whose works in the ART GALLERY include "A Venus" (1869).

MORRELL, JOHN BOWES (1873-1963) Liberal ALDERMAN and the son of a banker, J.B. Morrell served York twice as LORD MAYOR (1914-15 and 1949-50). He lived in York from the age of two, and was educated at BOOTHAM SCHOOL. He played a key role in the establishment of the CASTLE MUSEUM and the UNIVERSITY OF YORK, and initiated the revival of the MYSTERY PLAYS in 1951. He was co-founder of YORK CIVIC TRUST, a director of ROWNTREE & CO., and received the honorary FREEDOM OF THE CITY in 1950. The University Library is named after him owing to his association, along with DEAN Eric Milner-White and Oliver Sheldon, with the struggle for the University's foundation in the 1950s. The house at 111 WALMGATE, now the headquarters of the Council for British Archaeology, was named after him after he rescued it from demolition. He wrote the inspirational *City of Our Dreams*, about York, in 1940.

MOUNT, THE Street linking BLOSSOM STREET via Mount Vale to Tadcaster Road. It is the main road into York from the south and has been known by this name since at least the fourteenth century. The Mount was the site of a Royalist fort built on a mound to protect approaches to MICKLEGATE BAR prior to the SIEGE OF YORK during the ENGLISH CIVIL WAR. In 1742 Francis DRAKE wrote about the widening of The Mount in the *YORK COURANT*. Excavations revealed many human remains as the area was the site of a ROMAN cemetery, and Drake refers to hundred of skeletons being found.

MOUNT SCHOOL, THE Independent QUAKER girls' school in Dalton Terrace off The MOUNT, founded by ESTHER TUKE. It began in 1785 in the original FRIENDS' MEETING HOUSE, moving to Trinity Lane off MICKLEGATE. Esther was headmistress until her death in 1794. In 1796 the school moved to Tower Street where it remained until 1814. The school was re-established in 1831 in CASTLEGATE, moving to its present site in 1857. The Mount was one of the first schools to send girls to university. Judi DENCH and the authors Margaret Drabble and A.S. Byatt attended the school.

MULBERRY HALL Timber-framed building in STONEGATE. It is one of the country's leading china, porcelain and glass shops. The building dates from 1434, and has been a shop since the eighteenth century. The name is probably a version of Mulbrai or Mowbray Hall, indicating a connection with the noble Yorkshire family of Mowbray, who owned land off Little Stonegate.

MULTANGULAR TOWER York's only remaining ROMAN tower, marking the western corner of their walled fortress. It is located in the MUSEUM GARDENS and was part of the reconstruction of the defences by CONSTANTINE

THE GREAT in cAD310. The tower was incorporated into the present city WALLS until the removal of a section of wall near BOOTHAM BAR in 1833, to make way for ST LEONARD'S PLACE. The first twenty feet (6m) of the distinctive ten-sided tower are Roman and the top dates from the thirteenth century. Alongside the tower is a small section of Roman wall. The tower was called Elrondyng until it was realised it was a Roman tower in the eighteenth century.

MUNSTER City in Westphalia, north-west Germany, twinned with York in 1957. Its origins date back to AD805, when there was a *monasterium*, or place of learning, there. Munster's St Paul's Cathedral, or *Dom*, is now mostly thirteenth-century. Despite having 272,000 inhabitants plus 50,000 students, many more than York, Munster was deemed appropriate owing to its name translating as "minster". York is also twinned with DIJON in France and the FANTEAKWA district in Ghana.

MUSEUM GARDENS Large park between Museum Street and MARYGATE next to the river OUSE. As early as 1825 the YORKSHIRE PHILOSOPHICAL SOCIETY had earmarked the area of the KING'S MANOR riverbank as ideal for the grounds of its museum. The site now includes the YORKSHIRE MUSEUM, the OBSERVATORY, the HOSPITIUM, the ruins of ST MARY'S ABBEY and ST LEONARD'S HOSPITAL, the MULTANGULAR TOWER and the ANGLIAN TOWER. Peacocks and squirrels also added to the attraction of the Botanical Garden. The park was originally intended for the use of Society members only, but the gardens were opened to the paying public after Princess (later Queen) VICTORIA visited in 1835, at a time when city parks were a rarity. Free entry on Bank Holidays and at Whitsuntide proved to be a successful experiment in the 1840s. The financial pressure of maintaining the Gardens and Museum saw control pass from the Society to the CITY OF YORK COUNCIL in 1961. Entrance is now free to all.

MYSTERY PLAYS York Mystery Plays as performed today originated in the late fourteenth century, though as early as the twelfth century there was talk of gathering props to perform them. They were then known as the Corpus Christi Plays, as they were performed on the Feast of Corpus Christi which fell in May or June. The authors are unknown. The term "Mystery Play" was coined long after the discontinuation of the cycle in 1580, suppressed by the Protestant church owing to the plays' Catholic spirit. Their name is a reference to the GUILDS who were responsible for the Plays' production, "mistery" being derived from the Latin *ministerium*, meaning trade or craft. The Plays consisted of a lengthy series of short scenes from the Testaments, each performed by a different Guild as WAGON PLAYS, moving from TOFT GREEN through MICKLEGATE, CONEY STREET and STONEGATE, and finishing at PAVEMENT. They conveyed the meaning of the Bible to a largely illiterate population. In 1951 the Plays were revived in modified form and performed at ST MARY'S ABBEY, and they have been performed every three or four years since. They are traditionally performed on a four-yearly cycle. In 1992 and 1996 the MYSTERY PLAYS were held at the THEATRE ROYAL and in 2000 in the MINSTER.

MYTON, BATTLE OF Fought in 1319 fourteen miles (22.5km) north-west of York. On the orders of EDWARD II, an untrained "army" of merchants, peasants and some three hundred priests led by William Melton, ARCH-BISHOP OF YORK (1317-42), took on the SCOTS and were defeated by forces led by Sir James Douglas. Sir Nicholas Fleming was the first and only (and probably the last) LORD MAYOR to be killed in battle. The Scots referred to the slaughter as the "CHAPTER" of Myton, so great was the number of priests killed. Active combat for clergymen and Lord Mayors was not uncommon at the time.

N

NABURN LOCKS Locks built in 1757 to regulate the river OUSE. The building of the locks meant that the tide no longer reached York and limited the size of vessels travelling up river from the North Sea via the river Humber. They are situated six miles (9.7km) downstream from the confluence of the Ouse with the river FOSS.

NATIONAL CENTRE FOR EARLY MUSIC Situated in the former ST MARGARET'S CHURCH off WALMGATE, this award-winning £2m Centre is dedicated to early music. The twelfth-century church became redundant in 1974. In 2001 grants from the Arts Council Lottery Fund (£1.5m), CITY OF YORK COUNCIL, English Heritage and other charitable foundations enabled the establishment of the Centre. It now provides a permanent base for the annual YORK EARLY MUSIC FESTIVAL. Early music can be defined as music played in its original style and occasionally on original instruments. Although the principal activities of the York Early Music Foundation are performance, recording, education and research, it also has particular strengths in special needs education and new technology, and is open to the public.

NATIONAL RAILWAY MUSEUM World's largest railway museum, situated in Leeman Road near the RAILWAY STATION. The National Railway Museum houses the country's largest collection of railway stock and memorabilia. It opened in 1975. Prior to this a small railway museum had existed off Queen Street nearby. The collection includes 1.4 million negatives, 350,000 engineering drawings, 300,000 tickets, 7500 posters, 3300 models, 300 nameplates, 280 items of rolling stock and one lock of Robert STEPHENSON's hair. The museum's most famous locomotives are the MALLARD, a replica of STEPHENSON'S ROCKET, and since 2001 the only Japanese Bullet Train outside Japan. During school holidays a road train runs between DUNCOMBE PLACE and the museum.

NAVE of the Minster Open space on entrance into the MINSTER, rarely used for services. The nave occupies the western end of a cathedral. York's nave is the widest in England at 264 feet (80m) long by 100 feet (30.5m) wide. It was built between 1291 and c1340. Traditionally it is a cathedral's meeting place and in the Middle Ages it was frequently used for markets. The roof vaulting is constructed of oak beams. The nave contains some of the finest medieval STAINED GLASS in the world, dating mainly from the fourteenth century. It has a seating capacity of 2000. On a pillar between the WEST DOORS stands a statue of ST PETER, holding a key, which was given to the Minster in 1884. The coronation scene in the film *Elizabeth* (1998) was filmed here, although in reality Elizabeth I was crowned at Westminster Abbey.

NESTLE ROWNTREE *See* ROWNTREE & CO.

NEVILLES Probably the most powerful baronial family in fifteenth-century England, prominent in the WARS OF THE ROSES. Their feud with their cousins the PERCYS, and the clash at HEWORTH MOOR in York, helped to spark off the WARS OF THE ROSES. The most famous Neville was Warwick the Kingmaker, Richard Neville (1428-71), who was instrumental in putting EDWARD IV of the HOUSE OF YORK on the throne in 1461, only to later quarrel with the king and defect to the Lancastrian side. He was defeated and slain by Edward's forces at the Battle of Barnet.

NEVISON, WILLIAM "SWIFTNICKS" (1639-1684) Highwayman born in Pontefract, West Yorkshire, nicknamed "Swiftnicks" by CHARLES II. The dramatic ride in one day from London to York in 1676, as recounted by Daniel DEFOE, was made by Nevison if anyone, rather than Dick TURPIN. The purpose of the legendary ride was to establish an alibi, as he had been witnessed committing a robbery at dawn in London. Nevison asked the LORD MAYOR of York, who was enjoying a game of bowls on the green behind ST MARY'S ABBEY, for the time. The alibi proved successful and he was cleared. However his life of crime continued and he was eventually found guilty of attempted murder. Nevison was taken to the GALLOWS at York's TYBURN and hanged in May 1684, apparently exceptionally drunk. Defoe immortalised Nevison as "Mr Nicks" in his book *A Tour Through the Whole Island of Great Britain* (1724-26).

NEW DROP, THE York GALLOWS from 1801 to 1862. York's principal gallows, known as TYBURN, was pulled down in 1801 and a new scaffold was erected within the PRISON walls of the CASTLE, facing ST GEORGE'S FIELD. This became known as the "New Drop". Those about to be executed spent their last night in the CONDEMNED CELL of the Castle. The next morning they were led out onto the scaffold, followed by their own coffin. They would be faced by a crowd of jeering onlookers, controlled by soldiers, there being no police force before the 1830s. Perhaps the New Drop's most infamous victim and largest crowd-puller was wife-poisoner William Dove. He was executed in August 1856, watched by a crowd of over 15,000 people. Special excursion trains brought people into York to watch public hangings.

NEW EARSWICK Village three miles (4.8km) north of York, founded in 1902. It was conceived as a "Model Village" by JOSEPH ROWNTREE, following his son BENJAMIN SEEBOHM ROWNTREE'S report (first published in 1899 and updated in 1901) into poverty in the city. Fellow QUAKER and CHOCOLATE manufacturer George Cadbury had created the village of Bournville in Birmingham, built in 1901, which was undoubtedly an influence. New Earswick was built on 150 ACRES of land and the idea was to provide a "garden village" of low-rent quality housing, with a happy and healthy community. The village included a social centre, a school and playing fields, though no pub, Quakers being opposed to the consumption of alcohol. Each Sunday Catholics, Anglicans, Methodists and Quakers were able to meet in the social centre at different times. The Anglicans built their own church in 1912 and the Methodists in 1927, both receiving assistance from the Joseph Rowntree Trust. The village's current population is approximately 3000.

NEW WALK Riverside walk, stretching from TOWER PLACE to the MILLENNIUM BRIDGE. Created in the 1730s, it originally led from SKELDERGATE BRIDGE down river to the confluence of the OUSE and the FOSS. It was planted with elms and developed by the city CORPORATION to raise the status of York to that of a leading social centre, complementing the ASSEMBLY ROOMS, the RACECOURSE and the MANSION HOUSE. The New Walk was extended after the first BLUE BRIDGE was built in 1738. Situated on the New Walk is the LADY WELL, built in 1752 by John CARR.

NEW YORK The theory that the American city is named after the city of York is only partially correct. In 1664 the English king CHARLES II claimed the Dutch colonists' settlement New Netherlands, forcing director-general Peter Stuyvesant to divide up the area. A province containing the whole area from the west side of the Connecticut river to the east side of Delaware Bay, together with the whole of Long Island was created. Charles granted it to his brother JAMES (II), the eighth DUKE OF YORK. On 8 September 1664, the English flag was raised above the area's seat of government at Fort Amsterdam, renaming it Fort James. New Amsterdam thus became New York, after the Duke.

NEWCASTLE, DUKE OF (1592-1676) Royalist military commander of the northern counties under CHARLES I during the ENGLISH CIVIL WAR. He attempted unsuccessfully to defend the city during the SIEGE OF YORK. He was opposed to Prince RUPERT'S decision to pursue the Parliamentarians to MARSTON MOOR. Following the Royalist disaster at the battle, and York's fall, he abandoned the king's cause and lived in Europe until the Restoration of CHARLES II in 1660.

NEWGATE MARKET York's daily market, situated between PARLIAMENT STREET and the SHAMBLES since 1964. It is open every day except Christmas Day, Boxing Day and New Year's Day. The market's previous home (since 1836) had been PARLIAMENT STREET, and prior to that it was PAVEMENT, with the city's fish market around the corner in FOSSGATE. On the first day of the Parliament Street market, the traders picked up their wares and moved back to Pavement. For this defiance they were fined and the traders, in response, made an effigy of the magistrate and burnt it.

NEWSPAPERS York's first newspaper, the *YORK MERCURY*, was launched in 1719. Its major successors were the *YORK COURANT* in 1728 and the *YORK HERALD* in 1790. The *Herald* absorbed the *Courant* in 1848. The *Herald's* owners, the Hargroves, founded the *EVENING PRESS* in 1882.

NINTH LEGION ROMAN founders of EBORACUM (York). The Legio IX Hispana, so-named after its services in Spain, was one of four legions of 5000 men who arrived in Kent in AD43. Under the command of VESPASIAN's son QUINTUS PETILIUS CERIALIS, Governor of Britain at the time, in AD71 they created a base at York from which to fight. The Ninth Legion is better known for the myths that surround it than for anything it actually achieved. The last record of its time in York is from AD107 and the lack of information after this time has led to the romantic legend of a "Lost Legion". In reality, the Ninth Legion was replaced by the SIXTH LEGION and returned to the continent in AD122. The GHOSTS seen by Harry MARTINDALE in the TREASURER'S HOUSE in 1953 were thought to be soldiers of the Ninth Legion.

NORMAN HOUSE Remains of a twelfth-century NORMAN house, located in a yard at 52 STONEGATE. The arched window and wall suggest a sizeable hall, while the use of stone and evidence of decorative plastering indicate an owner of some wealth. Whilst looking up at the remains one is actually "inside" the house, the oldest domestic dwelling in the city.

NORMANS Eleventh-century conquerors of England, from Normandy in northern France. Following their victory at the Battle of Hastings in 1066, the Norman WILLIAM THE CONQUEROR led the country through a turbulent time of devastation and later expansion. The northern Anglo-Scandinavian earls would swear obedience to William, yet rebel as soon as he left the region. This resulted in William's HARRYING OF THE NORTH in 1069, when York was set on fire and the MINSTER severely damaged. After this time the city was rebuilt and flourished. ARCHBISHOP OF YORK Thomas of

BAYEUX built a new Minster between 1080 and 1100. Castles on BAILE HILL and at CLIFFORD'S TOWER were constructed, as well as ST MARY'S ABBEY and the KING'S FISHPOOL. William the Conqueror commissioned the DOMESDAY BOOK and the Norman period lasted until the middle of the twelfth century.

NORTH CHOIR AISLE of the Minster Dating from the late fourteenth and early fifteenth centuries, the aisle contains the memorial to Prince WILLIAM OF HATFIELD, son of EDWARD III, the only royal person to be buried in the MINSTER. His precise burial place in the Minster is unknown. In bay five is the St William Window depicting incidents in the life of ST WILLIAM OF YORK, by John Thornton, who was responsible for the GREAT EAST WINDOW. The window is currently undergoing a five-year period of restoration, but most of it is still visible. There is also an exhibition of panels, dating from 1993, embroidered by the Minster Broderers' GUILD and based on the birds and beasts which can be seen in the Minster. The office of the MINSTER POLICE is located here.

NORTH EASTERN RAILWAY HEADQUARTERS Large red brick building located between Station Road and TANNER ROW, currently used by GNER. It was built between 1890 and 1906 by William Bell, the company's architect. The North Eastern Railway was created in 1853 by the amalgamation of three of the region's major companies. A WAR MEMORIAL to employees of the Company killed in the two WORLD WARS stands on Station Road alongside the building, and a Book of Remembrance can be inspected in the headquarters.

NORTH NAVE AISLE of the Minster Passageway to the left of the NAVE on entering through the WEST DOOR. The two best-known windows date from 1320, the Pilgrimage Window (bay four, more popularly known as the Monkey's Funeral Window) and the Bellfounders' Window (bay five, showing the craft of bell-making).

NORTH TRANSEPT of the Minster Area to the north of the CHOIR SCREEN. The ceiling is more clearly made of wood than that of the NAVE. The North Transept contains the spectacular FIVE SISTERS WINDOW (c1250), the ST NICHOLAS CHAPEL, the ASTRONOMICAL CLOCK (1955) and the chiming HINDLEY CLOCK (1749), and leads to the CHAPTER HOUSE.

NORTHUMBERLAND, EARL OF (1528-72) Thomas PERCY, the Catholic seventh Earl, was publicly beheaded in PAVEMENT. He had led a rather farcical northern rebellion against the Protestant Queen Elizabeth I. His HEAD was spiked on MICKLEGATE BAR, though quickly removed by a supporter and buried at HOLY TRINITY CHURCH in GOODRAMGATE. The head was then returned to the BAR for a reward by another less than loyal supporter. Northumberland's decapitated GHOST is said to haunt the churchyard, in hapless pursuit of his head.

NORTHUMBRIA ANGLO-SAXON kingdom (AD604-c870) of which York was the capital. The kingdom was one of seven, the Saxon Heptarchy, prior to the NORMAN Conquest. In the seventh century the Saxon kingdoms Deira and Bernicia were merged to form Northumbria, of which EDWIN became king in 616. EOFORWIC, or York, was originally within Deira. Following the VIKING invasions of 866, Northumbria was once again divided into two kingdoms, Bernicia from the Firth of Forth as far as the river Tees in the south, and Deira, later JORVIK, from the Tees to south of the river Trent, near Leicester. In the eleventh century before the Norman Conquest, the Earls of Northumbria, who governed northern England, had their residence in Earlsborough off MARYGATE.

O

OBSERVATORY Astronomical observatory in the centre of the MUSEUM GARDENS, half hidden by trees. It was completed in 1833 for the members of the YORKSHIRE PHILOSOPHICAL SOCIETY. Thomas COOKE, the optical scientist, made the four-and-a-half-inch (11cm) telescope which it originally housed. As well as its role as an observation point for the night sky, the Observatory also served as time-keeper for the city, by accurately plotting the movement of the stars. Enthusiasm for the Observatory, however, was soon to wane as its proximity to the lights of the city made observation difficult. The problem was exacerbated by the unwelcome arrival of industrial pollution. It is only open to the public through application to the Yorkshire Philosophical Society.

ODEON CINEMA in classic Art Deco style, situated in BLOSSOM STREET. It was built in 1937 and typifies a modern building of the era.

OGLEFORTH Narrow street linking GOODRAMGATE to CHAPTER HOUSE STREET. Its name is recorded as Ugelford in 1109 after the Danish name Ugel, probably meaning "Ugel's Place". One of the four gates into MINSTER CLOSE was situated here. Despite the walls around Minster Close being taken down in 1550, the gate was still standing in 1786. Part of the unusual seventeenth-century brick DUTCH HOUSE remains. Between 1547 and 1858 ARCHBISHOP HOLGATE'S SCHOOL was situated in Ogleforth.

OLD WHITE SWAN Pub in GOODRAMGATE, known to have been an inn since at least 1703. Once a complex of at least nine separate buildings, the Swan has in its time housed a barber's shop, a poultry market, a pigsty and a coaching house. Extensive refurbishments in 1983 earned an architectural award. The inn may have been favoured by the gentry, hence the stone steps in the courtyard, used to board stagecoaches.

OLDE STARRE INN *See* YE OLDE STARRE INN

OSWALD (c605-641) ANGLO-SAXON king of NORTHUMBRIA. He was the nephew of EDWIN and between AD627 and AD633 built a stone MINSTER around the wooden church of Edwin's baptism.

OUR FATHER CHAPEL in the Minster Small chapel located in the NORTH NAVE AISLE. There is a "Touch & Hearing" model of the MINSTER here for the visually impaired.

OUR LADY'S ROW *See* LADY ROW

OUSE Major river through York, which begins twelve miles (19.2km) north at Ouse Gill Beck, where the river Swale joins the river Ure. The Ouse (pronounced "ooze") flows south to the river Humber and the North Sea and is fifty-seven miles (92km) long. For centuries, until the arrival of the RAILWAYS, York was a major port and KING'S STAITH and QUEEN'S STAITH were the landing areas for trade. In 1733 the NEW WALK was created as a riverside promenade. NABURN LOCKS were built in 1757 and the Ouse was no longer tidal through York. There are six bridges over the river in the city, including OUSE BRIDGE, LENDAL BRIDGE and the new MIL- LENNIUM BRIDGE. The river was originally called *Uys* or *Ewi*, meaning "water". The Romans called it *Isis*. ANGLO-SAXON names include *Youre* and *Eurewic*, meaning "place of strength". The most devastating FLOODS to date in York were in November 2000, when the Ouse rose to seventeen feet ten inches (5.2m) above its normal level.

OUSE BRIDGE York's oldest bridge over the river OUSE, dating from 1820. There has been a bridge on this site since at least the ninth century. In 1154 a bridge collapsed under the weight of a crowd welcoming the ARCH- BISHOP OF YORK, later ST WILLIAM, to the city. No one was killed and this was considered to be a miracle. The next bridge was built in 1235 and had six arches. The medieval bridge had around thirty buildings on each side, including houses, shops, a courthouse and the KID- COTES PRISON. In 1268 a chapel to St William was built on the bridge. The first public toilets in England were installed on Ouse Bridge in 1367, with an attendant, and in 1380 a local merchant left an annual sum to provide lighting. In 1564, after a long winter and a heavy thaw, the bridge collapsed. Its replacement rose seventeen feet (5m) above the Ouse allowing boats to pass underneath. Until 1792, when Selby Bridge was built, Ouse Bridge was the only bridge between York and the North Sea. The city CORPORATION met in chambers on Ouse Bridge until 1810, when the bridge was demolished. Ten years later the present bridge took its place, designed by Peter ATKINSON Junior, which was a toll bridge from 1820-29. The first vehicle to cross free of charge was carrying timber for repairs to the MINSTER after the fire caused by Jonathan MARTIN.

P

PARAGON STREET Running alongside the city WALLS from FISHERGATE to Foss Islands Road, the site of York's cattle market from 1826 until the 1960s. The market covered the full length of Paragon Street on one side, with the cattle pens on the side by the walls. The area was redeveloped in 1964 and is currently the location of the Barbican Centre, which was officially opened by the DUCHESS OF KENT in 1991. It houses a modern leisure complex and a concert arena and in 2001 the UK Snooker Championship was held there.

PARLIAMENT STREET Wide street linking PICCADILLY and ST SAMPSON'S SQUARE. One of the city's two principal shopping streets along with CONEY STREET. Created by an Act of Parliament (hence the name) it was opened in 1836 and was intended to ease the crowded conditions of the thriving marketplaces in St Sampson's Square and PAVEMENT by creating a broad and capacious new street. The new street cut the old JUBBERGATE in two, creating Market Street to the south. It was the site of the city's market until 1964 when NEWGATE MARKET opened, and it is still used occasionally for specialist markets. The impressive redbrick Barclays Bank was purpose-built as a bank in 1901 in the Victorian Gothic style. The central FOUNTAIN was created in 1992 and redesigned in 2002.

PAULINUS (cAD580-AD644) Early Bishop of York. Paulinus was an Italian missionary who oversaw the construction of the first MINSTER. He arrived with Queen ETHELBURGA of Kent at the court of EDWIN of NORTHUMBRIA in AD625, baptising the king in AD627 in a wooden MINSTER. Paulinus had arrived in Britain in AD601 to help with the conversion of the island at the order of Rome. In reality much of the country was already Christianised and there is evidence of thriving Christian communities in Northumbria at least thirty years before he arrived. BEDE describes Paulinus as being tall, stooping, with a shock of black hair and a hawk-like face, "both venerable and terrifying in appearance". On Edwin's death in AD633, Paulinus left York. He died in Rochester, Kent.

PAVEMENT Street linking STONEBOW to PARLIAMENT STREET. The street's name perhaps dates from when it was paved in stone, unusual for the fourteenth century. It was once a busy, bustling marketplace. A market cross or covered market hall, built in 1672, stood here but was pulled down in 1813 in an effort to ease congestion. The building offered shelter for traders against the weather and had an upstairs hall. Pavement was also a convenient place for public gatherings such as proclamations, punishments and EXECUTIONS. An effigy of Oliver CROMWELL was burnt here in 1660 and the Earl of NORTHUMBERLAND was beheaded here in 1572. Sir Thomas HERBERT was born in the HERBERT HOUSE in Pavement.

PEASHOLME (or PEASEHOLME) GREEN Street linking STONEBOW to LAYERTHORPE BRIDGE. It was the site of the medieval pea fields of York, from which it derives its name. ST ANTHONY'S HALL, ST CUTHBERT'S CHURCH and the BLACK SWAN pub are located here. Peasholme Green has had many uses in its history, including as a pig market, a wool market and a haymarket.

PEASHOLME HOUSE Georgian house in St Saviour's Place, built by John CARR in 1752. It is currently a language school.

PECKITT, WILLIAM (1731-1795) Glass painter and stainer born in Husthwaite, north of York. He began practising in York in 1751 and his work can be seen in the SOUTH TRANSEPT of the MINSTER, the GUILDHALL and in glass panels owned by the ART GALLERY. He is buried in the church of ST MARTIN-CUM-GREGORY.

PEDESTRIANISATION York has one of the largest pedestrianised areas in Britain, which includes almost all the city centre. In his report of 1968 Lord ESHER suggested that the whole centre of the city should be closed to traffic. STONEGATE was the first street to be pedestrianised in 1971 and other key areas followed in 1987. Vehicles are only permitted to drive down certain streets at designated times.

PENTY & PENTY Influential firm of York architects. Walter Penty (1853-1902) was the father of Arthur Joseph Penty (1875-1937). Late Victorian York was dominated by two architects, Walter Penty and Walter BRIERLEY. The Lighthorseman pub in FULFORD Road was built by Penty in the 1870s on the corner of NEW WALK Terrace, and at TANNER'S MOAT two arches survive of Botterill's Horse Repository, stables he built in 1880. In the 1890s Arthur Penty joined his father at the family firm, designing the Bay Horse pub in MARYGATE in 1894 and LEETHAM'S MILL in 1895. He was influenced by the Arts & Crafts movement and with George Walton, one of Charles Rennie Mackintosh's Glasgow group, in 1898 he designed the interior of the ELM BANK HOTEL for Sidney Leetham. In SKELDERGATE Penty & Penty built the Terry Memorial ALMSHOUSES (1899) in front of LADY ANNE MIDDLETON'S HALL. They also built River Street, Colenso Street and Lower Darnborough Street in CLEMENTHORPE (1900-02). In 1902 Arthur Penty went to London, where he founded Elmdon & Co. furniture company with Fred Rowntree, and worked at Hampstead Garden Suburb.

PERCYS Powerful landowners and Earls of NORTHUMBERLAND, England's northernmost county. From 1309 their principal seat was the NORMAN Alnwick Castle, situated between Newcastle upon Tyne and Berwick upon Tweed. The Percys played an important role in the country's politics during the WARS OF THE ROSES and the fifteenth and sixteenth centuries. Their allegiances often shifted, being generally dictated by intense rivalry with their cousins and neighbours the NEVILLES. The head of Harry HOTSPUR, Sir Henry Percy, was put on a spike on MICKLEGATE BAR following his 1403 rebellion against HENRY IV. The fourth Earl of Northumberland, also a Henry Percy, deserted RICHARD III at the Battle of Bosworth, and in retribution was hanged from a tree by Richard's supporters near Thirsk, North Yorkshire, in 1489. The seventh Earl, Thomas Percy, was executed in PAVEMENT in 1572, following a Catholic rebellion against Queen Elizabeth I. Thomas Percy, cousin of the ninth Earl, Henry, was one of the chief conspirators of the 1605 GUNPOWDER PLOT. The male line of the Percys of Northumberland became extinct in 1670.

PETERGATE *See* HIGH PETERGATE, LOW PETERGATE

PHILIPPA, QUEEN (c1314-1369) Queen of England 1327-1369. She was born in Hainault, now in Belgium, and her 1327 marriage to her cousin king EDWARD III was the most significant ROYAL WEDDING at York MINSTER. The presence of Hainaulters resulted in the HAINAULT RIOTS. She bore eight sons and five daughters, the number of sons perhaps leading inevitably to conflicts and the WARS OF THE ROSES. The king and queen had several ROYAL RESIDENCES in the city, including at the CASTLE, the Franciscan Friary and the medieval ARCHBISHOP'S PALACE.

PHOENIX Pub in George Street next to FISHERGATE BAR, close to Dick TURPIN's grave in ST GEORGE'S CHURCHYARD. It was known as the Labour in Vain until the middle of the nineteenth century. Its present name probably comes from the Phoenix Iron Foundry, which was situated at the back of FISHERGATE POSTERN. The front bar was used as a set for a television play in 1973, *Days of Hope*, which was set in 1916.

PICCADILLY Street linking PAVEMENT to FISHER-GATE, named after the London street in 1840. Its most noteworthy building is the MERCHANT ADVENTURERS' HALL. There was no road there until the nineteenth century as the river FOSS reached the city walls at FISH-ERGATE POSTERN and there was a marsh between the river and what is now Piccadilly.

PIKEING WELL *See* LADY WELL

PILGRIMAGE OF GRACE Uprising during the reign of HENRY VIII, opposing the DISSOLUTION OF THE MONASTERIES and insisting on the return of England to Papal supremacy. It was the largest insurrection in England between the Peasants' Revolt (1381) and the ENGLISH CIVIL WAR (1640s). The rebellion began in October 1536 in Lincolnshire, and soon spread to Yorkshire under the leadership of local landowners including Robert ASKE. Aske gave the insurrection its name referring to the religious concept of grace, as its main purpose was spiritual. However, given the important economic role of the monasteries there were clearly other motives. Aske assumed Henry would comply to avoid civil war as support was widespread, the Pilgrims numbering over 35,000. Henry agreed to consider their demands, including having an elected Parliament in York, and said all Pilgrims would be pardoned. They agreed to disband, believing they had won a great victory. Within a month Aske went to London to see Henry, and was received with honour. Henry, however, went back on his word, finding Aske and other leaders all guilty of treason. Aske was executed at CLIFFORD'S TOWER and his body hanged in chains there for a year as a deterrent to other rebellions.

PIPE ROLLS *Documents constituting the nation's earliest surviving series of public records. They list the revenue and expenditure of the Crown, and were compiled locally by the SHERIFF. They are continuous from 1155 to 1831. The name simply describes their shape when rolled up. York's Pipe Rolls proved to be important sources of the city's history.*

PLAGUE The 1348-49 countrywide outbreak of Bubonic Plague or the Black Death is estimated to have killed a third of the country's population. York's POPULATION suffered accordingly. There were further outbreaks from 1549 to 1552 and in 1604. The only firm figures from these outbreaks are from 1604, when 3512 people are known to have died. In 1631 plague was in the area again, but the city BARS were closed and York escaped a major epidemic.

PLAGUE STONES Reminders of the PLAGUES that affected York can still be seen on HOB MOOR and in CLIFTON at the BURTON STONE. These probably date back to the outbreak of 1604. They contain holes that were filled with disinfectant vinegar. If an infected person wished to purchase food, they had to wash the coins in the vinegar. This was mistakenly believed to be protection against the disease as it was thought that it was passed on via money. In reality, fear of the plague only passed with increased hygiene standards resulting in decreasing numbers of rats and fleas.

POLICE STATION In 1836 the idea of having a police force reached York, the Metropolitan Police having been introduced in London by Robert Peel in 1829. An advisor from London suggested a force of three sergeants and twenty constables, but the city CORPORATION settled for one sergeant and twelve constables as York was supposedly a "religious and moral city". SILVER STREET was the location of York's first police station between 1841 and 1892, when the station moved to CLIFFORD STREET. The headquarters of North Yorkshire Police is now situated in FULFORD Road on part of the site of the old CAVALRY BARRACKS.

POPE JOHN PAUL II (1920-) The Pope visited the KNAVESMIRE on 31 May 1982, and addressed an audience of 210,000 people, more than the POPULATION of York. He was the first Pope to visit England and had survived an assassination attempt in Rome the year before.

POPPLETON ROAD SCHOOL Primary school situated on the corner of Poppleton Road and Water End, designed by Walter BRIERLEY in 1904. During WORLD WAR ONE an anti-aircraft gun against the ZEPPELIN

RAIDS was placed near the school. It was badly damaged during the BAEDEKER BLITZ of 1942.

POPPLETON TITHE BARN Barn in Upper Poppleton, three miles (4.8km) west of York, dating from c1542. Some call it Rupert's Barn as it is alleged that Prince RUPERT may have housed part of his army here on his way to the Battle of MARSTON MOOR in 1644. In 1660, Lord THOMAS FAIRFAX is said to have gathered here with his men before marching into York to announce the restoration of the monarchy and CHARLES II's accession.

POPULATION York's population, including its surrounding villages, currently stands at 178,000. Several ANGLO-SAXON chroniclers put York's pre-NORMAN Conquest population at a disputable 25,000. However, in the 1400s the city's population was said to be approximately 12,000, the Black Death of 1349 having killed around one third. York's fifteenth-century population made it second only to London (approximately 35,000). In 1901 the population is recorded as 83,058 having grown from 19,325 in 1801. Between 1841 and 1851 approximately 2600 Irish people emigrated to York, mostly to the WALMGATE area, escaping the Potato Famine in Ireland and arriving to work on the RAILWAYS.

PORTCULLIS Strong wooden-framed vertical grating, often with points shod with iron. It is designed to be lowered to protect the gateways of castles and city gates. It was originally a ROMAN invention, though takes its name from the Old French *porte coleise*. All four of York's main gateways or BARS employed a portcullis and an intact example, largely original and theoretically still operational, can be seen in MONK BAR. It was last used in 1953 at the time of the coronation of Queen ELIZABETH II. A fragment of the one which existed in MICKLEGATE BAR can still be seen. The portcullis in BOOTHAM BAR is a replica.

POST OFFICE York's main Post Office is situated in LENDAL, built on the site of the medieval Augustinian friary. The first Post Office was established here in 1703 and later the Mail Coach office and yard was built behind it, with stables for a hundred horses to carry the mail across the country. When the Penny Post was introduced in 1840 a great increase in postal business occurred. In 1884 a new, larger Post Office was built on the site of the original one.

POSTERN A small door in the walls of a castle, or a back door. In York the term is sometimes used to refer to a building marking the end of a particular stretch of the city WALLS. There is therefore a FISHERGATE POSTERN, the BARKER TOWER (North Street Postern), while SKELDERGATE POSTERN, demolished in 1808, and LAYERTHORPE POSTERN, demolished in 1829, formed part of the original layout of the walls.

PRECENTOR Member of staff of the MINSTER, with overall responsibility for the music. The Precentor lived in PRECENTOR'S COURT, near the West End of the Minster.

PRECENTOR'S COURT Narrow lane hidden away opposite the WEST DOORS of the MINSTER, next to the PUREY-CUST HOSPITAL. The lane leads to Fenton House, an eighteenth-century building belonging to the Minster and once the residence of the PRECENTOR.

PRINCE OF WALES' OWN REGIMENT OF YORKSHIRE York's home regiment, the result of an amalgamation of the East Yorkshire and West Yorkshire regiments in 1958. Their REGIMENTAL MUSEUM is in Tower Street. The Regiment dates back to the Fourteenth Regiment of Foot, founded in 1685 by JAMES II.

PRINCESS MARGARET'S ARCH Stone archway in EXHBITION SQUARE, created by breaking through the wall of ST MARY'S ABBEY in 1503. Its name comes from its use as the entrance for Princess Margaret, daughter of HENRY VII, who stayed in York on her way north to marry JAMES IV of Scotland.

PRINCIPIA The ROMAN fortress or military headquarters of EBORACUM, which was situated where the MINSTER now stands. The first wooden church built on this site by King EDWIN in AD627 was possibly constructed in the courtyard of the ruins of the Principia. During work to strengthen the CENTRAL TOWER of the Minster, between 1967 and 1972, the ROMAN COLUMN now located outside the SOUTH TRANSEPT was discovered. This work led to the creation of the UNDERCROFT, which is open to the public.

PRIORY STREET Wide street off MICKLEGATE, created in 1854 by George Townsend ANDREWS. The street was built in the former grounds of HOLY TRINITY Priory and its creation led to the redevelopment of the BISHOPHILL area. There are three nonconformist CHURCHES in the street.

PRISONS There were prisons recorded in York from before the thirteenth century until 1929. There were two types of prison, "city prisons" for York inmates, and "county prisons", for those from the surrounding area. The chief County Prison, demolished in 1935, lay between CLIFFORD'S TOWER and the river FOSS, at York CASTLE. It was built in 1825. Also in the Castle area was the DEBTOR'S PRISON, built between 1701 and 1705 and used for both debtors and felons, and the FEMALE PRISON, built in 1780. All three prisons in this area ceased to be used as such in 1929. Earlier city prisons were the KIDCOTES and another debtors' prison, both of which closed in the early nineteenth century, on OUSE BRIDGE, the fourteenth-century Forest Prison (for poachers apprehended in the FOREST OF GALTRES) in DAVYGATE, and the Peter Prison, on the site of what is now the YORK ARMS pub near the MINSTER. The main City Prison was located alongside BAILE HILL between 1807 and 1838, before it relocated to the Castle area.

PUMP YARD or PUMP COURT Small courtyard at the northern end of the SHAMBLES, near NEWGATE MARKET. Methodist John WESLEY preached from the window of a house to a crowd below in 1757.

PUNCH BOWL Pub in STONEGATE. Although the frontage is the result of refurbishment in 1931, the pub is one of York's oldest inns. There are records of soldiers staying here in the 1750s, and the licence is probably much earlier. The name "Punch Bowl" is of seventeenth-century political origin. While the Tories enjoyed sack (a dry white Spanish wine) and claret, the Whigs preferred the much sweeter drink of punch.

PUREY-CUST HOSPITAL Private hospital which opened in 1915 next to PRECENTOR'S COURT. It was built on the site of the old sub-deanery in MINSTER CLOSE and the entrance is opposite the WEST DOORS of the MINSTER. The building was designed by Walter BRIERLEY, and was named after the long-serving DEAN of the Minster, Arthur Percival Purey-Cust (1828-1916), who was Dean from 1880 until his death.

Q

QUAKERS Nonconformist Christians who have had an enormous influence on York. Their official name is the Society of Friends and the name Quaker comes from the spiritual "trembling" experienced during meetings. Quakerism was founded by George Fox (1624-91) in 1647 in Leicestershire. In 1651 he preached in the MINSTER and was forcibly ejected. The Act of Toleration of 1689 put an end to the persecution of Quakers for non-attendance at Church of England services. York's Quaker families such as the TUKES and the ROWNTREES have become synonymous with social justice, welfare and the quality of life of the people of York. Quakers founded The RETREAT HOSPITAL, The MOUNT SCHOOL,

BOOTHAM SCHOOL and the village of NEW EAR-SWICK. The FRIENDS' MEETING HOUSE is situated off CASTLEGATE.

QUEEN'S STAITH Quayside opposite KING'S STAITH, situated at the bottom of MICKLEGATE by OUSE BRIDGE. Butter Staith, which stood alongside, was built in 1760 and used for shipping butter to London until the mid-nineteenth century. The BUTTER MARKET was located near the church of ST MARTIN-CUM-GREGORY. Queen's Staith was rebuilt in 1810 and used mainly for the coal trade, and referred to as Coal Staith. The staith was used as a landing area for industry associated with the river until the 1980s.

QUINTUS PETILIUS CERIALIS (First century AD) Commander of the NINTH LEGION who founded EBO-RACUM (York) in AD71 when the ROMANS moved north from Lincoln to suppress the BRIGANTES. The Governor of Britain, he was the son-in-law of VESPASIAN.

QUIRE in the Minster *See* CHOIR

R

RACECOURSE York Races have been held on the KNAVESMIRE since 1731 and take place from May to October. In 1530 there was a race on CLIFTON Ings to win a small golden bell, presented by the LORD MAYOR. However, racing at Clifton ended owing to the land often being flooded. By the late sixteenth century races were held on ACOMB Moor. At first the races involved one owner racing his horse against that of another. CHARLES I visited in 1633, when his horse lost. Modern racing, with several horses running, only became popular in the eighteenth century. In 1731 Simon Scrope of Danby wrote: "Tomorrow we set out for York to see the new horse course, lately made on Knavesmire, and to join in the great goings of the week, the life of which no town or city can compare with for gaiety, sport and company all of one mind." John CARR built the grandstand in 1754, now part of the County Stand. York was voted "Racecourse of the Year" in 2001 by the Racegoers' Club and the Racehorse Owners' Club. It is a flat racing track, rather than a steeplechase in which horses leap over fences. The August EBOR meeting is the most prestigious.

RAILWAY STATION York's current station, built between 1871 and 1877, is actually its third railway terminus. The first, a temporary wooden structure in Queen Street, just outside the city WALLS, opened in 1839. The first proper station opened in 1841, in TANNER ROW. Although offices have now been built on the site, the façade of the old station is still visible. Two archways remain, cut in the city walls in 1839 and 1845 to accommodate the tracks. The present station was built by William Peachy and Thomas Prosser. At the time it was the largest in the country and was seen by some as "a monument to extravagance", with its 800-foot-long (244m) glass and iron roof and platforms that eventually grew to be nearly 1700 feet (518m) long by 1910. The station was severely damaged during the BAEDEKER BLITZ of April 1942. The roof collapsed in parts and an empty express train was destroyed.

The NATIONAL RAILWAY MUSEUM now occupies the site of the old depot adjacent to the station.

RAILWAYS The railways first arrived in York in 1839. The city's position halfway between London and Edinburgh, along with the efforts of the "Railway King" George HUDSON, ensured its prominence during the so-called "Railway Mania" of 1845-47. Hudson, chairman of the Midland Railway, and his intense rival George LEEMAN, chairman of the North Eastern Railway, were the two major figures in York's nineteenth-century railway development. The former's questionable accounting practices led to his exposure and disgrace in 1849. Nonetheless, York had by then become the railway capital of the north. The present RAILWAY STATION, built between 1871 and 1877, is said to be one of the great buildings of Victorian England. The NORTH EASTERN RAILWAY HEAD-QUARTERS, now GNER, has been situated in Station Road since 1906. The NATIONAL RAILWAY MUSEUM, in Leeman Road, opened in 1975. Privatisation of the network in the mid-1990s resulted in the closure of York's Carriageworks, in Holgate Road, in 1995.

RED DEVIL Traditional sign for a printer's shop which can be seen above 33 STONEGATE. It serves as a reminder of Stonegate's long association with printing and the book trade. There exist plentiful theories as to why the sign was used to indicate a printer's shop, and apprentice printers are still sometimes referred to as "printers' devils". Printing was known as the "black art" owing to its dirty nature, hence a junior apprentice might be called the "red devil". Another theory is that the apprentice, collecting type from a customer, would sometimes mischievously rearrange the letters. The apprentice also had the unenviable task of feeding melted lead to cast letters into a fiery pot, in an atmosphere of sparks and brimstone reminiscent of Hell. Further evidence of Stonegate's link with the book trade can be found in the sign of the GOLDEN BIBLE and the statue of MINERVA, the ROMAN goddess of wisdom and drama, in MINSTER GATES.

RED HOUSE Large house in DUNCOMBE PLACE, built between 1702 and 1704 by the architect William ETTY. It was once the residence of Sir William Robinson, a former LORD MAYOR and MP for York. When Sir William parted from his post, the city CORPORATION wanted to use the house as the official Mayor's residence, but he refused to move so the MANSION HOUSE had to be built. Lawrence STERNE based the character of Dr Slop in *Tristram Shandy* (1760-67) on Dr John Burton, Chief Physician to the County Hospital, who lived in the Red House after 1740. The Red House currently contains an antiques centre and café.

RED INDIAN Statue of a Native American above 74A LOW PETERGATE, the traditional sign for a tobacconist's shop, tobacco having originated in North America. The business no longer exists and nor does the statue, having been stolen in 2002. It has been stolen before but later returned to its rightful place, and it is to be hoped that it will return once again.

RED LION Pub in Merchantgate, a street linking WALMGATE to PICCADILLY. Until 1912 the pub was all but concealed behind the now demolished Black Horse pub. Both pubs were alongside the old pig market, near FOSS

BRIDGE. Owing to a name change in the nineteenth century it is difficult to trace the Red Lion's licence back before 1800, though the building itself is clearly a great deal older. There are thirteenth-century foundation stones and the timber frames, both inside and out, are of a similar period. Upstairs there is a priest hole, dating from the sixteenth century. Given the age of the building, historical tales are plentiful. One story is that the notorious highwayman Dick TURPIN once escaped from an upstairs window. Like many pubs including YE OLDE STARRE INN and the BLACK SWAN, the Red Lion claims to be York's oldest.

RED TOWER Brick-built defensive tower on the city WALLS, alongside Foss Islands Road. It was built in 1490 when HENRY VII ordered the strengthening of the city's defences. The Red Tower was damaged in 1644 during the SIEGE OF YORK and fell into disrepair. In the early eighteenth century it became known as Brimstone House because it was used for the manufacture of gunpowder. It was being used as a stable in 1800 but was restored in 1858, when the present roof and windows were added.

REFORMATION King HENRY VIII placed himself at the head of the Church of England and broke with the papal authority of Rome through the Act of Supremacy of 1534. As a result of these actions, the PILGRIMAGE OF GRACE of 1536 and the DISSOLUTION OF THE MONASTERIES of 1536-40 took place.

REGIMENTAL MUSEUM Small museum situated in Tower Street, opposite CLIFFORD'S TOWER. It is the museum of the Royal Dragoon Guards and the PRINCE

OF WALES' OWN REGIMENT OF YORKSHIRE, and contains a fascinating insight into over 300 years of military history.

REREDOS of the Minster Ornamental screen covering the wall behind an altar. The reredos originally behind the HIGH ALTAR is now in ST STEPHEN'S CHAPEL.

RETREAT, THE Psychiatric hospital in HESLINGTON Road, built in 1796 under the supervision of Peter ATKINSON Senior. When William TUKE was nearly sixty years old he became concerned about the rights of the mentally ill, following the death of a QUAKER woman in BOOTHAM PARK HOSPITAL, then the Asylum, in terrible conditions. Tuke resolved to establish a hospital for Quakers where a kind, humane environment was the priority. He found a site near Heslington and began building The Retreat in 1795. Its official title was "The Retreat for Persons afflicted with Disorders of the Mind" and the first patients were admitted in 1796. The first Superintendent died within two months of the opening of the hospital so Tuke took over, appointing George Jepson to succeed him in 1797. The pioneering work begun by Tuke at The Retreat brought about enormous changes in attitudes towards the mentally ill, which spread throughout the world. In 1908 Walter BRIERLEY built Lamel Beeches, the residence for the Hospital Superintendent.

RICHARD I (1157-1199) King of England 1189-99. Reputedly the only Plantagenet king never to visit York, Richard "the Lionheart" spent less than a year of his reign in England. Nonetheless, his succession had a significant influence on one of the most shameful events in

York's history. Generous gifts offered by London's Jewish community at Richard's coronation at Westminster Abbey in September 1189 resulted in anti-Semitic feeling spreading as far as York, and the subsequent MASSACRE OF THE JEWS in CLIFFORD'S TOWER in March 1190.

RICHARD II (1367-1399) King of England 1377-99. A king with many failings, Richard II was nonetheless extremely popular in York, visiting the city no less than nine times. He presented York with its first mayoral SWORD OF STATE in 1387, and granted several CHARTERS, including one in 1396 which made York an independent county. Following a bitter quarrel with Londoners in 1392 and an outbreak of the plague there, he stayed in York for six months, bringing his government offices with him, and is thought to have wanted to make York the CAPITAL OF ENGLAND. The Sword of State, the MACE and the CAP OF MAINTENANCE he presented to York still appear on the city's COAT OF ARMS. A great benefactor to the MINSTER, he presented to it a notable relic, namely the remains of one of the Holy Innocents slaughtered by Herod. In 1398 he watched the MYSTERY PLAYS from a purpose-built enclosure near the Minster. His popularity in York outlived him and precipitated ARCHBISHOP OF YORK Richard SCROPE's rebellion against Richard's successor HENRY IV in 1405.

RICHARD III (1452-1485) King of England 1483-1485. Despite the image created by both history and by SHAKESPEARE, Richard III was undoubtedly an extremely popular king in York. As Duke of Gloucester, he would visit

York as many as six times a year, staying at the Augustinian Friary in LENDAL, where the main POST OFFICE now stands. After becoming king in July 1483, Richard's royal progress took him to York, entering the city via MICKLEGATE BAR in August 1483. He stayed at the now demolished Archbishop's Palace, next to York MINSTER. His son EDWARD OF MIDDLEHAM was invested as Prince of Wales in the Palace on 8 September 1483. Richard was a great benefactor to the Minster, where he intended to be buried, and founded the COUNCIL OF THE NORTH, which was later based in York. His death on Bosworth Field, in August 1485, was much mourned in York, being recorded in the city records as follows: "…King Richard, late mercifully reigning over us, was thrugh grete treason…piteously slain and murdred, to the great hevynesse of this citie…." The RICHARD III MUSEUM is located in MONK BAR.

RICHARD III MUSEUM Small museum housed in MONK BAR. The central exhibition puts RICHARD III "on trial", charged with the crime for which history condemns him, the murders of the "Princes in the Tower". Visitors are invited to give their own verdict. Also within the museum are the LITTLE EASE prison, a rare example of a working PORTCULLIS and a reconstructed execution chamber with a re-enactment of the executions of 1483. It is believed that the uppermost room was added at the request of King Richard himself in 1484.

RICHARD OF SHREWSBURY (1473-1483?) Second son of EDWARD IV and Elizabeth Woodville, and one of the "Princes in the Tower". As the fifth DUKE OF YORK, his was the first instance of the second in line to the throne being granted the title.

RICHARD, DUKE OF YORK (1411-1460) Third DUKE OF YORK, grandson of EDMUND OF LANGLEY and also of Roger de Mortimer, and a descendant through both of EDWARD III. He held the protectorate during HENRY VI's first bout of madness from 1454 to 1455. Following the Yorkist victory at Northampton in 1460 he claimed, and was granted, the succession. However, as the saying goes, "Richard of York gave battle in vain…." Shortly afterwards he was defeated and killed by the forces of Queen Margaret (Margaret of Anjou, French wife of Henry VI, known as the "she-wolf of France") at Wakefield, West Yorkshire. His head, with a paper crown on it, and that of his son Edmund, were placed on spikes above MICKLE-GATE BAR. "Off with his head, and set it on York gates/ So York may overlook the town of York" (Margaret of Anjou, *Henry VI* part 3 Act I Scene III). SHAKESPEARE was inaccurate in suggesting that "York may overlook the town of York", as the HEADS placed on Micklegate Bar looked outwards, away from the city, in order to act as a warning to those entering the city.

RIDINGS, YORKSHIRE *See* YORKSHIRE RIDINGS

RIVER HOUSE Victorian building in Museum Street with a balcony overlooking the river OUSE. It was originally the Yorkshire Club for gentlemen. The club's initial premises were established in 1835 in ST LEONARD'S PLACE "for the nobility and gentry of the county". The new club on Museum Street was built following the opening of LENDAL BRIDGE in 1863. Country gentlemen would ride to York from their estates, leave their horses at the nearby Botterill's Horse Repository in TANNERS' MOAT and stay at the club overnight. Becoming something of an anachronism in the twentieth century, the club enjoyed a revival with the opening of the UNIVERSITY OF YORK in 1963. Having no suitable buildings of their own at first, the university staff used the premises for meeting and entertaining. From 1963 they moved to the KING'S MANOR and HESLINGTON HALL. A long-term lease expired in the 1980s and the Yorkshire Club went out of business, running in name only and hiring other buildings for occasional functions. River House is currently a restaurant.

RIVER TRIPS Trips on the river OUSE, with commentary, are available from February until November. The trips depart from KING'S STAITH throughout the day from 10.30am and from LENDAL BRIDGE boatyard ten minutes later. The trips last for approximately one hour, and include key sights such as York MINSTER, CLIFFORD'S TOWER, ST MARY'S ABBEY, the MULTANGULAR TOWER, BISHOPTHORPE PALACE and the MILLENNIUM BRIDGE. There are also evening floodlit cruises from March until October and GHOST cruises during the peak season. It is also possible to hire a self-drive motorboat from King's Staith landing between March and November.

ROBIN HOOD Legendary outlaw possibly from the twelfth century. His name is associated with both the LITTLE JOHN pub and ROBIN HOOD'S TOWER. However, he has only a very tenuous connection with the city of York. The anonymous poem "The Gest of Robyn

Hode" dating from c1400, upon which much of the legend is based, has Robin helping out a "Sorrowful Knight" forced to mortgage his estates to the treacherous Abbot of ST MARY'S ABBEY. Elsewhere, one Robert Hod is recorded as a fugitive of York Assizes in 1225, while Thomas Gale, DEAN of York 1697-1702, left among his papers an epitaph allegedly inserted on Robin Hood's grave. The grave is situated at Kirklees Abbey, Mirfield, West Yorkshire. The earliest literary reference to Robin Hood is in William Langland's *Piers Plowman* (c1377). Other writers place him either in the thirteenth or fourteenth centuries, or more popularly at the time of RICHARD I, from 1190 onwards. One of the commanders of York CASTLE during the thirteenth century is reputedly the model for the Sheriff of Nottingham, Robin Hood's chief adversary.

ROBIN HOOD'S TOWER Corner tower on the city WALLS between BOOTHAM BAR and MONK BAR. The present tower was built in 1889 on the site of a previous one. The original tower was known as the Bawing Tower in around 1370, the Frost Tower (after William Frost, LORD MAYOR of York 1396-1404) by 1485 and ROBIN HOOD's Tower since the early 1600s. Quite how the Tower acquired its present name is unknown. It may be due to the presence of the medieval FOREST OF GALTRES, which stretched as far as this particular section of wall until the seventeenth century. At some stage it was also referred to as the Elbow Tower, perhaps suggesting the use of a bow and arrow.

ROCKET *See* STEPHENSON'S ROCKET

ROMAN BATH Pub situated in ST SAMPSON'S SQUARE. An inn from at least 1783, acquiring its name from the discovery of a section of first-century ROMAN baths during refurbishment in 1930. The baths were probably military and ran under the present Church Street. They are open to the public. The pub had previously been known as the Barrel Churn, the Cooper, the Barrel and the Mail Coach.

ROMAN COLUMN Fourth-century stone column located outside the SOUTH TRANSEPT of the MINSTER. It once stood in the Great Hall of the ROMAN PRINCIPIA, then occupied by the SIXTH LEGION. It was found in 1969 during excavations of the CENTRAL TOWER and given by the DEAN and CHAPTER to YORK CIVIC TRUST, who erected it in 1971 to mark the 1900th year of the city's foundation. York Guides often create some amusement by suggesting that it is upside down, though this is vehemently denied.

ROMAN GATEWAYS The four gateways to York's PRINCIPIA were the Porta Principalis Dextra, where BOOTHAM BAR now stands, the Porta Principalis Sinistra in what is now KING'S SQUARE, the Porta Praetoria in what is now ST HELEN'S SQUARE, and the Porta Decumana, to the west of MONK BAR. The site of the Porta Decumana is revealed by a small mound visible in the embankment of the present city WALLS, close to Monk Bar.

ROMAN PALACE Historian Francis DRAKE believed that the ROMAN palace (or *domus palatina*) was situated in what is now BEDERN. It was perhaps here that

SEVERUS (Emperor AD193-211) gave his two sons his dying wishes, and CONSTANTIUS CHLORUS (Emperor AD293-306) died. CONSTANTINE THE GREAT (Emperor AD306-337) may have been invested here by the Roman Legions. Some partisan local historians have claimed Constantine was born here, though his birthplace is more likely to have been Naissus or Nis in Serbia.

ROMAN REMAINS Roman ground level was approximately fifteen feet (4.5m) below the existing ground level, the present city having effectively been built upon its own remains. Nonetheless much is still visible. The MULTANGULAR TOWER in the MUSEUM GARDENS, sections of wall in ALDWARK and in the city LIBRARY grounds, and the remains of a bath house in the cellar of the ROMAN BATH pub are all easily accessible. Elsewhere, parts of the present city WALLS often follow the Roman defences. The UNDERCROFT of the MINSTER reveals evidence of the PRINCIPIA, a column from which is on display outside the SOUTH TRANSEPT. Several of York's streets have been highways for nearly 2000 years. STONEGATE (Via Praetoria), PETERGATE (Via Principatis) and CHAPTER HOUSE STREET (Via Decumana) are all examples of these. The Minster is situated upon the foundations of the Legion's headquarters, the Principia. The YORKSHIRE MUSEUM also houses a collection of Roman archaeology, including a huge stone head of Emperor CONSTANTINE. New finds occur regularly, with cemetery sites in FISHERGATE, The MOUNT, at the RAILWAY STATION and elsewhere outside the Roman walls, including at HEWORTH.

ROMAN ROADS The three principal ROMAN roads of EBORACUM (York), leading to their fort or PRINCIPIA, were the Via Principalis, now PETERGATE, the Via Praetoria, now STONEGATE, and the Via Decumana, now CHAPTER HOUSE STREET. The roads lay at least six feet (1.8m) below the current thoroughfares.

ROMANS Originally citizens of Rome in western Italy, Rome having been founded in 753BC. Their Empire at its peak incorporated the majority of Western Europe, and stretched as far east as Syria and as far south as North Africa and Egypt. Their first attempt to conquer Britain (Britannia) was by Julius Caesar (c102-44BC), who made incursions in both 55BC and 54BC. However, it was not until AD43 that Emperor Claudius sent an invasion force under Aulus Plautius to attempt a full conquest. The major cities to emerge included Londinium (London), EBORACUM (York), Camulodonum (Colchester), Aquae Sulis (Bath), Deva (Chester), Lindum (Lincoln), Verulamium (St Albans) and Corinium Dobunnorum (Cirencester). In cAD275 the ANGLO-SAXONS began threatening the south and east coasts of England, resulting in much re-fortification. Rome effectively abandoned the province cAD410, with Emperor Honorius refusing to aid the Romano-British against renewed Anglo-Saxon attacks. Apart from major construction of roads, walls and stone buildings, the Romans (unlike the Anglo-Saxons or the VIKINGS), recorded their history in great detail. The Romans arrived in York in AD71 and departed cAD410.

ROMANUS, JOHN (Thirteenth century) John Romanus the Elder was the CANON and Sub-DEAN of the MINSTER. An agreement for the transfer of land at JEWBURY was made in around 1230 between him and the JEWS OF YORK and his copy of the agreement survives in the Minster archives. Some of the money from the sale of land may have been used for the NORTH TRANSEPT of the MINSTER (c1220-45) and the FIVE SISTERS WINDOW, sometimes called the Jewish Window as it contains not pictures but geometrical designs consistent with the Old Testament prohibition of images. This may mean that Jewish money helped to pay for the MINSTER.

ROOF BOSSES *See* BOSSES in the Minster

ROSE WINDOW of the Minster One of the most impressive windows in the MINSTER, located in the SOUTH TRANSEPT. It is also known as the Wheel Window. The stonework dates from 1240 and the window may have originally contained *grisaille* glass like that of the FIVE SISTERS WINDOW. The Rose Window is twenty-two feet (6.7m) in diameter. It contains petals of red and white roses dating from c1515, each five feet (1.5m) long, showing the union of the two royal houses of York and Lancaster following the WARS OF THE ROSES. The central medallion dates from 1793, painted by William PECKITT, depicting a sunflower. This may have replaced a marigold as the window was once called the Marigold Window. The window was painstakingly restored by York Glaziers' Trust after the MINSTER FIRE of 1984. The glass was cracked and loosened by the fire but none of it fell out as the window had been re-leaded twelve years before.

ROUGIER STREET Street linking Station Road to George HUDSON Street, built between 1838 and 1846.

The comb-maker Joseph Rougier set up his York business there in the 1820s and by the 1860s it was the largest horn workshop in Britain. Horn was used to make buttons and jewellery as well as combs. Rougier was from a French Huguenot family, Protestants who had fled persecution in France. Rougier's workshop closed in 1931, due to competition from modern materials such as plastic.

ROWNTREE, BENJAMIN SEEBOHM (1871-1954) Son of JOSEPH SEEBOHM ROWNTREE, who conducted a major survey of the city's poor in 1899. The survey concluded that 3000 working-class families in York still lived in poverty, particularly in HUNGATE and WALMGATE. This constituted a quarter of the city's POPULATION. Rowntree employed a team of researchers to visit over 11,000 families in the city. He made the important connection between poor housing and ill health, and he worked out what the poverty line was, or the level of income needed to survive. Rowntree updated his groundbreaking work, *Poverty: A Study of Town Life*, in 1901. By 1908 the CITY OF YORK COUNCIL had begun to improve the worst areas of York. Whole streets were condemned as unfit for human habitation and demolished, leading to the redevelopment of the STONEBOW area. The social research begun by Benjamin Seebohm Rowntree is continued by the JOSEPH ROWNTREE FOUNDATION.

ROWNTREE, HENRY ISAAC (1838-1883) Younger brother of JOSEPH SEEBOHM ROWNTREE, and co-founder of ROWNTREE & CO. Henry Isaac Rowntree joined fellow QUAKER William TUKE's confectionery business in CASTLEGATE in 1860, buying the cocoa and CHOCOLATE department two years later. He moved the manufacturing process to a new factory at TANNERS' MOAT by LENDAL BRIDGE in 1869.

ROWNTREE, JOHN STEPHENSON (1834-1907) Brother of JOSEPH SEEBOHM ROWNTREE. He served as LORD MAYOR from 1880 to 1881. In 1848 he started the first QUAKER Adult School in Hope Street, off WALM-GATE. The aim was "to apply the teaching of the Bible to everyday life and the problems of society". The school moved in 1857 to a room in LADY PECKETT'S YARD, behind the original ROWNTREE & CO. shop and house. Rowntrees' schools and social clubs developed rapidly at the beginning of the twentieth century.

ROWNTREE, JOSEPH SEEBOHM (1836-1925) QUAKER and one of York's most influential figures. He was born above the family's grocery shop at 28 PAVE-MENT. At the age of fourteen his father (Joseph Rowntree Senior) took him to Ireland to witness the worst effects of the Potato Famine, which caused over one million deaths. The trip had a profound effect, instilling in the boy a life-long compassion for his fellow man. At twenty-one he and his elder brother JOHN STEPHENSON ROWNTREE taught an Adult School behind the family shop in LADY PECKETT'S YARD. In 1869 he joined his younger brother, HENRY ISAAC ROWNTREE, to work in his Cocoa, CHOCOLATE and Chicory Works at TANNERS' MOAT, taking over the accounts of what became ROWN-TREE & CO. He gave the workforce a library, a welfare worker and concerts. It was with this paternal system in mind that the village of NEW EARSWICK was built. His aim was to improve the living conditions of the whole city. Rowntree was an active member of the Temperance Society and wrote pamphlets such as *The Temperance Problem and Social Reform* (1900). In 1911 he received the FREEDOM OF THE CITY. On his death the northern edition of the *Daily Mirror* carried his funeral across the whole front page, leaving just a small corner to announce "New York shaken by Earthquake".

ROWNTREE & CO CHOCOLATE and confectionery business based in Haxby Road. The present site, however, is not the original. HENRY ISAAC ROWNTREE joined fellow QUAKER William TUKE's confectionery business in CASTLEGATE in 1860, buying the cocoa and chocolate department two years later. He moved the manufacturing process to a new factory at TANNERS' MOAT in 1869. In 1881 they began making gum and pastilles which proved so successful, producing four tons a week by the late 1880s, that by 1883 the workforce had doubled. It was originally known as Rowntree & Co., becoming Rowntree Mackintosh in 1969, and, since 1988, Nestlé Rowntree. The current factory was built on nine ACRES of land in 1890 to deal with an expanding workforce. There was a riverside warehouse in North Street, opposite ALL SAINTS CHURCH, which closed in the 1950s.

ROWNTREE FACTORY LIFE When ROWNTREE & CO. was based in TANNERS' MOAT bizarre anecdotes were plentiful. In the 1870s employees kept records of their hours and took their pay from a hat circulated by the foreman. Honesty was strongly recommended because in the event of there being insufficient money to pay the last person, all the cash would have to be replaced and the hat circulated again. The factory also had a parrot and a donkey, the latter for deliveries. Steam pipes were run into the stables so that the donkey could enjoy a Turkish bath. JOSEPH SEEBOHM ROWNTREE's enthusiasm for social activity for his workforce resulted in a disastrous outing to Whitby in the 1880s. Excessive drunkenness ensued, resulting in employees having to be escorted to their train home by the police. Joseph's firmly held beliefs in the evils of alcohol resulted in further excursions being cancelled.

ROWNTREE FAMILY QUAKER family of enormous importance in York's social and economic development. Joseph Rowntree Senior originally ran a family grocery business in PAVEMENT. Two of his sons HENRY ISAAC ROWNTREE and JOSEPH SEEBOHM ROWNTREE were responsible for the expansion of the ROWNTREE & CO. CHOCOLATE and confectionery business. Another son JOHN STEPHENSON ROWNTREE, along with Joseph Seebohm Rowntree, helped found adult schools and social clubs. Grandson BENJAMIN SEE-BOHM ROWNTREE conducted a survey of the city's poor in 1899, looking at income, diet and housing. Despite the success of their business, the emphasis was always upon improving social conditions and the general quality of life of working people. There was also an awareness of the significance of leisure. The Rowntree legacy also includes the JOSEPH ROWNTREE FOUNDATION, JOSEPH ROWNTREE SCHOOL and ROWNTREE PARK.

ROWNTREE PARK Public park located between CLEMENTHORPE and the MILLENNIUM BRIDGE, covering twenty-four ACRES. The park was created as a memorial to workers of ROWNTREE & CO who "fell and suffered" in WORLD WAR ONE. It was designed by architect Fred Rowntree (1860-1927) and opened in July 1921. The main gates are probably eighteenth-century and were given by the company in 1955 as a memorial to the efforts of York's citizens in WORLD WAR TWO. With its play area and extensive amenities the park remains extremely popular with children.

ROWNTREE WHARF *See* LEETHAM'S MILL

ROYAL OAK Pub in GOODRAMGATE, an inn since at least 1783. Formerly the Blue Pigg and the Blue Boar, it became the Royal Oak in 1819. The pub has an Elizabethan-style brick and timber frontage.

ROYAL RESIDENCES The early medieval kings would generally stay at York CASTLE when visiting the city. HENRY III, EDWARD I, EDWARD II and EDWARD III all stayed there. RICHARD II and other kings stayed at the now demolished Franciscan Friary, remains of which can still be seen alongside TOWER PLACE, between CLIFFORD'S TOWER and the river OUSE. A king might also stay at the now demolished ARCHBISHOP'S PALACE behind the MINSTER or at the HOSPITIUM in the grounds of ST MARY'S ABBEY. From HENRY VIII onwards the king would generally stay with whoever was willing to accommodate him. In the seventeenth century

JAMES I opted for the KING'S MANOR whilst CHARLES I stayed at Sir Arthur Ingram's house in DEAN'S PARK.

ROYAL WEDDINGS There have been three royal weddings in York MINSTER. In 1251 Alexander III of Scotland married Princess Margaret, daughter of HENRY III. In 1327 EDWARD III married PHILIPPA of HAINAULT and in 1961 the DUCHESS OF KENT was married there.

RUPERT, PRINCE (1619-82) Nephew of CHARLES I, born in Prague, a staunch supporter of the king during the ENGLISH CIVIL WAR and the SIEGE OF YORK. In June 1644 he was sent by Charles to relieve the city. Learning of his imminent arrival, the Parliamentarians temporarily abandoned the siege, moving south-west towards MARSTON MOOR. The flamboyant Rupert arrived outside York amidst wild celebrations on 1 July, persuading the garrison to join him in pursuit of the enemy. The ensuing battle the following day, however, resulted in a heavy defeat for the Royalist forces. The darling of the "Cavaliers" was forced to flee and went to Lancashire. York fell a fortnight later. Rupert is alleged to have spent the night of 1 July 1644 at POPPLETON TITHE BARN, although this is unlikely.

S

ST ANDREW'S HALL Redundant church in St Andrewgate, off COLLIERGATE near KING'S SQUARE. The church was built in the late fourteenth century and closed in 1559. In 1576 it was known to have been used as a pigsty, and it was reputedly a brothel in the 1730s. In 1842 it was used for the infants of ST PETER'S SCHOOL. Major restoration work was carried out in 1991, hence the modern roof, and the hall is now used by the congregation of an evangelical church.

ST ANTHONY'S HALL *See* BORTHWICK INSTITUTE of Historical Research

ST CRUX Church hall on the corner of PAVEMENT and the SHAMBLES, built on the site of the original St Crux church in 1888. The original church was recorded in the DOMESDAY BOOK and was demolished in 1887. The hall incorporates part of the wall of the church. It is currently used as a café.

ST CUTHBERT (d.AD687) Important saint in the north of England who was consecrated Bishop in the newly rebuilt stone MINSTER in 685. He was the Prior of Lindisfarne monastery from 664 to 676 and is commemorated in the Cuthbert Window in the Minster. His bones are kept in Durham Cathedral.

ST CUTHBERT'S CHAPEL of the Minster Small military chapel located in the SOUTH NAVE AISLE and dedicated to the Yorkshire Volunteers Regiment in 1982.

ST CUTHBERT'S CHURCH Redundant church in PEASHOLME GREEN, mentioned in the DOMESDAY BOOK. There is evidence of an ANGLO-SAXON church, but the present building dates from the fifteenth century. Due to be made redundant in the sixteenth century, it was saved in 1545 by Sir Martin Bowes, the Lord Mayor of London who was originally from York. Bowes begged the LORD MAYOR of York to spare his ancestral place of worship. In return for this favour, Bowes gave a large amount of money to the city to be distributed to poor citizens at Martinmas (the feast of St Martin). It is believed that a secret passageway once linked the church to the BLACK SWAN pub across the street. The parents of General WOLFE are said to have worshipped at the church. It is currently used as administrative offices by ST MICHAEL-LE-BELFREY CHURCH.

ST DENYS' CHURCH Situated in WALMGATE, St Denys' is said to be York's unluckiest church. The tower once had a spire 120 feet (36.5m) high, damaged during the SIEGE OF YORK in 1644 and described in 1680 as "shot thro'...in the late warr". The spire was then struck by lightning in 1730, partially destroyed in a gale, and removed for good in 1798. The tower was rebuilt without its spire in 1847. The first church on the site is recorded in 1154, and there is a rare NORMAN porch. It contains the city's oldest STAINED GLASS dating from c1160, remarkable given the church's accident-prone history.

ST GEORGE'S CHAPEL of the Minster Small military chapel situated in the SOUTH TRANSEPT. It was dedicated to the PRINCE OF WALES OWN REGIMENT in 1926.

ST GEORGE'S CHURCH Catholic church in George Street, off WALMGATE, built in 1850 by Joseph HANSOM. It was built to cope with the influx of Irish immigrants to the area following the Potato Famine in Ireland of the 1840s. The parishioners of ST WILFRID'S CHURCH had raised money to build a new church as they had been using a hall in BLAKE STREET, but when the Irish immigrants began to arrive in York it was agreed that St George's should be built first. The funds raised to build St Wilfrid's were used to build St George's, and St Wilfrid's was not built until 1864. Sister Mary XAVERIA of the BAR CONVENT taught the first children at St George's Primary School.

ST GEORGE'S CHURCHYARD Burial ground in George Street off WALMGATE where Dick TURPIN is buried. The churchyard belonged to the original St George's Church, upon which site the Catholic St George's was built. The first church was destroyed during the SIEGE OF YORK in the ENGLISH CIVIL WAR and was never rebuilt.

ST GEORGE'S FIELD Small park at the confluence of the OUSE and the FOSS, to the south of SKELDERGATE BRIDGE. It was once the site of St George's Chapel, used by medieval monarchs for worship during their stays in the city at one of the ROYAL RESIDENCES. The only trace of the chapel which remains is the name. The nearby CASTLE MILLS were granted to the Knights Templar, knights of a military religious order founded in 1118 by Crusaders, so-named as their house was close to the Temple of Solomon in Jerusalem. Given the Crusaders' association with St George, the area was named after him. The Knights Templar were suppressed in 1309-12, and twenty-four Knights were imprisoned in York CASTLE, the Chapel and the Castle Mills being taken over by the crown. In response to a legendary tourist question the area does not mark the site where St George slew the dragon.

ST HELEN *See* HELEN or HELENA, ST

ST HELEN'S CHURCH Church in ST HELEN'S SQUARE opposite the MANSION HOUSE. The earliest record of a church on this site is in 1235. The current church was made redundant in 1547. The church was due to be demolished in the early 1550s owing to its ruinous state, but was restored in 1553. In 1745 the churchyard was sold to create part of ST HELEN'S SQUARE and the graves were moved to a tiny plot on DAVYGATE, now a seating area. So many corpses had been buried in St Helen's Square that a small hill had grown in the centre of York and it had become increasingly difficult for carriages to pass. In 1603 a fountain of wine was built near the church for the visit of JAMES I. The view from the street is of William ATKINSON's rebuilt facade of 1875.

ST HELEN'S SQUARE Small square incorporating ST HELEN'S CHURCH, BETTY'S Tea Rooms and the MANSION HOUSE. The present square was built in 1745 and was the site of the original shop owned by TERRY'S in 1757. The road was widened when the churchyard of ST HELEN'S was moved to DAVYGATE in 1745. Originally the square was a narrow junction where STONEGATE, Davygate, BLAKE STREET and CONEY STREET met. It was once the site of the York Tavern, which later became Harker's Hotel, demolished in 1929 when the square was widened. The current Harker's Bar occupies the building of the former Yorkshire Insurance Company, built in 1846 by George Townsend ANDREWS.

ST JOHN THE EVANGELIST CHURCH Redundant church in MICKLEGATE. It was first recorded in 1194, though a window remains from the earlier NORMAN period. The timber-framed top of the tower dates from 1646. The church closed in 1934 and was threatened with demolition in the 1950s. It was the location of the York Arts Centre between 1968 and 1999 and is currently unoccupied.

ST JOHN'S CHAPEL of the Minster Small military chapel in the NORTH NAVE AISLE, alongside the NORTH TRANSEPT.

ST LAWRENCE'S CHURCH Situated in Lawrence Street, near WALMGATE BAR, the church dates from the twelfth century, having a NORMAN archway. Everything apart from the tower is nineteenth-century as the church was badly damaged during the SIEGE OF YORK.

ST LEONARD'S HOSPITAL Once the largest hospital in England, founded in the tenth century. Remains of what was once its chapel can be seen near the entrance to the MUSEUM GARDENS alongside the LIBRARY. It once covered the whole area between the Museum Gardens and the THEATRE ROYAL. The hospital owed much of its development to the financial generosity of royalty. It was founded by King ATHELSTAN after his victory at Brunanburh in 937. WILLIAM II gave a grant to the hospital before King Stephen rebuilt it and changed the dedication from ST PETER to St Leonard. This royal interest did not prevent the hospital from being closed in 1539 during the DISSOLUTION OF THE MONASTERIES. The Theatre Royal and the RED HOUSE were built on the remains of its gatehouse. The modern St Leonard's Hospice in Tadcaster Road is named after the original hospital.

ST LEONARD'S PLACE Crescent of houses designed by George Townsend ANDREWS. For its creation 350 feet (107m) of the city WALLS, between BOOTHAM BAR and the MULTANGULAR TOWER, were demolished by the City CORPORATION between 1833 and 1834, thereby linking GILLYGATE to BLAKE STREET. The jagged end of the removed section of the Walls can be seen alongside the KING'S MANOR. The buildings are currently used as offices by the CITY OF YORK COUN- CIL. In St Leonard's Place a short section of ROMAN wall is visible opposite the THEATRE ROYAL.

ST MARGARET'S CHURCH Redundant church in Percy's Lane off WALMGATE which houses the NATIONAL CENTRE FOR EARLY MUSIC. The church is first recorded in 1180 and has a NORMAN porch with carvings of the signs of the Zodiac, which was moved here from the war-damaged church of St Nicholas in Hull Road in 1644, after the SIEGE OF YORK. St Margaret's was enlarged in 1851.

ST MARTIN-CUM-GREGORY CHURCH Redundant church in MICKLEGATE, first mentioned in the DOMES- DAY BOOK. Hereabouts was the site of York's BUTTER MARKET from the late seventeenth century until c1834. Originally there were two churches, the church of St

Martin, situated in St Martin's Lane, and the church of St Gregory, in Micklegate near Barker Lane. The parishes were joined in 1585 but St Gregory's was later demolished. The remaining building has a thirteenth-century nave and fourteenth-century STAINED GLASS. There is a piece of stained glass depicting the white boar badge of RICHARD III. William PECKITT is buried in the church. At present it is often used for book fairs and jumble sales.

ST MARTIN-LE-GRAND CHURCH Church in CONEY STREET, severely damaged during the BAEDEKER BLITZ in 1942. Dating from the eleventh century, it now combines both fifteenth-century and twentieth-century features. The south aisle of the original church remains, and a paved garden acts as a shrine of remembrance to the fallen of the two WORLD WARS and all those who died in the air raid. The modern English organ was a gift of the German government. The new East Window and the Last Supper sculpture are modern, and there is a fine fifteenth-century window. The St Martin Window had been removed for safety before World War Two and has since been reinstated in the north wall. The nineteenth-century clock on the exterior overlooking CONEY STREET is topped by the LITTLE ADMIRAL, with the face of Father Time on one side.

ST MARY'S ABBEY Ruins of what was once one of the wealthiest abbeys in England can be seen in the MUSEUM GARDENS. It was a Benedictine monastery founded by WILLIAM II in 1088. The Abbey later had its own walls dating from 1266, some of which survive and can be seen in BOOTHAM and MARYGATE. The walls were built by Simon de Warwick (Abbot 1258-96), who would have resided in what is now the KING'S MANOR. York citizens objected to the Abbey's imposition of taxes on fairs held in BOOTHAM, and violent protests resulted in de Warwick obtaining permission from HENRY III to enclose the Abbey with a defensive wall. Like the FIVE SISTERS WINDOW in the MINSTER, St Mary's Abbey is mentioned in Charles DICKENS' novel *Nicholas Nickleby,* the monk in the story living there. Relations did not always run smoothly between the Abbey community and those living near it. The abbot had a wide jurisdiction over the whole area outside the city WALLS leading to conflicts and violence as people resented his power. In 1539 the Abbey was closed during HENRY VIII's DISSOLUTION OF THE MONASTERIES. From 1951 until 1988 the MYSTERY PLAYS were performed there. Further remains of the Abbey can be seen inside the YORKSHIRE MUSEUM, where the Chapter House archway has been reconstructed.

ST MARY'S CHURCH, BISHOPHILL JUNIOR Located in the lanes behind MICKLEGATE, this church is first recorded in 1194. However, it is clearly earlier, undoubtedly having the oldest surviving church tower in York, dating from the ANGLO-SAXON period of the early eleventh century. ROMAN brick was reused in its construction, making it the earliest surviving church architecture of any substance in York. The majority of the existing building dates from the twelfth and thirteenth centuries, and the two bells were made locally in the fifteenth century. Originally it was the partner of Bishophill Senior church, which was demolished in 1963.

ST MARY'S CHURCH, CASTLEGATE Redundant church, once one of the largest and most prestigious churches in the city. The discovery of a dedication suggests that it was the site of an ANGLO-SAXON "mynster" or place of learning. The octagonal tower and spire were added in the fifteenth century. The spire is 160 feet (49m) high and can be seen from all over the city. The York Story, a museum, was located in St Mary's between 1975 and 2001. The church is currently unoccupied.

ST MARY'S SQUARE Small square at the heart of the COPPERGATE Centre, the location of the JORVIK CENTRE and ST MARY'S CHURCH, CASTLEGATE.

ST MARY'S TOWER Defensive tower in the walls of ST MARY'S ABBEY, on the corner of BOOTHAM and MARYGATE. It was built in 1324 and is thirty feet (9m) high with an octagonal interior. During the SIEGE OF YORK in 1644 it was attacked and severely damaged by the Parliamentarian forces. On 16 June a mine was exploded beneath the tower. The records of religious houses were stored in the tower and these were destroyed by the explosion. Fortunately copies had been made, which are now stored in the Bodleian Library in Oxford. The troops entered the grounds of the KING'S MANOR but were beaten back. Forty men were killed and 216 captured. After the ENGLISH CIVIL WAR the tower was so clumsily rebuilt that it is possible to see the join. It is now used by a singing academy.

ST MICHAEL-LE-BELFREY CHURCH Situated in Deangate, alongside the MINSTER. A church is known to have stood on this site since 1294. Guy FAWKES was baptised here on 16 April 1570 and his father is buried here. The most popular item in the church is an enlarged section of the births register, illuminating the name of Guy Fawkes. Built between 1535 and 1536, St Michael-le-Belfrey is unique among York CHURCHES as all its architecture dates from the same period. The reason for its close proximity to the Minster is that ordinary people were expected to belong to and attend a parish church rather than the Minster.

ST MICHAEL'S CHAPEL of the Minster Small chapel located in the SOUTH TRANSEPT of the MINSTER. It contains three thirteenth-century tombs, of ARCH-BISHOP OF YORK Walter DE GRAY, Godrey de Ludham and Sewal de Bovil. There is also a monument to the DEAN of York, Augustus DUNCOMBE (c1815-80).

ST MICHAEL'S CHURCH Redundant church in SPURRIERGATE, which links CONEY STREET to Nessgate. A church is known to have stood here in ANGLO-SAXON times. The interior dates from the thirteenth century but was largely rebuilt in the nineteenth century. The church once had a tower from which the so-called "curfew bell" was rung every night at eight o'clock between 1872 and 1931. However no curfew was actually being imposed, it was merely a custom. The tower was pulled down in 1968 as modern building work had rendered it insecure, and its clock was placed on the church wall where it can still be seen. The church was once owned by ST MARY'S ABBEY, but after the DIS-SOLUTION OF THE MONASTERIES it reverted to the crown. It is now a café, the Spurriergate Centre, run by a Christian community.

ST NICHOLAS CHAPEL of the Minster Small chapel situated in the NORTH TRANSEPT, dedicated to the patron saint of children. Given St Nicholas's traditional association with Christmas, the kneeling cushions dating from 1983 depict the twelve days of Christmas. There is a gilded wooden screen, along the bottom of which are panels which open to reveal the names of women of the British Commonwealth who died in WORLD WAR ONE. The FIVE SISTERS WINDOW was restored in their memory in 1924.

ST OLAVE'S CHURCH Located in MARYGATE alongside the Abbey WALLS. The first church on the site was founded in the mid-eleventh century, and the powerful Earl SIWARD may have been buried there. Then it was called St Olaf's, named after the patron saint of Norway and a great-grandson of ERIC BLOODAXE. By the time of the DOMESDAY BOOK a NORMAN noble, Alan, Earl of Brittany (a cousin of WILLIAM THE CONQUEROR) had given it to Stephen, a monk from Whitby, to use as a base for what was to become ST MARY'S ABBEY. Although St Olave's looks like a fine example of a fifteenth-century church, it was in fact entirely reconstructed in the 1720s, having suffered great damage whilst being used as a gun battery by the Parliamentarian forces during the SIEGE OF YORK. Among those buried in its churchyard is York artist William ETTY.

ST PETER Apostle and patron saint of the MINSTER. He was handed the keys of Heaven by Jesus and the two crossed keys, which can be seen so often around the city, are therefore his symbol, giving the CROSS KEYS pub in GOODRAMGATE its name. The Peter PRISON was in the Minster precinct.

ST PETER'S SCHOOL Independent school in CLIFTON, the fourth oldest in England according to the scholar BEDE. It is said to have been founded in AD627. The first MINSTER founded in the same year by PAULINUS is thought to have had the original St Peter's School, a song school, alongside it. In the eighth century the scholar ALCUIN became a pupil, taught by ARCHBISHOP EGBERT. Alcuin later became a master at the school and created a library which attracted scholars from all over Europe. St Peter's survived the VIKING invasion of AD866 and went on to flourish. From 1289 the boarders were housed at ST MARY'S ABBEY. In a report of 1411 it was recorded that "an occupation of the boys at St Peter's was the visiting of taverns", and one boy was put in the STOCKS for playing football too close to the Minster. After the closure of St Mary's Abbey in 1539 the school moved to an old hospital outside BOOTHAM BAR, which was later badly damaged during the SIEGE OF YORK, when the school moved to BEDERN. In 1844 the school moved to its present site in CLIFTON. Its old boys include Guy FAWKES, John BARRY and the actor Greg Wise.

ST SAMPSON'S CHURCH Redundant church in Church Street, near ST SAMPSON'S SQUARE. It is first mentioned in 1154. Only a handful of churches in the world are dedicated to the Welsh St Sampson (d.AD535), who became Bishop at the Cathedral of Dol in Brittany, France.

His connection with York is unknown, though it is the only church in the city dedicated to an early British saint. The church was severely damaged in the SIEGE OF YORK and said to be "shot thro' and thro'...". In 1842 all of the building, with the exception of the tower, was destroyed in a fire. It was rebuilt in 1848 and became a social centre for the over-sixties in 1974. A hidden cloistered garden lies behind the main building.

ST SAMPSON'S SQUARE Small square at the northern end of PARLIAMENT STREET. The city's oldest market, the Thursday Market, was held here. During the SIEGE OF YORK, the attacking Parliamentarian army "shot well-nigh forty hot Fiery Bullets" one of which "slew a maide in Thursday Market…". The last market hall was built in 1705 and demolished in 1815, having become the haunt of "shady characters and people of lax morals". The market, along with the market on PARLIAMENT STREET, moved to NEWGATE in 1964.

ST SAVIOURGATE Street linking COLLIERGATE to St Saviour's Place, the location of the UNITARIAN CHAPEL, the Methodist CENTENARY CHAPEL, the ARC, and LADY HEWLEY'S ALMSHOUSES. It was described by historian Francis DRAKE in 1736 as "one of the neatest and best-built streets in the city."

ST SAVIOUR'S CHURCH Redundant church in ST SAV-IOURGATE, now home to the ARC or Archaeological Resource Centre. The church was first recorded c1090 as the property of ST MARY'S ABBEY. Most of the present church dates from rebuilding work carried out in 1844, but the tower dates from the mid-fifteenth century.

St Saviour's became the property of the CITY OF YORK COUNCIL in 1955. After use as storage for the CASTLE MUSEUM, it became the ARC in 1990. It contains a monument to the architect Thomas ATKINSON.

ST STEPHEN'S CHAPEL of the Minster Small chapel located in the East End of the MINSTER, to the north of the LADY CHAPEL. The fourteenth-century STAINED GLASS window depicts St Stephen, St Christopher and St Laurence holding a gridiron, a reference to his execution by grilling. Also within the chapel are stalls (seating) by Robert "Mousey" THOMPSON, and a bust of Mother Teresa of Calcutta. The clay REREDOS behind the altar originally stood behind the HIGH ALTAR in the CHOIR. It was moved to the chapel in 1937. The Victorian treatment of the ROMAN soldiers curiously sporting moustaches is noteworthy.

ST WILFRID OF YORK (AD634-709) Bishop of York (664 and 669-677). He was educated by St Aidan in the renowned monastery of Lindisfarne in NORTHUMBRIA and became Abbot of Ripon in 664. That year he attended the Synod of Whitby, where he defended the Roman church against the Celtic Christians. He was appointed Bishop of York and ordained in Gaul (France), but was exiled twice for quarrelling with King Ecgfrith of Northumbria. On both occasions the Pope supported him and he was reinstated. He was a learned priest who was loyal to Rome and founded Benedictine monasteries throughout England. The scholar ALCUIN described him as being "filled with light from Heaven". Wilfrid died at Oundle in Northamptonshire.

ST WILFRID'S CHURCH Catholic church in DUN-COMBE PLACE, completed in 1864. It is a classic example of Victorian gothic architecture. The church appears to break the rule of no building in York being taller than the MINSTER, particularly when approaching it from LENDAL BRIDGE, but this is a deliberate optical illusion. Along with ST GEORGE'S CHURCH near FISHERGATE BAR, it is one of only two Catholic churches within the city WALLS.

ST WILLIAM OF YORK (c1100-1154) ARCHBISHOP OF YORK, canonised in 1227. A great-nephew of King Stephen and probably a great-grandson of WILLIAM THE CONQUEROR, William Fitzherbert's royal connections helped him rise rapidly in the church. He was appointed TREASURER of the MINSTER, and was subsequently elected Archbishop in 1141. However his appointment was not approved by the Pope, and he was deposed in 1147. In 1153, he was unanimously re-elected by the CHAPTER of York, and this time received Papal approval. His return to the city was greeted by a huge crowd gathered on the timber OUSE BRIDGE. The bridge collapsed yet no one drowned and it was seen as a miracle. Within a month William mysteriously died, possibly poisoned by a resentful Archdeacon. He was buried in the nave of the NORMAN Minster, and tales of miraculous cures at his tomb soon spread. The DEAN and Chapter did not discourage the cult, and he was canonised in 1227. His remains have subsequently been moved a number of times, including after the destruction of his shrine in 1538 following the REFORMATION. During the renewal of foundations to the CENTRAL TOWER between 1967 and 1972, his remains were interred in the St William Shrine in the CRYPT. There is a St William Window (c1421) in the Minster's NORTH CHOIR AISLE.

ST WILLIAM'S COLLEGE Black and white timbered building in COLLEGE STREET near the East End of the MINSTER. The building was begun in 1465 on the orders of EDWARD IV as a home for the Minster's Chantry Priests. The priests' principal responsibility was the dubious practice of receiving payment in advance for praying for the souls of their deceased benefactors. The REFORMATION ended the role of the priests and the College was used as shops, a town house and tenements. The building housed the printing press of CHARLES I during the ENGLISH CIVIL WAR. The windows to the street were added in the 1800s while the building was in use as shops, and the courtyard porch and staircase were built in the seventeenth century, when it was a private house. Restoration began in 1906, co-ordinated by Frank GREEN, after some years of neglect. The College is dedicated to ST WILLIAM OF YORK. Currently it is a restaurant and visitor attraction. The GHOST of a seventeenth-century murderer, whose younger brother was wrongfully hanged for his crime, is said to pace the building's corridors at night.

SAXONS *See* ANGLO-SAXONS

SCARBOROUGH BRIDGE York's second bridge over the river OUSE, built in 1844 as a RAILWAY bridge and footbridge, which can be seen from LENDAL BRIDGE. Curiously the walkway was originally situated between the two tracks but this was thought to be unsafe and it was moved. The bridge allows trains to go directly between York and Scarborough.

SCARCROFT SCHOOL Primary school on Scarcroft Green built in 1896, designed by Walter BRIERLEY and considered to be his best building.

SCOTT, SIR WALTER (1771-1832) *See* MICKLEGATE BAR

SCOTS Such was the enmity of the city of York towards the Scots, who habitually invaded the north of England, that in 1501 the city CORPORATION ordered that a huge door knocker be fixed to BOOTHAM BAR. Any Scot who wished to enter the city must knock first and then only be admitted on the approval of the LORD MAYOR, the Warden or the Constable. They were imprisoned if they entered without permission. A local custom still has it as law that if a citizen of York catches a Scotsman at large after sunset within the city WALLS, he is entitled to shoot him with a bow and arrow.

SCROPE, ARCHBISHOP RICHARD (1350-1405) One of only two Archbishops to be executed, the other being Archbishop of Canterbury Thomas Cranmer (1489-1556). Scrope's crime was to lead a rebellion against HENRY IV, having originally supported the king on taking the crown from RICHARD II. Scrope became ARCHBISHOP OF YORK in 1398. In 1405 he published a manifesto, the *Articles of Impeachment*, condemning Henry IV, and gained a large local following. He was arrested and executed on a field belonging to the nuns of CLEMENTHORPE. He was seen to pray right until his beheading and begged his executioner to deal five blows to his neck in memory of the sacred wounds. He is now buried in the MINSTER. The Archbishop was unofficially "canonised" by York, with several miracles reported at his tomb in the Minster.

SCROPE, LORD HENRY (1376-1415) Nephew of Richard SCROPE, ARCHBISHOP OF YORK, and one of the HEADS displayed on a spike on MICKLEGATE BAR. Scrope was executed in Southampton, following his rebellion against HENRY V, and his head brought to York by royal orders.

SEVERUS, SEPTIMUS (AD146-211) ROMAN Emperor (AD193-211) born in North Africa (Leptis Magna, now in Libya), who died in York. He was the first black Roman Emperor. He arrived in the fortress of EBORACUM (York) in AD208 as the strengthening of the Roman WALLS was completed. Severus used the fortress as a base for campaigning against the tribes of the SCOTS. In bringing his court to Eboracum he raised the profile of the city, and accorded the civil settlement the highest rank of COLONIA. Eboracum became the capital of Northern Britain. Tradition has it that Severus was cremated just outside the Roman PRINCIPIA, and his ashes were placed in an urn and taken back to Rome by his family. The name of Severus Hill in ACOMB is misleading, more likely being named after a twelfth-century Abbot of ST MARY'S, Severinus or Savarus.

SEYMOUR, JANE (1505-37) Third wife of HENRY VIII. Jane's Catholic leanings allegedly led to the king making an insincere peace agreement with the northerners leading the PILGRIMAGE OF GRACE in 1536. He declared that his new bride, who he married in May 1536, would be crowned in York MINSTER. The York coronation never took place, as Jane was soon pregnant and died shortly after giving birth to Edward VI in October 1537.

SHAKESPEARE, WILLIAM (1564-1616) No fewer than eight of Shakespeare's plays (*Richard II, Henry IV parts 1 & 2, Henry V, Henry VI parts 1, 2 & 3* and *Richard III*) deal with the WARS OF THE ROSES period, with York inevitably featured. Both EDMUND OF LANGLEY and the Duke of Aumerle (the first and second DUKES OF YORK) appear in *Richard II*, while RICHARD DUKE OF YORK is in all three parts of *Henry VI*. Archbishop Richard SCROPE appears in both parts of *Henry IV*, prior to his execution. The heads of Richard Duke of York, Scrope and Harry HOTSPUR all end up on spikes on MICKLE-GATE BAR, with York's head specifically referred to in *Henry VI part 3*. The "sun of York" referred to in the famous opening lines of *Richard III* is a pun on the sun badge adopted by EDWARD IV, the handsome and successful son of Richard Duke of York.

SHAMBLES York's most famous medieval street, linking KING'S SQUARE to PAVEMENT. The narrow Shambles is the only existing street in the city to have been named in the DOMESDAY BOOK. Most of the buildings date from the fifteenth to the seventeenth centuries, although much restoration was undertaken in the twentieth century. It was the medieval street of the butchers, named after their "shammel" benches where meat was displayed. The benches can still be seen as well as can the meat-hooks. In 1316 the street was recorded as "Fleshammels". It was notorious for its poor sanitation and foul SMELLS. An open sewer ran down the middle of the street and there were slaughterhouses behind many of the houses. The Catholic martyr Margaret CLITHEROW lived in a house in the Shambles, and a shrine to her memory is housed at number thirty-five. In reality she may have lived at number ten, though given later changes in street numbers it is impossible to identify her house for certain.

SHED SEVEN York's most successful rock band, achieving fourteen chart hits between 1994 and 2001. The four-piece's biggest successes came with the singles *Going for Gold*, reaching number eight in 1996, *She Left Me on Friday*, number eleven in 1998, and *Disco Down*, which reached number thirteen the following year. Their first three albums, *Change Giver*, *A Maximum High* and *Let it Ride* all made the Top Twenty, while a greatest hits compilation, *Going for Gold*, achieved number seven in 1999. A label change from Polydor to Artful in 1999 saw them back in the singles charts in 2001 with *Truth be Told*, and in the album charts with *Cry for Help*.

SHERIFF Ceremonial civic role within the CITY OF YORK COUNCIL. The office of Sheriff is a legal one. He or she is a representative of the crown, and traditionally carries out duties in partnership with the LORD MAYOR.

SIEGE OF YORK Along with the BAEDEKER BLITZ, the most significant military attack upon the city. During the

ENGLISH CIVIL WAR York was garrisoned by forces loyal to CHARLES I, and was besieged by the Parliamentarians (Roundheads), between 23 April and 16 July 1644. The attackers were led by Lord FERDINANDO FAIRFAX and his son Sir THOMAS FAIRFAX, with their Scottish allies under the Earl of Leven. They were later assisted by the Earl of MANCHESTER. The city was garrisoned by 4000 men, commanded by the Earl of NEWCASTLE, while the besiegers had 30,000 men at their disposal. The arrival of the Royalist Prince RUPERT led the besiegers to flee to MARSTON MOOR. Following the Royalists' defeat at the battle, the siege recommenced and York fell on 16 July 1644. Ferdinando Fairfax was made Governor. The garrison were permitted to march proudly out of York through MICKLEGATE BAR, with their flags flying. CLIFFORD'S TOWER, WALMGATE BAR and ST MARY'S TOWER were among the buildings to sustain considerable damage. Evidence of this can still be seen at the latter two.

SILVER STREET Narrow street which leads from Church Street to NEWGATE MARKET. It was home to the medieval silversmiths and also to York's first POLICE STATION between 1841 and 1892.

SIWARD (d.1055) Earl Siward of NORTHUMBRIA is best known for his victory in battle over the Scottish king Macbeth in 1054. He may have been buried at ST OLAVE'S, a church which he founded in 1050. However, it is also claimed that the mound above the UNIVERSITY was once known as Siward's How, where he is said to have had a pagan burial. Siward dedicated the church to Olaf, patron saint of Norway and its king from 1016 to

1029, who was converted to Christianity while in England fighting the Danes.

SIXTH LEGION The second and last of the ROMAN legions stationed in York, known as *Victrix* or Victorious. It replaced the NINTH LEGION in AD122, having been sent to Britain by the Emperor Hadrian.

SKELDERGATE Street running parallel with the river OUSE, joining MICKLEGATE to SKELDERGATE BRIDGE. Its Viking name means "street of the shield-makers" from the Old Scandinavian word, *skjaldari*. In medieval times the area near Micklegate was known as "Hagg's Court" (a hagg being an Old English word for a leech). Housing here was possibly worse than in the notorious WATER LANES across the river. The Victorian novelist Wilkie COLLINS, in his 1862 novel *No Name*, bemoaned the "dingy warehouses and joyless private residences of red brick" which comprised the street. There was access to the warehouses of QUEEN'S STAITH, important for York industry and trade. LADY ANNE MIDDLETON'S HALL and the YORVIK BRASS RUBBING CENTRE are located on the street.

SKELDERGATE BRIDGE The city's third major road bridge, which opened to traffic in March 1881, replacing a FERRY. It was opened by LORD MAYOR of York JOHN STEPHENSON ROWNTREE and was a toll bridge until 1914. Spanning the river from BAILE HILL to ST GEORGE'S FIELD, Skeldergate Bridge was designed by Thomas Page who also built LENDAL BRIDGE. Before it was erected it had to be redesigned so that it could open, allowing taller ships up river. It last opened in 1975 and the winding gears have since been removed.

SLAVE MARKET Following the ROMAN withdrawal (cAD410) ST SAMPSON'S SQUARE was apparently occasionally used as a thriving Slave Market. Warring ANGLO-SAXON factions would sell those captured in battle to be conveyed to Rome. Beautiful English girls and handsome youths would be sold to become companions of wealthy Romans, perhaps contributing to the increasing decadence of the empire. Pope Gregory I (cAD540-604) is said to have commented on the beauty of the English slaves on their arrival in Rome. BEDE recorded him as saying "Non Angli sed angeli" ("They are not Angles but angels"). Slavery also flourished in York from the VIKING period until NORMAN times.

SMELLS A succession of monarchs commented upon York's plentiful smells. The moat of the CASTLE was used as a rubbish tip, the gutters of the SHAMBLES ran red with blood and offal from the butchers' shops, the cattle and horse markets added to the problem, while sewage was simply thrown into the narrow streets from the upper storeys. Other contributors to the city's smells were the KING'S FISHPOOL and the river FOSS. Today, the city smellscape is dominated by the two CHOCOLATE factories with their heavy, sweet smell of cocoa, and the winter beet campaign of the British Sugar factory off Boroughbridge Road.

SNAWSELL, WILLIAM (c1415-c1495) Goldsmith, ALDERMAN, LORD MAYOR of York in 1468, and tenant of BARLEY HALL from 1466 to 1489. A leading York citizen, Snawsell represented the city when Lancastrian HENRY VI was briefly restored to the throne (1470-71) and had to buy a Royal pardon when the Yorkist EDWARD IV regained the crown. He subsequently became a friend of RICHARD III, and his name can be found at the head of the list of councillors who recorded the news of the king's death at Bosworth Field on 22 August 1485. The death entry, dated 23 August 1485, still survives in the CITY ARCHIVES. Reputedly master of the York Mint, Snawsell owned considerable property in North Yorkshire.

SNICKELWAY Narrow alley or passageway, of which there are many in York. Examples include MAD ALICE LANE and COFFEE YARD. Snickelways are also known as snickets, alleyways or passages and "snickelway" is a modern amalgam of some of these names (snicket plus ginnel plus alleyway), though "ginnel" is largely a West Yorkshire word rather than a York one.

SNICKLEWAY INN Pub in GOODRAMGATE, the building dating from the sixteenth century when it is believed to have been a brothel. An inn from at least 1769, it was once called the Anglers' Arms because of its proximity to the MINSTER Stoneyard. An angler, rather than being a fisherman, worked out the geometry for the stonework. The pub has also been known as the Painters' Arms, the Square and Compass and the Board. It became the Snickleway Inn in 1994 and it reputedly has more GHOSTS than any other pub in York.

SOCIETY OF FRIENDS OF RICHARD III *See* FRIENDS OF RICHARD III

SOUTH CHOIR AISLE of the Minster Passageway to the right of the CHOIR on passing the CHOIR SCREEN. It dates from the late fourteenth and early fifteenth centuries, and contains the sixteenth-century Crucifixion Window, brought from Rouen in France after the French Revolution, in the bay closest to the East End. It is also the location of the memorial of Thomas Lamplugh, ARCHBISHOP OF YORK (1688-91), by the sculptor Grinling Gibbons, with its curious two right feet. Also noteworthy is the memorial to Sir William Gee (d.1611) showing his two wives and his six children. The eulogy extolling his many qualities ends by stating he "had all these pleas [virtues], yet died". Alongside there is a memorial to Jane Hodson (1598-1636) who died aged thirty-eight having borne twenty-four children, and to Lieutenant Henry Lees, cavalryman, who curiously died after falling from his horse in 1876.

SOUTH NAVE AISLE of the Minster Passageway to the right of the NAVE on entering through the WEST DOOR. It contains the JESSE WINDOW (bay three) and a twelfth-century panel depicting the legendary story of St Nicholas and the Jew (bay seven). A Christian, wrongly acquitted of defrauding a Jew, was run over by a horse and cart and killed. His staff broke open, containing the money owed. The forgiving Jew begged St Nicholas to bring the Christian back to life, and when this happened the Jew converted to Christianity.

SOUTH PARADE Terrace of twenty houses off BLOS-SOM STREET. It was built between 1824 and 1828 to the designs of Peter ATKINSON Junior, who lived at number seventeen.

SOUTH TRANSEPT of the Minster Built under ARCH-BISHOP OF YORK Walter DE GRAY in the thirteenth century, the South Transept is well-known for the damage sustained in the MINSTER FIRE of 1984. It contains the ROSE WINDOW, which has glass from c1500, the tomb of Archbishop De Gray, the entrance to the UNDER-CROFT and the steps to the CENTRAL TOWER. It was restored between 1984 and 1988 and the new roof BOSSES can be seen either by looking up or in a large mirror at the centre of the Transept.

SPURRIERGATE Street joining Nessgate to CONEY STREET, where ST MICHAEL'S CHURCH is situated. Once known as "Little Conystrete", the name means "Spurmaker Street".

STAINED GLASS York is said to contain more than half of the country's finest stained glass, most of which is in the MINSTER. There are examples of stained and painted glass from every century since the NORMAN Conquest. The Minster glass has survived largely due to orders by Parliamentarian commanders FERDINANDO FAIRFAX and his son Sir THOMAS FAIRFAX, that no glass was to be destroyed after the SIEGE OF YORK in 1644. The FIVE SISTERS WINDOW was removed for safety during WORLD WAR ONE. Other outstanding examples of stained glass are in ST DENYS' CHURCH and ALL SAINTS, NORTH STREET. Restoration of York's glass is in the hands of the York Glaziers' trust, headed by Sir Peter Gibson. The Trust deals with the restoration of glass from any source, not just from York.

STAMFORD BRIDGE, BATTLE OF Battle eight miles (13km) east of York fought on 25 September 1066. English king Harold GODWINSON was forced to march north from his watch against WILLIAM THE CONQUEROR, and surprised the forces of Harald Hardradi, who had been victorious at the Battle of FULFORD, at Stamford Bridge. Hardradi and his ally Godwinson's brother TOSTIG were defeated and killed. The battle served to weaken Godwinson's army prior to the Battle of Hastings on 14 October 1066.

STATUTE OF YORK Legislation introduced by EDWARD II after summoning Parliament to York in 1322. The king's extravagant expenditure and inordinate attachment to certain favourites had led to his supporters limiting his authority in 1311. His cousin and chief opponent Thomas, Earl of Lancaster, effectively ruled the country between 1314 and 1316. Following Edward's forces' victory at the Battle of Boroughbridge, sixteen miles (26km) north-west of York, Lancaster was captured and executed. The king, who would periodically come to York to avoid his disgruntled barons, thus introduced laws granting him, at the very least, more freedom to debate his powers.

STEPHENSON, GEORGE (1781-1848) Railway engineer who, with his son Robert, designed and built STEPHENSON'S ROCKET, a replica of which can be seen in the NATIONAL RAILWAY MUSEUM. The original Rocket is in the Science Museum in London. The Rocket won a "contest of engines" in 1829, reaching a speed of thirty miles per hour (48.3km per hour). Stephenson was engineer on both the Stockton and Darlington Railway, which opened in 1825, and the Liverpool and Manchester Railway, which opened in 1830.

STEPHENSON'S ROCKET One of the most famous locomotives in the world, a replica of Stephenson's Rocket is housed in the NATIONAL RAILWAY MUSEUM. Built in 1826, the Rocket was the nineteenth engine built by George STEPHENSON and his son, Robert. In 1829 it won the Rainhill trials, a competition to find a steam locomotive for the Liverpool and Manchester Railway.

STERNE, LAURENCE (1713-1768) Author of *Tristram Shandy*, considered to be the first English novel. Sterne lived at Shandy Hall in Coxwold, seventeen miles (27km) north of York. He was the great-grandson of Richard Sterne, ARCHBISHOP OF YORK (1664-83), and his uncle was the PRECENTOR and a CANON at the MINSTER. Sterne lived for a time in a church house off STONEGATE. He became a vicar and in 1738 went to the parish of Sutton-on-the-Forest, eight miles (13km) north of York. He wrote a great many sermons, four volumes of which were published in his lifetime. In 1759 he began *The Life and Opinions of Tristram Shandy, Gentleman*, the first two volumes of which, printed by the GOLDEN BIBLE press, made him a celebrity. Between 1761 and 1767 he brought out a further seven volumes. Sterne was dogged by ill health for most of his life and often travelled abroad to recuperate. He always returned to Yorkshire to write the next instalment of his master-piece. He wrote *A Sentimental Journey* about his European travels, which was published three weeks before his death. The character of Dr Slop in *Tristram Shandy* was based on Dr John Burton, the Chief Physician to the COUNTY HOSPITAL, who lived in the RED HOUSE.

STOCKS Punishment for petty crimes from ANGLO-SAXON times to the early nineteenth century. The stocks comprised wooden structures into which the ankles or wrists were inserted through holes. The miscreant was thus publicly humiliated with onlookers having the oppor-tunity to throw rotten fruit, amongst other things, at them. York's only surviving stocks can be seen in HOLY TRIN-ITY churchyard in MICKLEGATE.

STONE CATS Curious black stone cats adorn a number of building in York, including a restaurant in WALMGATE and shops in CONEY STREET. They are the trademark of York-based architect Tom Adams (1930-), who appar-ently added a silhouette of a black cat to make his archi-tectural drawings stand out while a student at Birmingham. He chose a cat not as a retort to "Mousey" THOMPSON's mouse, but because he knew that Leonardo da Vinci had used a mouse. Adams runs a prop-erty agency called Tom Cat Properties.

STONEBOW Street created in 1955 linking PAVEMENT to PEASHOLME GREEN. Stonebow House was built in 1964 by Wells, Hickman & Partners. Perhaps a typical example of 1960s architecture, it is one of the ugliest buildings in York, a four-storey concrete office block above shops and a car park. Much of the HUNGATE area was demolished to create the street.

STONEGATE York's second most famous street after the SHAMBLES, linking MINSTER GATES to ST HELEN'S SQUARE. Stonegate has been a highway for nearly 2000 years and was originally the ROMAN Via Praetoria, leading to the legionary headquarters or PRINCIPIA. Its name, first recorded in the twelfth century, means "stone-paved street" rather than being a reference to the stone used to build the MINSTER which was carried up Stonegate from the river OUSE. Stonegate was for centuries associated with the book trade, with bookshops and printing presses including the GOLDEN BIBLE, and NEWSPAPERS were printed in COFFEE YARD. The street features architecture of every period from the NORMANS to the Victorians, and notable buildings include MULBERRY HALL.

STRAYS Ancient common lands of York, generally preserved for grazing the sheep and cattle of the freemen of the city. MICKLEGATE Stray is to the south-west of the city, comprising KNAVESMIRE and HOB MOOR, WALMGATE Stray is to the south-east, between FULFORD Road and HESLINGTON, BOOTHAM Stray is to the north, off Wigginton Road and MONK Stray is to the north-east near HEWORTH. The CITY OF YORK COUNCIL gradually gained control of them during the twentieth century, their original purpose having lapsed. York had numerous other common lands, but many were lost in the

Acts of Enclosure in the 1820s when the strays were redefined. Each stray had its own herdsman or Pasture Master, the last retiring in 1965.

STUART, HENRY BENEDICT (1725-1807) Self-proclaimed DUKE OF YORK 1725-1788. He was the JACOBITE "Shadow Duke", the second son of the "Old Pretender", James Francis Edward Stuart. Henry never actually set foot in England, following the Jacobite defeat at Culloden, near Inverness in the Scottish Highlands, in 1746. Nonetheless he claimed the title of Duke of York and indeed, that of Henry IX of England on the death of the "Young Pretender", Charles Edward Stuart, in 1788. He took Roman Catholic orders after Culloden and called himself Cardinal York, taking his place at the Vatican. He is buried at St Peter's in Rome.

SWEYN FORKBEARD (d.1014) Sweyn I, King of Norway, Denmark and later England (1013-14). He was the father of King CANUTE, and was so nicknamed because of his long cleft beard. Forkbeard died at Gainsborough in Lincolnshire and is said to have been buried in York.

SWEYN II (c1020-1076) King of Denmark and nephew of King CANUTE, who laid claim to the throne of England. In 1069 he sent 200 longships down the river OUSE and united with ANGLO-SAXON forces in an attempt to capture NORMAN York. The Norman Commander, William Malet, in an attempt to clear fighting ground, set fire to some houses. The result was the destruction of around a third of the city, including the MINSTER. There was a mass slaughter of the Normans and for a few weeks there was a Norse northern English kingdom. However, when Anglo-Saxon rule was proclaimed, Sweyn returned to Denmark. A furious WILLIAM THE CONQUEROR sent his forces towards York to inflict the HARRYING OF THE NORTH. Nonetheless, Sweyn led the last VIKING raid on York to plunder the city and the ruins of the Minster in 1075.

SWINEGATE Street linking Church Street to GRAPE LANE, so-called because it was the location of a pig market in medieval times. Further remains of the ROMAN military baths found below the ROMAN BATH pub were discovered here in the 1930s. The new Swinegate Quarter is the area defined by PETERGATE, Grape Lane and Church Street. In 1968 Lord ESHER's report stressed the importance of redevelopment of the city centre. However, it was not until the early 1990s that the area was redeveloped. It now contains shops, restaurants and small businesses.

SWORD OF STATE Traditionally a monarch has to touch York's ceremonial sword when entering the city through MICKLEGATE BAR. The custom began following RICHARD II's visit to the city in 1387 when he gave the Sword of State to LORD MAYOR William de Selby. Richard II's sword vanished after 1736 and was replaced by a sword made in 1416 for Sigismund, Emperor of Bohemia. Sigismund was a Knight of the Order of the Dragon whose most famous member was Vlad Dracule, the inspiration for Count Dracula. Another sword was presented by Sir Martin Bowes after his request to the Lord

Mayor to save ST CUTHBERT'S CHURCH from demolition was granted. The sword is held blade upwards for civic processions unless the monarch is present when it is held blade downwards in submission. Sigismund's sword is the one currently used and is usually kept in the MANSION HOUSE.

T

TANNER ROW Street linking North Street to TOFT GREEN. It was part of the ROMAN civilian settlement, the COLONIA, and their main road to the south-west. It is currently the location of the Great North Eastern RAILWAY headquarters, in the buildings of the second RAILWAY STATION, and originally the site of Lady Hewley's hospital, built in 1700.

TANNERS' MOAT Short street linking ROUGIER STREET to Wellington Row. It was the site of York's leather industry (tanning) in ROMAN, ANGLO-SAXON and VIKING times, hence its name. Tanners' Moat was originally an inlet of the river OUSE. The area by LENDAL BRIDGE was leased by the GUILD of Tanners in 1476. By the late 1860s it was the site of the ROWNTREE & CO. cocoa factory. Botterill's Horse Repository was situated here and its arches, dating from c1880, are still visible.

TEMPEST ANDERSON HALL York's first purpose-built lecture hall, located in the MUSEUM GARDENS alongside the YORKSHIRE MUSEUM. The hall was built in 1912 and named after Dr Tempest Anderson, who had been President of the YORKSHIRE PHILOSOPHICAL SOCIETY. The hall was constructed with the money he bequeathed the Yorkshire Museum. Public lectures are still held there.

TERRY'S One of the two main contributors to York's CHOCOLATE heritage, along with ROWNTREE & CO. The company's history can be traced back to 1767, when the confectionery firm Bayldon & Berry was founded. The firm was originally based in BOOTHAM, before moving to ST HELEN'S SQUARE in 1824. Joseph TERRY married into the Berry family in 1823. Following William Bayldon and George Berry's departures from the business, Joseph took sole control in 1828. The building in St Helen's Square where the manufacturing process took place still bears his name. By 1840 Terry's was supplying confectionery to over seventy cities throughout the country. On Joseph Terry's death in 1850 three of his sons, Joseph Junior, Robert and John took over the business. In 1864 a new site in CLEMENTHORPE next to SKELDERGATE BRIDGE was developed, which took over the manufacturing side in 1886. A larger site was soon required and between 1924 and 1930 a new factory was developed in Bishopthorpe Road, alongside the RACECOURSE. Terry's are perhaps best known for their *All Gold* plain chocolates, launched in 1931, and *Chocolate Orange*, launched in 1932. The company became Terry's Suchard in 1993, and is now Kraft Foods. Its prominent clock tower can be seen from the MILLENNIUM BRIDGE.

TERRY, JOSEPH (1777-1850) Important figure in York's CHOCOLATE and confectionery industry. Unlike their competitors the ROWNTREES, the Terrys were High Anglican, rather than QUAKER. As one historian put it "CRAVEN'S was maternal, Rowntree's paternal, and TERRY'S feudal". Joseph Terry was born in Pocklington, thirteen miles (21km) south-east of York, and came to the city as an apprentice apothecary at a business in SPURRIERGATE. He went on to set up as a chemist in WALMGATE. In 1823 he became involved in the confectionery trade by marriage into the Berry family, but it was one of his five sons, Joseph Terry Junior, who made what was to become Terry's Suchard (now Kraft Foods) into a major concern. Joseph Terry Senior was knighted by Queen VICTORIA for his services to industry.

THEATRE ROYAL York's principal theatre, situated in ST LEONARD'S PLACE. The first theatre on this site opened in 1744 on part of the ruins of ST LEONARD'S HOSPITAL. Remains of the hospital walls are visible from the foyer of the present building. It opened as the New Theatre, not becoming the Theatre Royal until 1769. Under the management of Tate Wilkinson, who took charge from 1766 until his death in 1803, the standard was raised to that of a London playhouse. However, the Victorian era saw a decline in its fortunes. Competition from music halls and later CINEMAS caused further decline and successive managers went bankrupt. Since 1935 York Citizens Theatre Trust has managed the theatre. From 1877 to 1889 the Gothic frontage was built and the modern foyer was added in 1967. York's residents visit it most often during the annual two-month pantomime starring Berwick KALER. In 1992 and 1996 the MYSTERY PLAYS were held at the Theatre Royal. Other York theatres include the GRAND OPERA HOUSE, the ROWNTREE THEATRE and the Riding Lights Theatre in Friargate.

THOMAS OF BAYEUX *See* BAYEUX, THOMAS OF

THOMPSON, ROBERT "MOUSEY" (1876-1955) Carpenter known by a distinctive trademark. He was born in Kilburn, North Yorkshire and made tables, stools and altar pieces. His signature was that of a mouse carved onto his work, as early in his career he had described himself as "poor as a church mouse". Examples of his work can be found inside the archway of ST WILLIAM'S COLLEGE and in the MINSTER. The business still exists in Kilburn.

THREE CRANES One of York's oldest pubs, located in ST SAMPSON'S SQUARE. It has held its licence since 1749. The pub's sign depicting three cranes or birds is misleading. The pub took its name from the lifting cranes used to move traders' wares for the Thursday Market held here until 1964.

THREE-LEGGED MARE Pub in HIGH PETERGATE, owned by the YORK BREWERY, which opened in 2001. Its curious name is somewhat macabre. It refers to a triangular hanging GALLOWS, a design dating from the early seventeenth century. This gallows was used for EXECUTIONS at the KNAVESMIRE. To "ride the three-legged mare" became a slang term meaning to be hanged.

THREE TUNS Pub in COPPERGATE, an inn since at least 1782. It was formerly known as The Yorkshireman Coffee House, and later The Yorkshireman. Its name is derived from the old coat of arms of the Vintners or wine makers. A "tun" was traditionally the largest storage cask for beer, containing 216 gallons (982 litres).

THURSDAY MARKET Former name of ST SAMPSON'S SQUARE.

THURSTAN (c1070-1140) ARCHBISHOP OF YORK (1114-40). Thurstan helped to establish Fountains Abbey in North Yorkshire, but is best remembered for his unlikely role in winning the Battle of the Standard. England had been weakened by the civil wars between the NORMAN cousins Stephen and Matilda, when DAVID I of Scotland invaded the north of England in 1138. Thurstan led the York forces to battle under four holy standards or banners depicting saints, and was victorious at Cowton near Northallerton, twenty-eight miles (45km) north of York.

TITANIC Two York men perished when the famous ocean liner, the *Titanic*, sank on the night of 15 April 1912 on its maiden voyage across the Atlantic. J. Foley, a forty-four-year-old storekeeper, and C. Stagg, a thirty-seven-year-old steward, lost their lives in the disaster.

TOFT GREEN Street linking TANNER ROW to Bar Lane and MICKLEGATE. During the city's ROMAN period Toft Green was part of the civilian COLONIA, perhaps the site of baths and a temple. During the Middle Ages it was the site of a profitable pig market and from 1228 a friary stood here. From the twelfth century until c1344 it was known as the King's Tofts, a toft being a measure of land belonging to the crown. Citizens would practice their archery there after church and the medieval kings assembled their troops there prior to marching out of the city. Toft Green was also known as Pageant Green as carts and sets for the MYSTERY PLAYS were kept here, and it was the starting point of the Plays. From 1841 to 1871 it was the location of the second RAILWAY STATION. The first train departed on 6 April that year for Copmanthorpe, less than three miles (4.8km) away. Toft Green is currently the site of the YORK BREWERY.

TOSTIG (d.1066) Treacherous younger brother of English king Harold GODWINSON, Tostig ruled from York as Earl of NORTHUMBRIA (1055-65). His harsh rule "depriving of life and land all those…weaker than he", as recorded in the *Anglo-Saxon Chronicle,* resulted in open rebellion in York in 1065. His brother showed little inclination to help him, and he sailed to Europe. He returned with the Norwegian king Harald HARDRADI, winning a comprehensive victory over the new Earl of Northumbria, Morcar, at the Battle of FULFORD on 20 September 1066. Five days later, however, Godwinson's forces surprised the victors at STAMFORD BRIDGE, and in the ensuing battle both Hardradi and Tostig were killed.

TOURISM York is one of Britain's three most popular tourist destinations, along with London and Edinburgh. Tourism is undoubtedly one of the most important industries in the city. International tourism is essentially a post-WORLD WAR TWO phenomenon, though prior to this the arrival of the RAILWAYS in the 1830s resulted in a vast increase in visitors to the city. Until the early twentieth century tourism was so popular that it supported at least three companies producing picture postcards, as few people owned a camera. Even before this in the eighteenth century the more affluent would come to York to visit the theatre, the RACECOURSE or the ASSEMBLY ROOMS. From late Victorian times onwards, York was also a popular destination for cycling clubs. In 1971 the city celebrated the 1900th anniversary of its foundation as EBORACUM and energetic promotion by city councillors resulted in a huge influx of visitors to York. The city's tourist trade was further boosted by the opening of the JORVIK CENTRE in 1984, and media attention following the fire in York MINSTER in the same year. York currently has approximately four million visitors annually.

TOWER PLACE Narrow lane running from Tower Street to the DAVY TOWER, behind the only remaining wall of the medieval Franciscan friary. The friary, built c1230, housed EDWARD II's Parliament of 1322, the Parliaments of EDWARD III, and was used as a ROYAL RESIDENCE by the early medieval kings, notably RICHARD II. It was demolished following the DISSOLUTION OF THE MONASTERIES of the sixteenth century. The eight terraced houses were built in 1828.

TOWN CRIER York's current Town Crier, John Redpath, unlike his predecessors is freelance rather than being employed by the CITY OF YORK COUNCIL. He has been Town Crier since 1990. Although the origin of the role is unclear, it is assumed that Town Criers have existed since towns began, owing to the lack of NEWSPAPERS and to general illiteracy. Their traditional role was to announce events of state, such as the death of a monarch. "Bellmen" are depicted on the Bayeux Tapestry (c1070, depicting the events of the NORMAN Conquest and the Battle of Hastings), and the cry "O Yea!" is in fact "*Oyez*", Norman French for "Harken" or "listen".

TOWTON, BATTLE OF The bloodiest battle fought on English soil, marking a turning point in the first phase of the WARS OF THE ROSES. It took place in a village twelve miles (19km) south-west of York, in a snowstorm on Palm Sunday 29 March 1461. A Lancastrian army of nearly 60,000 stood ready to fight 50,000 Yorkist men. By evening the Yorkist army were victorious, claiming York, the north and the crown for EDWARD IV. It was said that the rivers ran red with blood. No accurate records remain but some historians put the death toll at over 40,000 (at least 25,000 Lancastrians and 10,000 Yorkists). The first fleeing Lancastrians destroyed a bridge over the river Wharfe in order to give HENRY VI and Queen Margaret more time to escape. By doing so they probably condemned at least 12,000 of their men to death.

TRAMS The York Tramway Company was formed in 1880. The first tram line ran from FULFORD to the city centre, and the trams were horse-drawn. The importance of the route contributed to the creation of CLIFFORD STREET in 1880-81. The first electric tram ran from Fulford to Nessgate in 1910, and York RAILWAY STATION was the tramway centre. In 1911 HOLGATE

BRIDGE was built to link ACOMB to the city centre by tram. The trams began losing money after WORLD WAR ONE, and were completely superseded by buses in 1935.

TRANSEPTS of the Minster The NORTH TRANSEPT and the SOUTH TRANSEPT are the earliest parts of the MINSTER, built between 1220 and c1253. Transepts are the two wings of the cruciform cathedral.

TREASURER of the Minster Keeper of the MINSTER's wealth. The first treasurer, Ranulph, was appointed c1091 by Thomas of BAYEUX. A Treasurer's varied tasks included not only taking care of the treasure but also overseeing the building works. For his work he was paid the largest salary after the DEAN. Treasurer William Cliff resigned in 1547 following the REFORMATION, giving the understandable reason that no treasure remained. He was rewarded for putting up little resistance to HENRY VIII's reforms by being appointed Dean of Chester. The post was not re-introduced until 1936. It is one of the Minster's four most important posts along with the ARCH-BISHOP, the Dean and the PRECENTOR.

TREASURER'S HOUSE Mansion located in Minster Yard. It stands on the site of the house of the medieval TREASURERS, and the name is virtually all that survives from that period. The medieval house, which incorporated GRAY'S COURT, was built on ROMAN foundations, hence the famous GHOSTS seen by Harry MARTIN-DALE in 1953. Following the abolition of the post of Treasurer in 1547 after HENRY VIII's REFORMATION, the house became the property of the crown, and was owned by two ARCHBISHOPS, Robert HOLGATE and

Nicholas Heath, before it became the property of Thomas Young, Archbishop of York (1561-68) and President of the COUNCIL OF THE NORTH. The Young family owned the house until 1648. Thereafter, owners included Sir THOMAS FAIRFAX and Dr Jaques Sterne, uncle of Laurence STERNE. From a window in the house astronomer John GOODRICKE observed the night sky in the eighteenth century. The house was extensively remodelled in both the seventeenth and eighteenth centuries. Much of the present interior is due to restoration by Frank GREEN, who bought the house in 1897, giving it to the National Trust in 1930. It is open to the public.

TREATY OF YORK Agreement signed in York in 1237 between the English and the SCOTS. The kings of Scotland had longstanding ambitions to acquire areas of NORTHUMBRIA in northern England. The Scottish king Alexander II and HENRY III reached a settlement offering the former English estates if he abandoned his claims. Good relations appeared to last, as at Christmas 1251 Henry's young daughter and Alexander's even younger son were married in York MINSTER.

TRIFORIUMS of the Minster High arcades or walkways located above the arches of the NAVE, CHOIR and TRANSEPTS of the MINSTER.

TUDOR, HENRY *See* HENRY TUDOR

TUKE, ESTHER (d.1794) Wife of WILLIAM TUKE and the founder of the QUAKER school for girls which later became the MOUNT SCHOOL. The school was established in 1785 in Trinity Lane off MICKLEGATE. The Tukes lived there and Esther was the headmistress for the rest of her life.

TUKE, MARY (1695-1752) QUAKER who established a small grocery shop in WALMGATE. For seven years she fought the GUILD of MERCHANT ADVENTURERS who wanted to prevent her from trading. She was deemed ineligible for membership of the guild as she was not the widow or daughter of a member. She was fined several times but eventually given permission to trade in 1732. In 1733 she moved her shop to CASTLEGATE, near the FRIENDS' MEETING HOUSE. Her son WILLIAM TUKE took over on her death, by which time they were highly successful dealers in the lucrative commodity of tea. In 1860 HENRY ISAAC ROWNTREE joined the company and two years later bought the cocoa and CHOCOLATE department from Tuke & Co. Their bestselling item was Tuke's Superior Rock Cocoa, renamed Rowntree's Prize Medal Rock Cocoa. The company became ROWNTREE & CO.

TUKE, SAMUEL (1784-1857) Grandson of WILLIAM TUKE, Samuel took over the family business in 1818, running it until 1852, during which period there were many changes. On Samuel's death the firm's head office transferred to London. In 1860 HENRY ISAAC ROWNTREE joined the company in York, leading to the establishment of ROWNTREE & CO. The Tukes supported the abolition of the slave trade and in 1807 Samuel Tuke donated money to reformer William Wilberforce's successful campaign to win a Parliamentary seat in Yorkshire. Samuel Tuke was a teacher at one of the first Adult Schools in

York, which began in 1816. In 1818 William Tuke had proposed a "middle class" school for QUAKER boys, but he
died before its establishment. In 1822 the school began
in a house known as "The Appendage" in Lawrence
Street. BOOTHAM SCHOOL moved to its present site in
BOOTHAM in 1846, having been established in 1829. As
well as involvement in the management of The RETREAT,
Samuel was also a Governor of York Asylum, now
BOOTHAM PARK HOSPITAL.

TUKE, WILLIAM (1732-1822) Leading QUAKER who is
best remembered as the pioneering founder of The
RETREAT hospital. The son of MARY TUKE, he began
to work in her shop in 1746 and took it over on her death
in 1752, by which time the Tukes were successful tea
dealers. William became a member of the MERCHANT
ADVENTURERS' GUILD and lived over the shop in
CASTLEGATE. After his first wife's death he became
more involved in Quaker affairs. In 1765 he married
Esther Maud, who established a Quaker school for girls
which later became the MOUNT SCHOOL. The Tukes
moved to Trinity Lane, off MICKLEGATE. William's son
Henry joined the business in 1770 and began to produce
cocoa and CHOCOLATE. When William was nearly sixty
years old he became concerned about the rights of the
mentally ill, after the death of a Quaker woman in
BOOTHAM PARK HOSPITAL, then the Asylum, in terrible conditions. What Tuke started at The Retreat brought
about enormous changes in attitudes towards the
"insane" which spread throughout the world. In 1818, at
the age of eighty-six, Tuke retired from the family business.

TURPIN, DICK (1706-1739) Infamous highwayman executed and buried in York. He was the son of an Essex innkeeper and an apprentice butcher, who joined a gang of cattle and deer-stealers in Epping Forest. When the gang disbanded he went into partnership with Tom King, a well-known highwayman. To avoid capture he went to Yorkshire, taking the name of Palmer and setting himself up as a horse-dealer. He was convicted at York ASSIZE COURTS in 1739 of horse theft, then a capital offence. He probably spent his last days in the CONDEMNED CELL, now part of the CASTLE MUSEUM, and was hanged at TYBURN on 7 April. After Turpin's execution a body-snatching surgeon dug up his corpse, which was rescued by a mob of locals from a garden in STONEGATE. His grave is in ST GEORGE'S CHURCH-YARD in George Street, near PICCADILLY. The fabled ride from London to York in a day was performed by "Swiftnicks" NEVISON if anyone. Turpin's famous mare, BLACK BESS, is a nineteenth-century romantic addition to the story.

TYBURN Site of public EXECUTIONS in York between 1379 and 1801. A large stone in Tadcaster Road alongside the KNAVESMIRE marks the spot. Private soldier Edward Hewison was the first to be executed here in March 1379. He had raped a servant of Sheriff Hutton Castle as she made her way to York. The last execution was of Edward Hughes, a soldier of the Eighteenth Light Dragoons who was also convicted of rape, in August 1801. More famous hangings included those of "Swiftnicks" NEVISON in 1684, and Dick TURPIN in 1739. Tyburn was decommisioned in 1801, with the opening of the NEW DROP at York CASTLE. The Tyburn gallows, known as the THREE-LEGGED MARE, was finally removed in 1812. Public executions, generally outside the Castle and always great crowd-pullers, continued until 1868. York's last execution, in private at the Castle, was in 1896.

U

ULPH'S DRINKING HORN in the Minster Relic in the UNDERCROFT of York MINSTER. Ulph, or Ulf, was a powerful Anglo-Danish earl, probably in the tenth or early eleventh century. The relic is a large decorated ivory drinking horn with the inscription "Ulf, a prince in Western Deira, gave this horn with his lands". Deira was an ANGLO-SAXON kingdom occupying east and central Yorkshire before becoming part of NORTHUMBRIA. The traditional story behind the inscription is that Ulph gave all his lands to the Minster, having been outraged to overhear his greedy sons arguing over their potential inheritance. The horn, allegedly a thousand years old already, was given as proof of his intentions. It is said that the horn came from the Holy Land, although Byzantium (modern-day Turkey) is its more likely origin. The horn has lost its gold decoration over the years though it remains an interesting relic.

UNDERCROFT of the Minster Underground exhibition in the MINSTER, incorporating the CRYPT, the Foundations Museum and the Treasury. Clearly visible are the concrete supports and steel bolts used to underpin the CENTRAL TOWER. Major engineering work was undertaken between 1967 and 1972 to reinforce the foundations of the tower. The ROMAN remains of the PRINCIPIA were uncovered along with a ROMAN COLUMN. The foundations of the NORMAN Minster were also discovered. The Treasury includes ULPH'S DRINKING HORN as well as a collection of silver. An audio tour is included in the admission price.

UNITARIAN CHAPEL Nonconformist Protestant chapel in ST SAVIOURGATE. It was built between 1692 and 1693 as a Presbyterian chapel and later became a Unitarian chapel. It is the oldest of York's nonconformist churches still standing. Charles WELLBELOVED, the scholar and historian, was its Minister in the nineteenth century and is buried here.

UNIVERSITY OF YORK Located in HESLINGTON, two miles (3.2km) to the south-east of the city centre. The University opened in October 1963 with 216 students, following a local campaign initiated by YORK CIVIC TRUST. Eric JAMES, the first Vice-Chancellor, wrote the *Development Plan* with three colleagues. The University is situated in 180 ACRES of parkland surrounding an artificial lake. The original six colleges were ALCUIN, Derwent, GOODRICKE, Langwith, VANBRUGH and WENTWORTH, with James College opening in 1991 and Halifax College in 1996. When it opened the University was described by Nikolaus Pevsner as "probably the best of the new universities". Fast initial growth increased the student population to 2700 by 1972, with a full range of departments. Despite a period of economic uncertainty in the 1970s and 1980s both teaching and research achieved national recognition, reflected in recent league tables. It is now often referred to as "the Cambridge of the North". The development of York Science Park between 1990 and 2002 raised the University's profile in providing modern employment opportunities. There are now over 8000 students.

V

VANBRUGH, JOHN (1664-1726) Architect and dramatist born in London, who built CASTLE HOWARD in 1702 with Nicholas Hawksmoor. In 1705 Vanbrugh and Hawksmoor built Blenheim Palace in Oxfordshire. Vanbrugh's best-known plays are *The Relapse: Or Virtue in Danger* and *The Provok'd Wife*, both Restoration comedies. A college at the UNIVERSITY OF YORK is named after him.

VAVASOURS Catholic family from Weston, near Otley, West Yorkshire. The Vavasours owned the Peter's Post Quarry (later known as the Jackdaw Crag Quarry) near Tadcaster, twelve miles (19.3km) south-west of York. Among the buildings made from the quarry stone are York MINSTER, Selby Abbey, Beverley Minster and ST MARY'S ABBEY. As a rare privilege for granting the stone, the family were permitted to celebrate Mass in the chapel of their home of Hazlewood Castle, near the quarry, by Queen Elizabeth I. Mistress Ann Vavasour became Elizabeth I's favourite maid of honour, and tradition has her as the mysterious "dark lady" of SHAKESPEARE's sonnets. Thomas Vavasour commanded a ship during the Spanish Armada conflict of 1588, and a statue of William Vavasour is to the right of the exterior of the WEST DOORS of the Minster, holding a piece of stone from the quarry. However not all the Vavasours escaped persecution. The unfortunate Dorothy Vavasour, a friend of Margaret CLITHEROW, died in the KIDCOTES in 1587.

VENUTIUS (First century AD) King of the BRIGANTES, occupiers of areas of Northern England at the time of the ROMAN invasion of AD43. Conflict with his pro-Roman Queen CARTIMANDUA resulted in Roman intervention cAD69. His headquarters was at Stanwick near Richmond, North Yorkshire.

VESPASIAN (AD9-79) ROMAN Emperor AD69-79, who appointed his son-in-law QUINTUS PETILIUS CERIALIS to lead the expansion of Roman rule in North Britain which led to the establishment of the military base EBORACUM (York). Vespasian became Emperor following Nero's suicide, and one of his many achievements was the construction of the Colosseum in Rome during his reign.

VICTORIA (1819-1901) Queen of the United Kingdom 1837-1901. As the young Princess Victoria she visited the MUSEUM GARDENS in 1835, to the delight of the local people. However, in 1849 her visit as Queen to York's former RAILWAY STATION, in TANNER ROW, proved less than successful. Disappointed by the inadequate restaurant facilities at the small terminus, she vowed never to return to the city.

VICTORIA BAR Gateway in the city WALLS, constructed in 1838 as a link from the BISHOPHILL area to Nunnery

Lane. The gateway was paid for from public donations, raised by the CITY OF YORK COUNCIL under the control of George HUDSON. During its construction there was found to be an ancient, blocked gateway where the main archway is now. This was possibly the lost Lounlith POSTERN, a medieval entrance on the line of a street, Lounlithgate, which ran to what is now BAILE HILL.

VIKING KINGS Between AD866 and AD954 there were eleven VIKING rulers of the kingdom of JORVIK. These included IVAR THE BONELESS (reigned 866-73), Halfdan (reigned 873-77), Sihtric (reigned 921-27) and ERIC BLOODAXE (reigned 947-48 and 952-54). The kingdom was briefly under ANGLO-SAXON rule (927-39) having been captured by ATHELSTAN.

VIKINGS Scandinavian traders and warriors who ruled York from AD866 to AD954. Vikings gave York its name (from JORVIK) and their reorganisation of the ROMAN streets still survives. Vikings, a term meaning "traders" and made popular by the Victorians, were known as Danes by the ANGLO-SAXON people they attacked. Having raided monasteries since the 790s, a "Great Army", under IVAR THE BONELESS, captured York from the Anglo-Saxons in 866. York became the capital of the Viking kingdom of Jorvik, until ERIC BLOODAXE died in 954. The settlers lived mostly near the river FOSS, trading in leather, horn, and goods from Scandinavia, Europe, Greenland and even Moscow, which was founded by their kinsmen. Over forty of York's street names contain the word "gate", from the Danish *gata* meaning street. The Vikings' main street was probably PAVEMENT and the remains of many leather shops have been excavated here. Gothfrith, VIKING KING of Jorvik (883-95) was given a Christian burial in the MINSTER, and evidence of the Viking occupation has been found throughout York. Many homes were discovered in the COPPERGATE archaeological dig of 1976-81, resulting in the creation of the JORVIK CENTRE. York's Viking heritage is commemorated in the JOLABLOT festival each February.

VOLUNTARY GUIDES Fully trained voluntary guides who conduct free walking tours of the city every morning throughout the year, and in the early evening from April to September. Private tours can also be arranged. The guides are based at York's principal Tourist Information Office in the DE GREY ROOMS in ST LEONARD'S PLACE.

W

WAGON PLAYS Originally the MYSTERY PLAYS were performed on wagons taken around the city to specific streets such as STONEGATE and CONEY STREET. This format was revived in 1996 and the plays are performed on wagons every three or four years, most recently in 2002. The GUILDS would often be given appropriate pieces, the fishermen generally performing Noah's Ark and the wealthy MERCHANT ADVENTURERS the final piece, Judgement Day.

WALLACE, WILLIAM (c1272-1305) Hero of the SCOTS who lit the torch of the Scottish Wars of Independence.

The spectacular sacking of York, as depicted in Mel Gibson's 1995 film *Braveheart*, is Hollywood fiction. In reality, Wallace unsuccessfully besieged Carlisle Cathedral in Cumbria and got no further south than Cockermouth.

WALLS, ABBEY *See* ST MARY'S ABBEY

WALLS, CITY The current walls were built between the 1240s and the 1340s and enclose 263 ACRES. The full circuit, including gaps, is approximately two-and-three-quarter miles (4.4km). Originally a ROMAN wall enclosed their PRINCIPIA or fortress area, a total of fifty acres. These first walls were wooden, rebuilt in stone cAD107. A section of Roman wall can still be seen alongside the MULTANGULAR TOWER. The VIKINGS extended the Roman walls to what is now roughly the present circuit. The walls do not surround the city completely, the area between LAYERTHORPE BRIDGE and the RED TOWER being a swamp and later the KING'S FISHPOOL, defences in themselves. The money for the upkeep of the medieval walls came from a "murage tax" (*muri* meaning walls in Latin) and from renting out gateways and towers as homes. Even the grass of the ramparts was sold as hay. As York largely avoided industrialisation, the walls survived. Nonetheless, in the nineteenth century the city CORPORATION intended to pull them down, eventually dissuaded by passionate campaigners including William ETTY. The only section to be demolished was some 350 feet (107m) joining BOOTHAM BAR to the Multangular Tower. The wall walks are usually open from dawn until dusk.

WALMGATE Street leading from FOSS BRIDGE to WALMGATE BAR. It was originally called Walbergate, the major route south-east out of JORVIK. The street was historically one of York's poorest areas. Following the PLAGUE of 1631 those in receipt of poor relief were three times as many in the Walmgate ward than in other more prosperous wards. In 1846 the followers of John WESLEY identified BEDERN, HUNGATE, the WATER LANES and Walmgate as the four worst areas of the city, and appointed missionaries to work full-time there. Walmgate became York's Irish quarter in the mid-nineteenth century, the 1851 Census showing the Irish-born population was 1,928, having risen from 429 in 1841. The 1881 figures showed that one in every three children born in Walmgate would die before their first birthday. The street housed a cattle market in the early nineteenth century, prior to the construction of a purpose-built market nearby in PARAGON STREET. In 1800 there were twenty-six pubs in the street of which only two, the Spread Eagle and the FIVE LIONS, remain. The INL (Irish National League) CLUB closed in 2002.

WALMGATE BAR One of the four principal BARS of the city, Walmgate Bar is a twelfth-century stone archway which had a portcullis and fifteenth-century wooden gates. It is pocked with the marks of cannonballs and bullets dating from the SIEGE OF YORK in 1644, during the ENGLISH CIVIL WAR. The BARBICAN was rebuilt in 1648 and an inscription marking completion of this work was placed above the outer arch. The Bar was again restored in 1840 and a smaller side archway added. The larger side archway was added in 1862. The inner part of the Bar consists of a timber-framed Elizabethan house, which was the birthplace of John Browne, an artist, in 1793. The Bar was inhabited from the fourteenth century until 1959 and there was even a garden on the roof. Walmgate Bar is the only one of York's historic gateways still to have its barbican due to public opposition to its demolition in 1831. Its large outer doors were made of iron but have long since been removed. Despite plentiful signs warning of its height, the Bar is still frequently damaged by lorries. The house is currently used by the Calvary Chapel.

WAR MEMORIALS York's war memorials are located in DUNCOMBE PLACE, on SKELDERGATE BRIDGE roundabout, in DEAN'S PARK, in Station Road, in the MEMORIAL GARDENS, in Salisbury Road, on ACOMB Green and in the MINSTER. Those in Duncombe Place and alongside Skeldergate Bridge are BOER WAR MEMORIALS, while the archways in Dean's Park, all that remains of the medieval ARCHBISHOP'S PALACE, are dedicated to the army's Second Division. The Station Road memorial commemorates the 2236 employees of the North Eastern RAILWAY killed in WORLD WAR ONE and the 551 in WORLD WAR TWO. It was designed by Sir Edwin Lutyens, who was responsible for the Cenotaph in Whitehall, London. The memorial in Salisbury Road is in memory of the seventy-two men and three women of the Leeman Road district killed in World War One, and the Acomb Green memorial is dedicated to the seventy-seven men of the parish who died in the 1914-18 war. Memorials in the Minster include the ASTRONOMICAL CLOCK and the FIVE SISTERS WINDOW.

WARD, MARY (1585-1645) Influential woman of the Yorkshire Catholic resistance buried at St Thomas's Church, Osbaldwick in York. She was born near Ripon, North Yorkshire, to a family with a long history of opposition to Protestantism. Two uncles were implicated in the Catholic GUNPOWDER PLOT and were killed. Mary Ward founded the IBVM (Institute of the Blessed Virgin Mary) in 1609, opening schools for girls in Flanders. In 1631 the order was suppressed by the Pope, and Mary Ward was imprisoned in Munich on charges of heresy but eventually released. She returned to London in 1639 and in 1644, during the ENGLISH CIVIL WAR, she moved the IBVM to HEWORTH Hall in York. At her deathbed was the young Mother Frances Bedingfield, who established York's BAR CONVENT based on Mary Ward's principles.

WARS OF THE ROSES (1455-85) Intermittent English civil wars of the fifteenth century, in which York played a significant role. Legend has it that an argument in a garden of roses prompted the supporters of RICHARD DUKE OF YORK to pluck a WHITE ROSE, and those loyal to the Lancastrian HENRY VI a red one. In reality, the conflict was only first referred to by this name in 1762. Despite its theoretical length, the fighting occupied an aggregate time of just thirteen weeks. The conflict is often erroneously seen as being one between Yorkshire and Lancashire. It was in fact between two sets of feuding aristocrats, those of the HOUSE OF YORK and of the House of Lancaster. This misconception is perpetuated by the name given to cricket matches between the two counties being referred to as "Roses" clashes. The legend of the roses was perhaps compounded by the writings of Sir Walter SCOTT (1771-1832).

WATER LANES Three infamous lanes leading to the river OUSE from CASTLEGATE, notorious slums and dens of vice, were known as the Water Lanes. Finally cleared and rebuilt in the early 1880s, Kergate, Thrush Lane and Hertergate, as they were recorded in the twelfth century, were known as First, Middle and Far Water Lane in Victorian times. They were roughly on the lines of the present King Street, Clifford Street and Cumberland Street. Drawings of Kergate suggest that it would apparently have put the SHAMBLES to shame, with its narrowness and overhanging buildings sloping down to the river. Danish remains found when CLIFFORD STREET was built suggests that there was commercial activity in the area well before the DOMESDAY BOOK, although perhaps not of the same nature that outraged polite Victorian society.

WELLBELOVED, CHARLES (1769-1858) Senior Minister of the UNITARIAN CHAPEL in ST SAVIOUR-GATE from 1792 to 1858, he was also an archaeologist and wrote many books about the city's archaeology. He was one of the founders of the YORKSHIRE PHILO-SOPHICAL SOCIETY in 1822 and the York Institute in 1827, and raised funds for the restoration of the MIN-STER after the fire in 1829 started by Jonathan MARTIN.

WENTWORTH, THOMAS (1593-1641) Earl of Strafford and adviser to CHARLES I, Wentworth was the last President of the York-based COUNCIL OF THE NORTH between 1628 and 1633. Following an outbreak of the PLAGUE in 1631 he imposed restrictions on people's movement which helped contain the disease. He lived in the KING'S MANOR and was responsible for major developments there. However, one of the charges which led to Strafford's execution a year before the beginning of the ENGLISH CIVIL WAR was that he placed his own coat of arms on a royal palace. The arms can be seen today, on the arch leading to the second courtyard. A college at the UNIVERSITY OF YORK is named after him, as well as a street off Scarcroft Road.

WESLEY, JOHN (1703-1791) Clergyman and founder of Methodism, born in Lincolnshire. Methodism is a Protestant denomination which took root among sections of society who felt neglected by the Church of England. The Methodists broke away from the established Church in 1795. By the time of Wesley's death he is reputed to have travelled nearly 300,000 miles and preached 40,000 sermons. He visited York some twenty-six times, preaching in a meeting-house in PUMP YARD, Newgate, or in the open air until the PEASHOLME GREEN chapel was opened in 1759 in ALDWARK. The chapel was replaced in 1805 by the now demolished Wesleyan Chapel in New Street.

WEST DOORS of the Minster Double oak doors made in the 1840s to replace those lost in the MINSTER FIRE. The West Doors lead into the NAVE. The enthronement ceremony involves a new ARCHBISHOP OF YORK knocking three times with his staff before being welcomed and admitted by the DEAN. The stonework of the archway was completely replaced in 1998 by the Minster's masons and stonecarvers as part of a ten-year programme of restoration. The carvings depict the stories of Genesis. The three statues above the West Door are of

William de PERCY on the left, holding a piece of wood, having contributed wood for the Minster roof, ARCH-BISHOP OF YORK William de Melton (Archbishop 1317-42) holding a model of the cathedral, and William VAVASOUR holding a piece of stone from his Tadcaster quarry. Inside the Minster, to each side of the doors, are wooden panels inscribed with the names of all the Bishops and Archbishops of York, the Deans and the PRECENTORS.

WEST FRONT of the Minster Begun in 1291 and completed in the late 1350s, apart from the WESTERN TOWERS and the stonework surrounding the WEST DOORS. This is the view of the MINSTER seen when approaching from LENDAL BRIDGE, and Lop Lane was widened to create DUNCOMBE PLACE in 1860 to make the view even more impressive.

WEST WINDOW of the Minster *See* GREAT WEST WINDOW

WESTERN TOWERS of the Minster The two large towers above the WEST FRONT of the MINSTER were completed in 1473. The north-west tower contains the ten-and-three-quarter-ton bell BIG PETER, also known as Great Peter, the third heaviest bell in Britain. It was given to the Minster in 1845 by the churchwardens of York's city CHURCHES who raised the money after the 1840 MINSTER FIRE. Big Peter was recast in 1926. The south-west tower contains a belfry with fourteen bells. New bells were installed in 2000, dedicated to the late Queen Elizabeth, the Queen Mother. The towers are not open to the public.

WHIP-MA-WHOP-MA-GATE Short street leading from COLLIERGATE to PAVEMENT. It is York's shortest street at approximately thirty-five yards (32m) with the longest name. The curious name was rendered Whitnourwhatnourgate in the sixteenth century, it being an Old English joke on the street's bizarre size, roughly translating as "What a street! Call this a street?" Some authorities claim that the name has a darker meaning and that this tiny street was once the sight of public floggings. Over the years the name has been rendered in a variety of ways such as Whipnam Whapnamgate, Whipney Whapneygate and Whitman Whatmangate.

WHITE ROSE OF YORK Emblem of York and Yorkshire. It is debatable when it was first adopted, though all indications suggest the latter half of the nineteenth century. The WARS OF THE ROSES were not referred to as such until the 1760s and the white rose is not known to have been used as a symbol by any of the major Yorkist protagonists. The picking of roses in a garden instigated by RICHARD DUKE OF YORK is probably a legend embellished by Sir Walter SCOTT. YORKSHIRE DAY, the first of August, commemorates the Battle of Minden (1759) in Germany when victorious Yorkshire regiments picked white roses, and this may offer an explanation for the symbol. In 1844 when the Yorkshire Cricket Club was founded, they used a white rose as their emblem, though differing from the type more commonly known.

WILLIAM I See WILLIAM THE CONQUEROR

WILLIAM II (1057-1100) King of England 1087-1100. The son of WILLIAM THE CONQUEROR, who came to York to establish ST MARY'S ABBEY in 1088. He was also known as William Rufus ("red face") because of his ruddy complexion. Unpopular with his noblemen, he died, probably murdered, while hunting in the New Forest in Hampshire.

WILLIAM OF HATFIELD (1336-46) The only royal tomb in the MINSTER is of William of Hatfield (near Doncaster), the second son of EDWARD III and Queen PHILIPPA. It is located in the NORTH CHOIR AISLE. In reality, the memorial tomb is empty and was erected a short time after Prince William's death. The location of his actual grave in the Minster is unknown. The tomb typifies the medieval style of memorial, with the feet facing towards the east, preparing to sit up and view the Resurrection.

WILLIAM THE CONQUEROR (1028-87) King of England 1066-1087. The illegitimate son of Robert I ("The Devil"), Duke of Normandy in northern France, William "The Bastard" conquered England after defeating the ANGLO-SAXON Harold GODWINSON at Hastings on 14 October 1066. William claimed the throne as nominated heir of his cousin, the Anglo-Saxon king Edward the Confessor (King of England 1042-66). Resistance to his rule resulted in him building two wooden castles in York, BAILE HILL and CLIFFORD'S TOWER. Northern rebellions in 1069, including the murder of Robert de Comines (to whom he had given the Earldom of NORTHUMBRIA) at Durham, and the attack upon York of Anglo-Saxon forces with SWEYN II of Denmark, prompted his brutal HARRYING OF THE NORTH in 1070. He commissioned the DOMESDAY BOOK in 1086.

WOLFE, JAMES (1727-1759) British General who died taking Quebec in Canada from the French. Born in Westerham, Kent, it is believed he spent periods of his childhood at a house on PEASHOLME GREEN, now the BLACK SWAN pub. The building belonged to the family of his mother, Henrietta Thompson of Long Marston.

WOLSEY, THOMAS (1471-1530) Wolsey was appointed ARCHBISHOP OF YORK in 1514. However, he may well have never set foot in the city. Best known as Lord Chancellor to HENRY VIII, Wolsey was reluctant to further Henry's divorce from Catherine of Aragon, failing to obtain papal permission for it. He was subsequently charged with High Treason, and would almost certainly have been executed, had he not died prior to his trial. In 1529 he retired to Cawood Castle, ten miles (16km) south-west of York.

WOOL TRADE Wool was the basis of York's commercial prosperity until the 1480s. In 1336 two weavers from Brabant in Belgium settled in York under licence from EDWARD III. The wealth generated by the wool trade enabled the building of the MINSTER and financed the MERCHANT ADVENTURERS' voyages to Russia, the Mediterranean and the Middle East. Sheep raised on the lands of the extremely rich monasteries of North Yorkshire provided the wool.

WORLD WAR ONE (1914-18) York was bombed three times in May 1916 during German ZEPPELIN RAIDS. The KNAVESMIRE, Nunthorpe and PEASHOLME

GREEN areas were the most severely affected. WAR MEMORIALS to those killed in the war can be seen in the MEMORIAL GARDENS, on ACOMB Green, in Station Road, in Salisbury Street near Leeman Road, and in DEAN'S PARK. There are also memorials in the MINSTER.

WORLD WAR TWO (1939-45) York was bombed eleven times by the Germans during the Second World War, including the BAEDEKER BLITZ of 1942. WAR MEMORIALS are situated in the MEMORIAL GARDENS, on ACOMB Green, in Station Road, in DEAN'S PARK and in the MINSTER. HESLINGTON HALL was the headquarters of Bomber Command, whose station was at Elvington, six miles (9.7km) south-east of York, where the YORKSHIRE AIR MUSEUM now stands.

WORMALD'S CUT Small section of waterway leading from the river FOSS towards Navigation Road. Following plans to canalise the river FOSS in 1793, this industrial waterway was constructed in 1794 in order to serve Samuel Wormald's brewery and timber yard at the rear of WALMGATE. It later serviced LEETHAM'S MILL, the old grain warehouse of which still survives as ROWNTREE WHARF.

WRIGHT, AUSTIN (1911-1997) Sculptor born in Cheshire, who moved to York in 1937 and taught at BOOTHAM SCHOOL until 1949. At the age of forty-four he became a professional sculptor, holding successful exhibitions throughout England.

X

XAVERIA, SISTER MARY (1784-1864) Nun and teacher at the BAR CONVENT, who is buried in its cemetery. She was appointed Headmistress of the Convent's Poor School in 1830 prior to teaching the first children at ST GEORGE'S CHURCH school, which opened in 1852 off WALMGATE. The records of the Bar Convent describe her as being met by "a disorderly crowd of wild-looking little creatures for the most part barefooted, squalid and dirty, shouting and screaming". Having surveyed the scene for a few minutes, Sister Xaveria began to sing. Her deep rich voice "acted like magic upon the undisciplined audience. In a few moments they were standing silent and almost motionless." She remained at St George's School until 1860.

Y

YE OLDE STARRE INN Pub in STONEGATE. Its distinctive sign, dating from 1733, stretches across Stonegate and states that it is York's oldest inn. Although the Starre Inn dates from at least 1644, many pubs claim to be York's oldest, including the BLACK SWAN, the RED LION, and the GOLDEN FLEECE. During the ENGLISH CIVIL WAR, when it was not uncommon for a man to drink eight pints of beer per day owing to the impurity of the water, the landlord was a Royalist named William Foster. After the SIEGE OF YORK when the city fell to the FAIRFAXES and the Parliamentarian army, Foster found his pub full of Roundheads whom he refused to serve. An account of this was recorded in verse and now hangs on the wall in the pub.

YOMTOB OF JOIGNY (d.1190) Rabbi who died in the MASSACRE OF THE JEWS. In the 1180s York's Jewish community had invited Rabbi Yomtob of Joigny in France to teach in the city. On 16 March 1190, when the JEWS were trapped in CLIFFORD'S TOWER, Yomtob called upon them to commit suicide. The Rabbi killed about sixty men, including JOSCE, after they had first killed their wives and children. After he took his own life, a fire started by the Jews raged within Clifford's Tower, endangering the few survivors. They pleaded for mercy, agreeing to accept baptism. The waiting mob agreed but when the Jews left the Tower Richard MALEBYSSE and his men massacred them.

YORK ARCHAEOLOGICAL TRUST Formed in 1972, its aim is to rescue and record archaeological evidence from being destroyed by urban development. As an educational charity, the Trust provides archaeological services in York and the region. Hundreds of sites have been dug or monitored during development, and the results analysed, published and conserved. Its series of research books *The Archaeology of York* is now recognised as the fullest account of the archaeology of a single city. Its best-known excavation (1976-81) was at COPPERGATE, the site of the modern JORVIK CENTRE, which recreates and interprets the VIKING city and its people. The Trust also owns and manages the ARC (Archaeological Resource Centre) in ST SAVIOURGATE, which opened in 1990. The Trust's offices are located in OGLEFORTH.

YORK ARMS Pub in HIGH PETERGATE. The building is situated near the MINSTER on the site of the ancient Peter PRISON. The pub's history can be traced back to 1818, when it was known as the Chapter Coffee House. During the 1820s it was renamed The Eclipse. The York Arms was rebuilt in 1838, when it was known as The Board, but by 1843 it was trading once again under its original Chapter Coffee House name. It became the York Arms in the 1860s.

YORK BREWERY York's only brewery, based in TOFT GREEN. Throughout York's history there have been a number of breweries though the York Brewery is the first to brew beer commercially within the city WALLS since Hunt's Brewery in ALDWARK closed in the late 1950s. York Brewery's first brew was completed in May 1996. It has opened three pubs in the city, the Last Drop, the THREE-LEGGED MARE, and in 2002, the Rook and Gaskill in Lawrence Street. Tours of the brewery are available.

YORK CASTLE *See* CASTLE

YORK CITY SOCCER CLUB York's professional football club became a "soccer" club in 2002, the first in this country to adopt such a name. It was an attempt by new chairman John Batchelor, mindful of the potential of the US market, to emphasise a connection with NEW YORK. The club was founded in 1922, following private meetings in the BLUE BELL pub held by George Robinson. They initially played at Fulfordgate, off FULFORD Road, before moving to BOOTHAM Crescent in 1932. York City have developed something of a reputation as "giant killers", reaching the quarter-finals of the FA Cup in 1938, losing after a replay to Huddersfield Town. A record 28,123 people attended the goal-less draw at Bootham Crescent. York City also reached the semi-final in 1955, before losing, again after a replay, to eventual winners Newcastle United. More recent FA Cup feats include a home win over Arsenal (1-0) in 1985, and home draws with Liverpool (both 1-1) in 1985 and 1986. In 1995 they defeated Manchester United (4-3 on aggregate) in the Coca-Cola Cup. Their nickname is "The Minstermen" and they play in red and white.

YORK CIVIC TRUST Charity which protects York's historic buildings. It was established in 1946 with the aim of protecting "from dilapidation, disfiguration or destruction, buildings and open spaces of beauty and historic interest". The York Civic Trust was co-founded by John Bowes MORRELL, DEAN Eric Milner-White (1884-1963) and Oliver Sheldon of ROWNTREE & CO., and it purchases buildings in York of historical interest for renovation. The Trust has found uses for redundant CHURCHES, affixed plaques commemorating aspects of the city's history, and was responsible for the floodlighting of the MINSTER. They are indefatigable defenders of the city's heritage and funded the ESHER Report of 1967.

YORK COLLEGE College of sixth form, further and higher education in Tadcaster Road, one mile (1.6km) south-west of the city centre. The college has two sites, the other being in Sim Balk Lane nearby. Originally known as the York Institute, the college was based in BEDERN

from 1827 until 1845. It moved to a larger site in ST SAV-
IOURGATE and again in 1884 to purpose-built premises,
designed by Walter PENTY in CLIFFORD STREET. This
building also housed York's first LIBRARY. When the
library moved to a new building in Museum Street in 1929,
the Clifford Street building remained in use as the York
Institute. The Sim Balk Lane site opened in 1957 as
Ashfield Secondary Modern School, closing in 1985 and
becoming York Sixth Form College in 1999, when it
merged with the College of Arts and Technology on
Tadcaster Road. The Tadcaster Road college opened in
1955. The site also incorporates the College of Art and
Design, originally based in Lop Lane, now DUNCOMBE
PLACE, founded in 1842. There are currently over 13,000
students, both full-time and part-time. The Clifford Street
premises are now a nightclub and the site of the YORK
DUNGEON.

YORK COLLEGE FOR GIRLS Redundant girls' school
in LOW PETERGATE. The York College for Girls was
known originally as the Girls' Public Day School Trust,
which had its first intake of students in 1880. The school
closed in 1996 and the building is currently unused. The
building was formerly the home of Dr Alexander Hunter,
the first physician of the York Lunatic Asylum, now
BOOTHAM PARK HOSPITAL. The Georgian façade,
which dates from 1725 with alterations in 1770 and 1865,
has been superimposed on a much older half-timbered
building, once the Talbot Inn.

YORK CORPORATION *See* CORPORATION

YORK COURANT York NEWSPAPER founded in 1728 by John White, son of Grace White, who had established the *YORK MERCURY* in 1719. More successful than its predecessor, the *Courant* lasted until 1848, when it was absorbed by the *YORK HERALD*. The *Courant* is the direct ancestor of the present *EVENING PRESS*. The *Herald's* owner was William Hargrove, whose son William Hargrove Junior founded York's first evening paper, the *Yorkshire Evening Press*, in 1882. One of the *Courant's* biggest local stories was the burning of the MINSTER by Jonathan MARTIN in 1829.

YORK CRICKET CLUB Founded in 1784 and based at CLIFTON Park, off Shipton Road. The Club originally played on HEWORTH Moor and the KNAVESMIRE. From 1830 their premises were known as TOFT GREEN, though the ground itself was actually situated outside the city WALLS, behind what is now the RAILWAY STATION. After a brief demise in the late 1830s, the Club was revived in 1842, and rapidly prospered. A pavilion was built in 1851, and over 10,000 spectators watched the Club play Pontefract (West Yorkshire) in 1863. The building of the Railway Station (1871-77) forced them back to the Knavesmire, before cricket-loving Joseph TERRY Junior inspired a move to BOOTHAM Crescent in 1881. With the arrival of YORK CITY Football Club at the Crescent in 1932, the Club relocated to Wigginton Road, before the building of YORK DISTRICT HOSPITAL forced a move to the present location in 1966. Perhaps the most curious recorded event concerning the Club is their play-ing of two matches on the frozen river OUSE, following the harsh winter of 1861.

YORK DISTRICT HOSPITAL Situated in Wigginton Road, the hospital opened in 1976. It took ten years to plan and build, effectively replacing ten other HOSPITALS in the city and bringing acute and emergency care under one roof. Other hospitals remaining in York are BOOTHAM PARK, The RETREAT (both psychiatric hospitals) and the PUREY-CUST private hospital.

YORK DUNGEON Horror attraction situated in CLIFFORD STREET. The Dungeon gruesomely recreates the most macabre episodes of the city's past. Dick TURPIN, as well as PLAGUE victims and torture chambers, are among its highlights. There is also participation from actors.

YORK EARLY MUSIC FESTIVAL Annual festival of vocal, choral and instrumental music, based at the NATIONAL CENTRE FOR EARLY MUSIC near WALMGATE. The Festival was founded in 1977 and has a different theme every year. It attracts performers and audiences from all over the world, and many performances are broadcast by BBC Radio. As well as at ST MARGARET'S CHURCH, events take place throughout the city, especially at the MINSTER.

YORK HAM World-famous cured ham, which originated in York and can be bought from Scotts butchers in LOW PETERGATE. The ham is brined, dried and aged in sawdust for three months. The first sawdust was allegedly from the oak beams cut when York MINSTER was built. There is debate as to whether York Ham should be smoked or unsmoked.

YORK HERALD York NEWSPAPER, originally the *York Herald and County Advertiser*, founded in 1790. It absorbed the *YORK COURANT* in 1848, and the short-lived *York Telegraph* (founded in 1869) in 1874. The paper appeared as a morning daily from 1874, changing its name to the *Yorkshire Herald* in 1890, before becoming a weekly in 1936. In 1954 it amalgamated with the *Yorkshire Gazette*, a paper established in 1819 and published weekly since 1885. The *Gazette & Herald* was taken over by the *Yorkshire EVENING PRESS* in 1954 and is now based in the same offices in WALMGATE.

YORK, HOUSE OF *See* HOUSE OF YORK

YORK MERCURY York first NEWSPAPER, issued from Grace White's printing press in COFFEE YARD on 23 February 1719. It was a weekly single sheet, with the rather unwieldy full title of *The York Mercury, or a General View of the Affairs of Europe but more particularly of Great Britain, with useful observations about Trade*. In reality, it offered little local news, largely containing four-day-old extracts from London newspapers and the occasional local announcement. A story of May 1723 tells of a wife running away with another man. Her husband wished that she "immediately return to her said husband, she shall be kindly entertained, otherwise he desires that no person trust her, or entertain her at their peril." There is no follow up to this story in the surviving copies. The *Mercury* lasted until 1728, when it was succeeded by the *YORK COURANT*.

YORK MINSTER *See* MINSTER

YORK RACECOURSE *See* RACECOURSE

YORK RUGBY LEAGUE CLUB Formed in 1868 as an amateur Rugby Union club, before switching to Rugby League in 1897 and turning professional. Rugby is first thought to have been played in York by the pupils of ST PETER'S SCHOOL, though the school actually banned the "hooligan game" and the club was founded by ex-pupils. Their early fixtures were played on the KNAVESMIRE, before moves to the Yorkshire Gentleman's Cricket ground, now the site of YORK DISTRICT HOSPITAL, and to FULFORD. They moved to a site in Clarence Street in 1885, remaining there until 1989 when they moved to Monk's Cross, two miles (3.2km) north of the city centre. The club enjoyed their biggest successes, as losing finalists, at Wembley in 1931, and in winning the Second Division Championship in 1981.

YORK RUGBY UNION FOOTBALL CLUB Although Rugby Union has been played in York since the late nineteenth century, the present club was not officially formed until 1928. Initially playing on HOB MOOR, the club moved to its present home, Clifton Park off Shipton Road, in 1966. They have won the Yorkshire Challenge Shield three times (1949, 1964 and 1981), and gained promotion to the North-East Division One in the season 1988-89. Other successes include winning the North-East Division One Championship in 1991-92, and the North Division Two Championship in 1993-94. There are at present five senior sides, with teams for every age group, and with plans for competitive matches for girls in the season 2002-03.

YORK ST JOHN COLLEGE Higher Education College situated in LORD MAYOR'S WALK, previously the College of Ripon and York St John. It is affiliated to the University of Leeds. The original college opened in 1841, with only a handful of pupils, and was based in a house in MONKGATE, training male students for the ministry. In 1842 a nearby house began training women. The present building in Lord Mayor's Walk opened in 1846 for men, while the women students moved into the Monkgate premises. The women were relocated to a new college in Ripon in 1862. By this time the college's purpose was to supply teachers for Church of England elementary schools. ARCHBISHOP HOLGATE'S SCHOOL was based in premises to the left of the main drive, now the Holgate Building, from 1858 to 1963. At present the college offers a range of courses, mainly BA and BSc degrees, to both men and women, and has over 4000 students. The Ripon site was closed in 2001.

YORK STONE Fine-grained sandstone with a slate-like appearance. York Stone is in fact quarried in the Bradford, Halifax and Leeds areas of Yorkshire.

YORK WAITS An octet of minstrels, first recorded in 1304. Eight men were paid an annual wage of £4 to perform at ceremonial events throughout the year. One of these events was to serenade the heads of York's "most important houses" every Monday morning for five weeks after Christmas.

YORKSHIRE AIR MUSEUM Located on Halifax Way, Elvington, six miles (9.7km) south-east of York. A restored WORLD WAR TWO bomber command station, it was opened to the public in 1986. The exhibitions include the country's only complete Halifax Bomber and another forty-three aircraft.

YORKSHIRE CLUB *See* RIVER HOUSE

YORKSHIRE DAY The first of August is Yorkshire Day, commemorating the Battle of Minden, near Hanover in north-west Germany. On that date in 1759 the Anglo-Allied army under the command of Ferdinand of Brunswick fought the French. Despite the British infantry defeating the French cavalry to achieve a decisive victory, there were substantial losses amongst Yorkshiremen. The YORKSHIRE RIDINGS Society designated the first of August Yorkshire Day.

YORKSHIRE MUSEUM Located in the MUSEUM GARDENS. William Wilkins designed the building in 1829, originally to house the geological collection of the YORKSHIRE PHILOSOPHICAL SOCIETY. It was not designed for the paying public but by 1833 the museum was attracting 4000 visitors a year, including the future Queen VICTORIA in 1835. Due to a lack of funding and some negligence, many exhibits were lost or damaged. These included the loss of the first complete skeleton of the extinct giant Irish Elk. In 1942 damage was inflicted during the BAEDEKER BLITZ, when a bomb exploded nearby. Although the Museum received a large bequest in the will of Dr Tempest Anderson in the early twentieth century, the Yorkshire Philosophical Society agreed to hand over the museum to the CITY OF YORK COUNCIL in 1961. With the contribution of public money the museum has become a leading attraction, now housing the COPPERGATE HELMET and the MIDDLEHAM JEWEL. There are frequent temporary exhibitions. The W.A. Ismay Collection of Studio Pottery is the largest such collection in England and includes pots by David LLOYD-JONES. There is a GHOST story associated with the museum, as the book *Antiquities and Curiosities of the Church* occasionally projects itself from the shelves.

YORKSHIRE MUSEUM OF FARMING Situated in Murton, three miles (4.8km) east of York, alongside York Livestock Market. The museum illustrates the changes which have taken place in English farming practices over the last 150 years. The livestock building contains rare breeds of live animals, a 1930s vet's surgery with original fittings from author James Herriot's surgery in Thirsk, North Yorkshire, and a blacksmith's forge. The museum opened in 1982. In 1992 the Danelaw VIKING village opened in an adjoining site, and in 1998 the ROMAN Brigantium fort was added. Both attractions demonstrate farming practices from the relevant periods.

YORKSHIRE PHILOSOPHICAL SOCIETY Organisation now based in The Lodge, built in 1874 alongside the entrance to the MUSEUM GARDENS. The Society was founded in 1822 to promote the study of geology, botany, zoology and archaeology in the county of Yorkshire. The word "philosophical" is used in the original Greek sense of the word, meaning a systematic enquiry into the nature of the world. The Society was originally based in Low Ousegate in a now demolished building overlooking KING'S STAITH steps. In 1825 the Society acquired the site which is now the Museum Gardens, originally pasture with haystacks, cowsheds and pigsties. In 1829 they founded the YORKSHIRE MUSEUM, originally not designed for the paying public but to house the geological collection.

YORKSHIRE RIDINGS Old divisions of Yorkshire which converged at the EYE OF YORK. From around AD875 until local government reform in 1974, the county, the largest in England, was made up of the North, East and West Ridings. They stretched as far north as Middlesborough and as far south as Sheffield. York itself stands at the junction of all three, though as the capital of the county it was not in a Riding itself. York's gateways, or BARS, marked the paths into the Ridings. BOOTHAM BAR and MONK BAR lead to the North Riding, MICKLEGATE BAR to the West, and WALMGATE BAR to the East. There was no South Riding. There could only be three Ridings as the word is derived from "thridding", meaning dividing into three or thirds. The Yorkshire Ridings Society designated the first of August as YORKSHIRE DAY.

YORVIK BRASS RUBBING CENTRE Located in former ALMSHOUSES in SKELDERGATE, alongside LADY ANNE MIDDLETON'S HALL. Visitors can go to the centre and choose a brass replica from one of the largest private collections in the country. As part of this typically English pastime, a rubbing can be made of the brass.

YOUNG'S HOTEL Situated in HIGH PETERGATE opposite ST MICHAEL-LE-BELFREY CHURCH. The hotel claims to be the birthplace of Guy FAWKES, but this is unlikely as the building itself dates from 1700, nearly a century after Fawkes's death. It is more likely that his birth-place was a now demolished house in the garden to the rear of 32 STONEGATE, and behind Young's Hotel. The baptism of Guy Fawkes at St Michael-Le-Belfrey confirms this, as High Petergate was not in that parish, unlike Stonegate.

Z

ZEPPELIN RAIDS German bombardment of York during WORLD WAR ONE, by airships invented by Count Zeppelin in 1900. A total of nine people were killed and twenty-eight seriously injured, and there was considerable damage to property. The first and most serious raid occurred on 2 May 1916, when the city was completely unprotected. The airship flew over the KNAVESMIRE, bombing the Red Cross hospital, though there were no casualties. It bombed Nunthorpe Avenue where a woman was severely injured, then Upper Price Street, demolishing a house and killing the occupants. Thereafter it bombed PEASHOLME GREEN, where six people were killed. By the time of the second raid, York had a powerful searchlight and anti-aircraft gun placed near POPPLETON ROAD SCHOOL. The Zeppelin approached from the direction of FULFORD but was chased off by anti-aircraft fire, dropping some of its bombs near HEWORTH Church. The remainder of the airship's bombs fell on Low Moor, killing six horses. The third and final raid occurred on 27 November 1916 but did little harm, retreating as the searchlight quickly picked it up and it was blasted with shells.

ZOUCHE, WILLIAM DE LA (1276-1352) ARCHBISHOP OF YORK (1342-52). In 1346, while EDWARD III was in France, Archbishop Zouche left York with Queen PHILIPPA and an army to repel a Scottish invasion led by King David II. The SCOTS were defeated at the Battle of Neville's Cross near Durham. In 1349, when the PLAGUE reached York, Zouche, although wisely not in the city at the time, sent instructions to offer prayers. They clearly went unanswered as more than half the clergymen in Yorkshire died.

ZOUCHE CHAPEL in the Minster The Zouche Chapel is located in the SOUTH CHOIR AISLE of the MINSTER, and is named after William de la ZOUCHE, ARCHBISHOP OF YORK (1342-52). The chapel contains STAINED GLASS dating from the fifteenth, sixteenth and twentieth centuries. The glass features St Francis of Assisi, but there are mainly strange depictions of animals such as a procession of monkeys and a bear with a beehive on its head. It is perhaps best known for the sixteenth-century window featuring a bird on one leg attempting to entice a spider from its web. The chapel is reserved for private prayer.